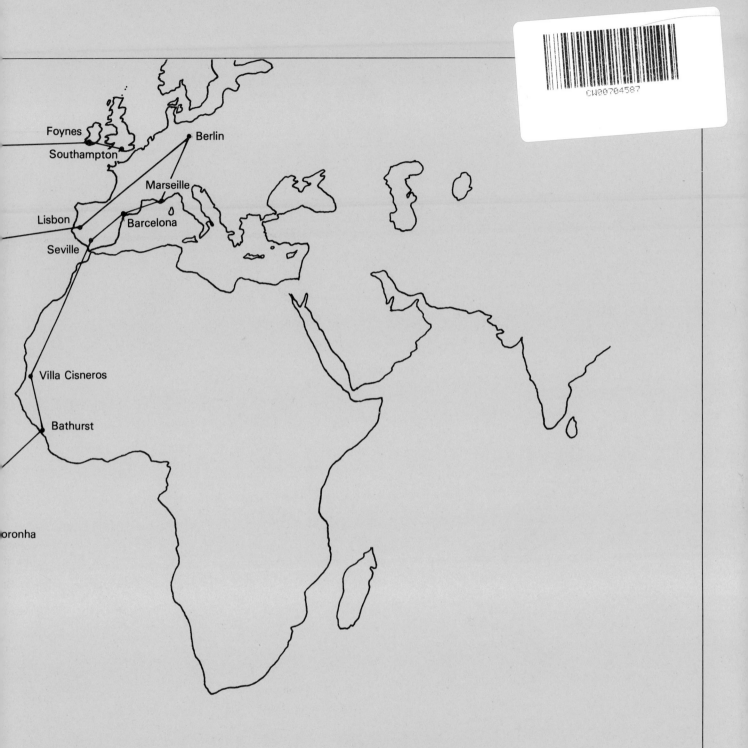

Foynes
Southampton
Berlin
Marseille
Lisbon
Barcelona
Seville
Villa Cisneros
Bathurst
oronha

**THE NORTH AND SOUTH
ATLANTIC AIR ROUTES
IN THE 1930s**

R.McM

THE SKY THEIR FRONTIER

The Sky their Frontier

The Story of the World's
Pioneer Airlines and Routes, 1920-40

Robert Jackson

ARCO PUBLISHING, INC.
New York

Published 1984 by Arco Publishing, Inc.
215 Park Avenue South, New York, NY 10003

Library of Congress Cataloging in Publication Data

Jackson, Robert, 1941-
  The sky their frontier.

  Includes index.
  1. Aeronautics, Commercial—History. 2. Air lines—
History. I. Title.
HE9774.J33 1984   387.7'065   83-25880
ISBN 0-668-06153-7

Printed in England.

Contents

Chapter One
Across the Atlantic

At 1.54 pm GMT on 6 July, 1919, the British rigid airship R.34 nosed down to her moorings at Mineola airfield, New York, at the close of the first ever flight from east to west across the Atlantic. She had left East Fortune, in Scotland, 108 hours and 12 minutes earlier, under the command of Major G. H. Scott, AFC. On board her were Brigadier-General E. M. Maitland, CMG, DSO, the officer commanding the British Military Airship Service, a crew of thirty, a kitten and a stowaway, an airman named Ballantyne.

She arrived at her destination unheralded, and on 10 July, after three hectic days of receptions and press interviews, she slipped away on the return flight. At 6.56 am on 17 July, after a flight of 75 hours and 2 minutes, she reached Pulham in Norfolk, adding to her honours by completing the first round trip of the Atlantic by air.

The R.34 was not the first to make a successful Atlantic air crossing, but she was the last of the first. There had been several gallant failures in 1919, as brave men sought to tackle and overcome one of the greatest natural obstacles in the path of aviation, and the two big successes had been well publicized. First of all, a Curtiss NC-4 flying-boat — one of a team of three, belonging to the U.S. Navy's Seaplane Division One — had reached Lisbon harbour on 27 May, after flying from Newfoundland via the Azores; her two companion aircraft, NC-1 and NC-3, had both landed short of their goal. The successful machine, commanded by Lieutenant-Commander A. C. Read, had spent ten days in Lisbon before going on to complete the last leg of her journey; her flying time had been 53 hours and 58 minutes, spread over twenty-three days.

Then, just under three weeks later, had come the most historic flight of all; the first non-stop crossing of the Atlantic from Lester's Field, Newfoundland, to Clifden in Galway by a converted Vickers Vimy flown by Captain John Alcock and navigated by Lieutenant Arthur Whitten Brown.

British rigid airship R.34, the first to make an east-west crossing of the Atlantic in 1919.

R.34 approaching to land at Pulham, Norfolk, after the Atlantic return flight.

To them went a *Daily Mail* prize of £10,000, knighthoods, the acclaim of the world and a coveted place in aviation history.

It might have been thought that these flights, and that of the R.34 after them, would have broken the dam and released a wave of aerial exploration over the Atlantic, but such was not the case. Crossing two thousand miles of ocean was one thing; putting the crossing to commercial use was another. A year after the R.34 made her flight, the airship remained the only vehicle capable of carrying a substantial number of people, or a cargo of reasonable size, across the Atlantic by air, and in Britain the rigid airship was viewed as a military rather than a commercial venture. The Germans might have inaugurated a commercial transatlantic service with either one of two Zeppelin rigid airship designs, the L.72 — originally designed for the German Navy and later transferred to France as the *Dixmude* — and the LZ.120 *Bodensee,* the first post-war commercial Zeppelin. This flew on 24 August 1919 and was luxuriously equipped for her time, having a refrigerator and a fully electric galley. However, no attempt was made at an Atlantic crossing with these craft, mainly because some of Zeppelin's directors felt that a successful and possibly record flight would unleash a lot of anti-German feeling so soon after the end of the war.

There remained only the adventurers, and in the early 1920s the adventurers were looking to other challenges; a flight to Australia, for example, or across Asia. After all, the incentive to make a non-stop Atlantic crossing had gone when Alcock and Brown took the prize. So nothing further happened for two years, until 30 March 1922, when two Portuguese aviators named Sacadura Cabral and Gago Coutinho took off from Lisbon Bay in a British-built Fairey IIID floatplane to attempt the first crossing by air of the South Atlantic.

On the first day, Cabral — who, appropriately, was descended from Alvarez Cabral, the discoverer of Brazil in 1500 — flew from Lisbon to Las Palmas, a distance of 800 miles, and on 3 April Coutinho navigated him on to St. Vincent in the Cape Verde Islands, a leg of 1,060 miles. The flight of 17 April involved a short hop of 125 miles between St. Vincent Island and Santiago Island; then, after refuelling, the aircraft set out the next day on the 1,100 miles flight to St. Paul Island, a miniscule speck of volcanic rock 500 yards by 300 in the middle of the Atlantic, where the Portuguese cruiser *Republica* was waiting with fuel.

It was now that luck deserted the two men. Faced with a strong headwind, their aircraft ran out of fuel short of the objective and ditched, smashing a float in the process. Fortunately, the *Republica* reached the scene quickly and rescued both men, together with the aero-engine, but the rest of the machine was damaged beyond repair and allowed to sink.

A second aircraft was shipped out, and in this the crew continued the flight to Fernando de Noronha Island, a hundred miles off the coast of Brazil, but once again a forced landing resulted in severe damage and this machine, too, had to be abandoned. Cabral and Coutinho eventually reached Rio de Janeiro on 16 June in a third Fairey IIID, having been en route for ten weeks. It was hardly the record-breaking achievement they had hoped for.

In 1924, after a lapse of two more years, there were three transatlantic attempts, one successful, one partially so and the third a failure. The failure involved four Italian airmen, Locatelli, Crosio, Fraccini and Farcinelli, who set off from Pisa in a Dornier Wal flying-boat on 25 July 1924. The Wal, built under licence by the Società di Costruzioni Meccaniche di Pisa and registered I-DEOR, was powered by two BMW VI engines, giving it a speed of 140 mph maximum; its range was 1,365 miles.

The Italians, making the transatlantic flight in stages, reached Reykyavik in Iceland, where they encountered two Douglas DT-2 'World Cruisers' which had been specially fitted out on the orders of the U.S. Army to undertake a flight around the world (see Chapter Three). Accompanied by these aircraft, the Dornier Wal resumed its flight on 21 August, heading for Greenland, its crew taking comfort from the fact that the icy waters over which they flew were patrolled by warships of the United States Navy, keeping a watchful eye on the around-the-world attempt.

It turned out to be just as well. The Dornier was faster than the Douglas aircraft and quickly out-distanced them, flying on alone in thick cloud. The weather grew steadily worse until, in the end, Locatelli was forced to land on the sea close to Cape Farewell. After three days, the silver glint of the aircraft's paintwork among the ice-floes brought the cruiser USS *Richmond* to the scene. The airmen were rescued, but the Dornier had to be abandoned.

The Douglas machines went on to complete their voyage, although — since a third aircraft had been forced to ditch off the Faroes — their transatlantic flight could only be called a partial success. The truly successful crossing of 1924 was made on 13 October, by a Zeppelin — the LZ.126.

Commanded by Hugo Eckener, LZ.126 took off from the Zeppelin works at Friedrichshafen on the morning of 13 October on a delivery flight to the United States. At 10 pm on the 15th the crew sighted the lights of Halifax, Nova Scotia, and in the early hours of the following morning the airship flew over Boston. At 9 am she moored at Lakehurst, New Jersey, after a flight of 77 hours, and was duly handed over to the United States Navy as the ZR-3. Her flight was a foretaste of things to come, when the great silver airships were to command the Atlantic skies for a brief span of years.

Named the *Los Angeles,* the LZ.126, alias ZR-3, was to make the only Atlantic flights of 1925. On 20 February, she embarked on a cruise from Lakehurst to Bermuda and back, covering a distance of 1,500 miles, and on 22 May she made a second trip to the island, commanded by Captain G. W. Steele USN. On this second occasion, she carried out a series of trials which involved mooring to the mast of a ship at sea.

Early in 1926, it was Spain's turn to explore a potential air route over the South Atlantic. On 22 January, a Dornier Wal crewed by Franco, de Alda, Duran and Rada set out from Melilla, in Morocco, and flew to Palos de Moguer on the first leg of a flight to Montevideo.

Major Scott, commander of the R.34, leaving the airship on returning to Pulham after the Atlantic crossing. Major Scott was later killed in the R.101 disaster.

At Palos it collected a passenger, a photographer named Alonso, and then continued to Las Palmas in the Canaries. On the 26th it reached the Porto Praya in the Cape Verde Islands, and five days later it arrived at Fernando de Noronha, having flown via Ribera de Inferno. On 31 January it made landfall at Pernambuco, on the mainland of South America, and flew on to Rio de Janeiro on 4 February; it completed its journey at Montevideo on the 9th.

A second attempt on the South Atlantic was made later that year by a Brazilian crew, de Barros, Cunha, Braya and Cinquini, who set out from Genoa on 17 October in a Savoia-Marchetti S.55 seaplane, a machine designed as a torpedo-bomber and minelayer for the Italian Navy. It was powered by two 750 hp Isotta-Fraschisni engines, mounted in tandem above the wing, and had a maximum speed of 164 mph and a range of 1,245 miles. Following much the same route as the earlier Spanish expedition, the Brazilian crew were beset by numerous delays for one reason or another and did not reach Fernando de Noronha until 28 April the following year.

The tempo of Atlantic exploration picked up dramatically in 1927. On 8 February, a trio of Italians — de Pinedo, del Prete and Zacchetti — set out to make the first flight around the periphery of the Atlantic in an S.55 named *Santa Maria*. They reached Rio de Janeiro on 26 February, after a relatively uneventful Atlantic crossing, and a month later they arrived in Cuba after a leisurely flag-showing flight northwards. Then, on 6 April, disaster struck when the aircraft caught fire at Roosevelt, Texas, and burnt out; it was another month before a replacement machine, the *Santa Maria II,* could be made available, and they continued their flight to New York in this on 8 May.

On 18 May their tour brought them to Chicago, and on the 20th they reached Newfoundland in readiness for their eastbound flight across the North Atlantic. They took off on 23 May, and after a flight of 1,500 miles they touched down on the sea 180 miles north-west of Horta, in the Azores. A recovery ship came to their rescue and, their fuel exhausted, they reached Horta on 26 May, after spending three uncomfortable days under tow. On 10 June, after a much-needed rest, they flew on to Ponta Delgada, from there to Lisbon and finally to Rome, their destination. Altogether, between 8 February and 16 June 1926, they had covered a distance of more than 25,300 miles.

While the Italians were still crossing the South Atlantic on the outward leg of their voyage, on 19 February, another attempted crossing had much less fortunate consequences. This time the starting point was Marina-di-Pisa, the aircraft was a Dornier Wal named *Uruguay,* and the four-man crew belonged to that country. They were Taddeo and Glanco Larre-Borges, who were brothers, and their companions d'Ibarra and Rigoli.

The aircraft reached Casablanca via Alicante, and on 2 March it took off on the next leg, to Dakar. However, engine trouble forced the pilot to make an emergency landing in the desert north of Cape Juby. The aircraft was wrecked and the crew captured by the Tuareg. Three days later, the Dornier was sighted by two French Aéropostale pilots, Jean Mermoz and Pierre Ville, who reported its position, and some time later two more pilots of the same company, Guillaumet and Riguelle, landed alongside to investigate. There was no sign of the crew, but as there were plenty of hoofmarks in the vicinity the Frenchmen realised what must have happened, and informed the authorities accordingly. Fortunately, the Dornier's crew were ransomed a few days later and released in reasonable shape.

Meanwhile, another South Atlantic flight had got away to a much better start. The crew were an experienced team: Sacadura Cabral, Sarmento de Beires, de Castilho and Gouveia, and their aircraft was a Dornier Wal named *Argos.* They had left Marina-di-Pisa on 13 January and flown to Lisbon, where the aircraft was thoroughly checked and provisioned for the Atlantic crossing. Preparations were almost complete when the aircraft broke loose from its moorings; it was recovered with some difficulty and there was a further delay while it was checked for damage. At this point, for reasons which are not clear, Cabral was replaced as flight commander by another Portuguese pilot named Duvalle-Portugal.

The *Argos* left Lisbon on 2 March and flew to Boloma in Portuguese Guinea. From there, it flew non-stop to Fernando de Noronha, arriving on 17 March after a 1,600-mile flight that lasted 18 hours 11 minutes. From here it flew on to Natal, reaching Pernambuco on 20 March and Bahia on 7 April, and three days later it arrived at Rio de Janeiro. The original plan had been to fly on to Argentina, but for some unspecified reason the next stage of the Dornier's journey took it on a northerly heading. On 6 June, during a flight along the coast between Belem and British Guiana, technical trouble forced the pilot to ditch; the crew were picked up by a yacht, but the aircraft was lost.

In the spring of 1927, there were once again plenty of incentives to rekindle interest in transatlantic flying. The main carrot that dangled temptingly before the noses of aviators was the Raymond Orteig prize of 25,000 dollars for the first non-stop flight between New York and Paris, or vice versa, but there were several others, including one of a similar amount for the first successful crossing to Dallas, Texas, in less than seventy-five hours.

The difficulties involved were still enormous. Engines were a little more reliable — but not much — than they had been when Alcock and Brown made their crossing eight years earlier, but there were no adequate methods of forecasting the unpredictable Atlantic weather, no blind flying instruments to help a pilot out of trouble if he was forced to fly through cloud, and no real aids to accurate long-distance navigation over nearly two thousand miles of featureless sea. Last of all, but by no means least, was the cost of fitting out an aircraft for a transatlantic attempt. No pilot could hope to do it without heavy sponsorship, and sponsors required a virtual guarantee of success.

The French, to their everlasting credit, tried hard and valiantly, despite a succession of tragedies. On 21 September 1926, a crew comprising René Fonck, France's top-scoring fighter pilot of the 1914-18 War, another Frenchman named Charles Clavier, Lieutenant L. W. Curtin, an American, and a Russian named Jacob Islamoff, had prepared to try for the New York—Paris crossing in a Sikorsky S.35; the heavily-laden aircraft had crashed on take-off, and Clavier and Islamoff had both been burned alive.

Now, early in 1927, there were two more French tragedies in quick succession. In the first, a Farman Goliath left St. Louis-du-Senegal on 5 May and headed out over the Atlantic; neither it nor its crew — Saint-Roman, Mouneyres and Petit — were seen again. Then, only two days later, came another blow that shocked and saddened the whole of France.

On 8 May, Charles Nungesser — another leading and well-loved air ace of the First World War — and his navigator, Francois Coli, took off from Paris in a Levasseur aircraft named *L'Oiseau Blanc* (White Bird). On its side, beneath the cockpit, it carried a macabre emblem that was Nungesser's personal symbol, one which had been painted on his fighter during the war: a heart bearing a skull and crossbones, a coffin and two funeral candles.

The aircraft took off safely, and as soon as it was airborne Nungesser jettisoned its undercarriage — a measure designed to save weight and cut down drag, for the Levasseur would have to fly into the teeth of the prevailing westerly wind. A small armada of aircraft accompanied it as far as the English Channel, then it continued alone until it was lost to sight against the western sky.

It vanished without trace, somewhere out there over the grey Atlantic wastes. All that remained of it was its undercarriage, preserved today in France's Musée de l'Air.

Thirteen days later, on 21 May, a Ryan Monoplane named *Spirit of St Louis* came slanting down out of the sky to land in darkness at Le Bourget, Paris. It had flown from New York in 33 hours and 30 minutes at an average speed of 107.9 miles an hour, and its shy and serious-looking young pilot, Charles Lindbergh, had flown into the pages of history. That historic flight, its drama told and retold so many times, needs no repetition here. For Lindbergh, the solo transatlantic crossing was only the beginning of an eventful career that encompassed fame and tragedy alike; it was not the end of his Atlantic flying, for he still had a major contribution to make in this area, as we shall see later.

At the beginning of the 1920s, following the first Atlantic air crossings, there had been a long hiatus. Nothing of the sort happened now; after Lindbergh, attempts on the Atlantic came thick and fast. It was as though every adventurous aviator was determined to get in on the act before the whole business of transatlantic flying became routine.

Two weeks after Lindbergh's exploit, on 4 June, another American — Clarence Chamberlin — set off from New York in a Bellanca monoplane named *Miss Columbia,* his intention being to go one better than Lindbergh by flying non-stop to Berlin. He was accompanied by his sponsor, Charles Levine. The flight was straightforward, although the Ballanca had to land at Eisleben, a few miles short of Berlin, when its fuel ran out. It had covered a distance of 3,905 miles non-stop in a time of 43 hours, 49 minutes and 33 seconds, establishing a new world record for distance in a straight line. It was a magnificent achievement, unfortunately overshadowed by Lindbergh's earlier effort.

An attempt to put the air crossing of the Atlantic on an embryo commercial footing came on 29 June, when a Fokker F.VII named *America* took off from New York bound for Paris, carrying the first transatlantic air mail. On board were Admiral Richard Byrd, the celebrated explorer and navigator, Bert Acosta, the pilot, Fokker test pilot Bernt Balchen, and George Noville, the wireless operator and engineer. The flight was made in appalling visibility, the aircraft flying through cloud over most of the route, and when it eventually reached France it was unable to land because of fog over Paris. After circling for a while, looking for a landmark, the crew decided to head back to the coast. The pilot groped his way down to make a forced landing in the shallows just off the beach at Ver-sur-Mer, Calvados, and the crew waded ashore, clutching 150 pounds of mail. They had been in the air for 46 hours and 6 minutes, and were utterly exhausted.

The next crew to cross the Atlantic, on 27 August, were also Americans; Edward Schlee and William Brock, who flew from Newfoundland to London in a Stinson monoplane named *Pride of Detriot* in 23 hours and 19 minutes. This was not solely an Atlantic attempt, for the two men subsequently flew on in stages to Tokyo; their aim was to fly around the world.

Although the airship R.34 had made an east-west non-stop crossing of the Atlantic, no aeroplane had yet done so, and it was for this purpose that a Fokker F.VIIa, bearing the British registration G-EBTQ and the name *St Raphael,* set out from Upavon in Wiltshire into the blustery morning of 31 August. The aircraft was the property of Princess Ludwig of Löwenstein-Wertheim and was painted silver and black. It was piloted by Lieutenant-Colonel F. F. R. Minchin, a very experienced long-distance pilot, and his navigator was Flying Officer Leslie Hamilton, RAF. The princess, who was an Englishwoman — the widow of a German prince who had been killed in the Spanish-American War of 1899 — travelled as a passenger.

The Fokker had to fight its way through strong headwinds right from the start. Halfway across the Atlantic a ship reported that it had seen the aircraft's lights, crawling across the dark, windy sky overhead. It was never seen again.

A week after this tragedy, on 6 September, another Fokker F.VII — named *Old Glory* and crewed by a Frenchman, Bertau, and two Americans named Hill and Payne — set out to try the east-west crossing. The aircraft bore a wreath, with the inscription: "Nungesser and Coli, you showed us the way; we have followed you." This aircraft and its crew, too, vanished without trace. Then, only twenty-four hours later, a similar fate befell two Canadians, T. B. Tully and J. V. Medcalf, who set out from Harbour Grace in Newfoundland in a Stinson-Detroiter named *Sir John Carling* to fly to London. Despite a lengthy air and sea search off the coast of North America, no trace of them or their aircraft was ever found.

Then, on 10 October, the run of tragedy seemed to break at last with a faultless crossing of the South Atlantic by two Frenchmen, Captain D. Costes and his navigator, Le Brix, who took off from Le Bourget in a Breguet XIXGR serialled 1685 and bearing the names *Nungesser et Coli.* The machine reached St. Louis-du-Senegal the next day after a flight of 2,870 miles, then on 14 October made the 2,100 mile flight to Natal in 18 hours and 5 minutes, achieving the first non-stop crossing between Senegal and Brazil. The Breguet flew on to Buenos Aires, arriving on 20 October, and used the Argentine capital as a base to make a South American tour, which took place between 1 and 22 November. Three days later the Frenchmen left Buenos Aires and flew on to New York, arriving there on 11 February 1928. So far, they had flown more than 22,300 miles. By the time they crossed the American continent to San Francisco, which they reached on 7 March, the total mileage had risen to over 25,000. From San Francisco, they took ship for Japan, where their odyssey continued.

In the North Atlantic, however, the bad luck continued. On 11 October, the day after Costes and Le Brix set off on their record-breaking flight, an American named Captain G. Haldeman left New York for Paris in a Stinson called *The American Girl;* his passenger was a New York show girl, Ruth Elder, and the flight was nothing more than a risky publicity stunt. During the flight the Stinson's engine seized and Haldeman ditched, having just managed to get out an SOS call. This was picked up by an oil tanker, the SS *Barendrecht,* which sent a lifeboat to the assistance of the two Americans and picked them up in heavy seas and icy darkness.

A few days later, a German crew flying a Junkers seaplane set out from Lisbon carrying a woman passenger, the famous Viennese actress Frau Dillenz. They also failed in their attempt, being forced to turn back to the Azores in the face of severe weather. At the same time, on 17 October, a rich American woman, Mrs Frances Grayson, set out from New York in a Sikorsky amphibian named *The Dawn,* determined to be the first woman to make the air crossing. The aircraft, piloted by Wilmer Stulz and navigated by Bruce H. Goldsborough, suffered the failure of the port engine over the Atlantic and had to turn back. Another attempt was made on Christmas Eve, this time with a different pilot: Oscar Omdal, veteran of many exploration flights inside the Arctic Circle. An engineer named Schroeder was also carried, and Goldsborough remained as navigator.

The weather forecast was fearsome: gales, snow, ice and hail. Surprisingly, the experienced Omdal decided to take off. Many hours later, the crew of a ship reported having heard the aircraft's engines in the darkness. After that there was nothing; *The Dawn* vanished along with its occupants, swallowed by the Atlantic.

Ironically — or perhaps fittingly — it was the pilot who had been replaced by Omdal, Wilmer Stulz, who became the first to take a woman over the Atlantic by air several months later. But before that happened, another woman had lost her life in the attempt. On 13 March, 1928, Elsie Mackay, the daughter of Lord Inchcape (at that time Chairman of P and O Lines) took off from RAF Cranwell in a Stinson Detroiter, the *Endeavour,* piloted by Captain W. R. Hinchcliffe, a highly experienced Imperial Airways officer. Five hours later, having made dreadfully slow progress in strong headwinds, the aircraft was sighted over south-west Ireland, heading out over the Atlantic, and that was the last seen of it or its occupants.

Then, on 17 June, Wilmer Stulz set out from Newfoundland in a Fokker F.VII floatplane named *Friendship.* It was a difficult crossing through rain, dense cloud and severe turbulence, but 20 hours and 40 minutes later the aircraft touched down safely at Burry Point, Wales. With Stulz were an engineer named Gordon and the first woman to make the air crossing of the Atlantic; she had navigated for most of the way. Her name was Amelia Earhart.

Meanwhile, in April, the first east-west non-stop crossing of the Atlantic by a heavier-than-air machine had also been completed. On 12 April, an all-metal Junkers W33L left Baldonnel, Dublin, carrying a crew of three; two Germans, Baron Gunther von Hünefeld and Captain Hermann Koehl, and an Irishman, Commandant James Fitzmaurice. To guard against icing, the fuselage of the aircraft — which was named *Bremen* — was coated with paraffin. The flight went well until the aircraft encountered the notorious Newfoundland fog banks, when its compasses began to behave erratically. Unable to fix their position, and growing increasingly worried about their fuel state, the crew decided to land close to a lighthouse which was fortuitously sighted through the murk on what was subsequently identified as Greenly Island, Labrador. The landing on the rocky, icy terrain was heavy, and the Junkers' undercarriage collapsed, destroying its chances of flying on to New York; nevertheless, it had made the crossing in 36 hours 30 minutes in the face of some very strong headwinds.

It may truthfully be said that this flight completed the phase of Atlantic air exploration; another, several months later, began the commercial phase. It was made by the new German airship *Graf Zeppelin,* descendent of the Zeppelins which might well have inaugurated commercial transatlantic flying nearly a decade earlier, had politics not intervened.

Herman Köhl, former head of Lufthansa night flying training (right), together with Commandant Fitzmaurice of the Irish Air Force (centre) and Baron von Hünefeld (left) who crossed the Atlantic non-stop from East to West in the single-engined Junkers W.33 'Bremen' on 12/13 April, 1928.

After a series of successful test flights, the *Graf Zeppelin* left her base at Friedrichshafen at 7.30 am on 11 October, 1928, carrying thirty-seven crew, twenty passengers, 62,000 letters and 100 specially-franked postcards. Because of bad weather, her commander, Hugo Eckener, had elected to fly the 6,000-mile route via Gibraltar, Madeira and Bermuda, keeping clear of the fogs and icing of the more northerly routes.

Flying via the Saone Valley and Barcelona, the airship reached Gibraltar at dawn the next day and headed out over the Atlantic in almost perfect conditions, a friendly north-easterly breeze pushing her along at a ground speed of nearly 100 mph. At 1.30 pm she reached Madeira and established contact with a radio station in the Azores, which warned her of bad weather ahead. At 6 am the following morning she ran into a bad squall, running through driving rain and severe turbulence that smashed some crockery, badly frightened the passengers and — more seriously — ripped the fabric that covered the under-surface of the port stablizing fin. It was flapping in the slipstream, threatening to jam the elevator, so as soon as the squall was behind them several crew members climbed out onto the framework of the fin to repair the damage.

Further squalls were encountered later in the flight, but the *Graf Zeppelin* negotiated them successfully and, at 10 am on 15 October, she cruised over Chesapeake Bay and headed for Washington, flying low over the city before turning north for New York. Shortly after dark, after a flight that had lasted 111 hours and 43 minutes, she moored safely at Lakehurst to a tremendous reception from a crowd of over 20,000 people.

The return flight to Germany from Lakehurst began at 2 am on 29 October. On this occasion the airship carried 24 passengers and over 100,000 letters and postcards, and Eckener had decided to fly home via the northern route. In the afternoon she ran into savage squalls of rain and hail, followed by a wall of dense fog. Eckener nosed the ship through it after fixing his position, but she was gripped by a strong southerly wind and blown nearly 300 miles to the north of her intended track, as far as Newfoundland. Eckener made the appropriate corrections and stuck to a north-easterly heading for a while to escape the southerly wind as quickly as possible, then, at Latitude 54° North, he turned south-east, heading for the mouth of the English Channel. Later, he altered his course still further south to avoid storms, and at 6 pm the next day the *Graf Zeppelin* made landfall on the French coast at the mouth of the River Loire.

The airship reached her moorings at Friedrichshafen at 7.06 am on 1 November 1928, having made a record-breaking flight of 71 hours and 7 minutes. She had carried a small number of fare-paying passengers in both directions (in fact, most of her passengers had been specially-invited VIPs) and, having proved herself despite one major drawback — her lack of speed — she seemed to have laid the foundation for a regular airship service across the Atlantic, if the money and support could be found for the Zeppelin Company to build bigger and more powerful ships.

In the following year, as part of around-the-world voyage, the *Graf Zeppelin* repeated her transatlantic performance. Leaving Friedrichshafen on 1 August, she made the crossing to Lakehurst — her starting-point for the flight — in 95 hours and 26 minutes. The flight back across the Atlantic, started a week later, was made in 55 hours 22 minutes, the airship arriving at Friedrichshafen on 10 August. Nineteen days later she was back at Lakehurst, having completed her around-the-world odyssey, and on 1 September she crossed the Atlantic for a third time in a month, reaching Friedrichshafen on the 4th after a flight of 67 hours 20 minuters. On this final leg of her long journey she carried 63 passengers and crew, as well as 1,800 pounds of mail and freight.

The airship had shown itself to be quite capable of carrying a worthwhile load of passengers and cargo across the Atlantic, and Eckener exploited its success by embarking on a fund-raising campaign in American business circles with a view to establishing a regular airship service on the transatlantic route. To prove his point still further, he also planned a prestige flight to South America; this eventually took place on 18 May 1930, when the *Graf Zeppelin* flew from Friedrichshafen to Seville and then non-stop to Pernambuco, arriving on the 24th. She began her homeward run four days later, flying back to Germany by way of Lakehurst and the North Atlantic route.

With the exception of one violent rainstorm encountered over the South Atlantic, this flight was completely free of incident and in fact pioneered what was to be a very successful regular service to South America, which began in 1932. In that year the *Graf Zeppelin* made nine flights across the South Atlantic, three of them to Rio de Janeiro, where a big airship shed was eventually built by the

The rigid airship R.101, the craft that killed Britain's hopes of introducing airships on the Empire routes when it crashed at Beauvais in October 1930.

firm of German engineers and made ready for use in 1935. In the meantime, the *Graf Zeppelin* made nine more flights to South America in 1933, followed by twelve in 1934 and sixteen in 1935. The number of passengers carried on this route increased steadily; in 1933 it was 300, in 1934 400, and the following year 720, as well as 31,000 pounds of freight and mail. By the end of 1935, the Zeppelin Company was looking forward to the future with confidence, for the *Graf Zeppelin* was soon to be joined on the transatlantic routes by a faster and more powerful sister ship: the *Hindenburg*.

Besides, Germany's only potential competitor on the transatlantic airship routes, Great Britain, had been wiped out of the running under tragic circumstances several years earlier. In the mid-1920s, the British Government had authorized the construction of two airships to investigate commercial possibilities over long-distance routes, mainly to India. (Pre-occupation with the Empire routes to the Far East, in fact, was to lose a lot of ground for the British in subsequent transatlantic exploitation). The airships, designated R.100 and R.101, were to be built respectively by the Airship Guarantee Company, a subsidiary of Vickers, and the Air Ministry airship establishment at Cardington, and airship bases were also to be set up in Egypt, India and Canada.

The R.101 was the first to fly, on 14 October 1929, and subsequent test flights revealed numerous technical snags and design faults. The R.100, which flew for the first time in November, soon emerged as the better of the two ships, with good all-weather operational stability and a maximum speed during trials of 81 mph. By July 1930 she had completed seven test flights, most of them successful, and had logged 150 hours' flight time. She was now ready to undertake the first of the 'Empire' proving flights, and since the R.101 was scheduled to make a flight to India — once the more serious snags had been ironed out — it was decided that the R.100 should follow her illustrious predecessor, the R.34, by making an east-west trip across the Atlantic.

At 2.50 am on 29 July, 1930, the R.100 left her mooring mast at Cardington and set course for her destination, Montreal. Her commander was Captain R. S. Booth, with Captain G. F. Meager as his First Officer and Squadron Leader E. L. Johnston as navigator. Also on board were Sir Dennis

Burney, Nevil Shute Norway, Lieutenant Commander Prentice, Flight Lieutenant Wann, RAF, and Major G. H. Scott, who had commanded the R.34 on her historic flight and who was now the officer in charge of flying operations at Cardington.

The airship made an uneventful flight across the Atlantic, although she ran into a severe storm near Quebec and lost a substantial amount of fabric from her fins. The trouble was patched up within two hours and the R.100 cruised on to her destination, mooring at St Hubert Airfield, Montreal, at daybreak on 1 August after a flight of 78 hours 51 minutes. With 42 crew and 13 passengers on board, she had covered a distance of 3,300 miles at an average speed of 42 mph. She stayed at Montreal for a fortnight before taking off on the west-east transatlantic flight on 13 August. With the prevailing winds behind her she made good time, reaching Cardington at 10 am GMT on 16 August after a flight of 56 hours 30 minutes. Afterwards, she was taken into her shed and preparations were made to give her a thorough overhaul in readiness for more long-range flights.

But the R.100 was destined never to fly again. Less than two months later, on 4 October 1930, the Ministry ship, R.101, set out for India. Among those on board were Lord Thomson, the Air Minister, Sir Sefton Brancker, the Director of Civil Aviation, and Major Scott. In the early hours of the following morning, with the passengers and most of the crew in bed, she mushed into a hillside near Beauvais, France, and almost instantly became a blazing inferno from stem to stern as five and a half million cubic feet of hydrogen exploded. Of the 54 people on board there were only six survivors, all of whom had miraculous escapes.

In an attempt to shorten mail delivery time across the Atlantic, a Heinkel He 12 was catapult-launched from the luxury liner 'Bremen' and flew to New York on 22 July, 1929.

The older He 12s and He 58s were replaced on the North Atlantic mail route by Junkers Ju46s in 1932, these aircraft being launched from the liners 'Bremen' and 'Europa' at a point in the ocean up to 750 miles from their destination.

The tragedy — one of the most unnecessary in the history of aviation, for there had been plenty of warnings that the R.101 was not ready to undertake the flight — marked the end of rigid airship development in the United Kingdom. The R.100 was grounded and was eventually sold as scrap for £450; a good and promising airship sacrificed because of the disaster that overwhelmed a bad one.

This left the *Graf Zeppelin* as the only vehicle capable of making an Atlantic air crossing in one hop in comparative safety. As far as heavier-than-air machines were concerned, the best that could be hoped for in 1930 was some sort of compromise of the kind the French had investigated in April 1928, when a Lioré-et-Olivier H198 seaplane had been catapulted from a ramp fitted to the stern of the liner *Ile de France* and then flown 430 miles to New York with a load of mail, saving twenty-four hours on the normal sea time. The Germans carried out similar experiments a year later; on 22 July 1929, Heinkel He 12 D-1717, piloted by von Studnitz, was catapulted from the liner *Bremen* 250 miles from New York, and on 1 August it was launched from the same vessel at a similar distance from the French coast to complete the return mail flight to Germany. This technique was later developed and used successfully on the South Atlantic mail run, as we shall see — but it did not solve the problem of carrying passengers across the ocean.

Nevertheless, although the airlines lacked the tools to make commercial transatlantic flying a reality in 1930, some dialogues were already taking place between airline managers which were to

The twelve-engined Dornier Do X, built in 1929, was the biggest aircraft in the world in its day. Planned for transatlantic service, it made demonstration flights in North and South America, but the design was too unwieldy and it never entered service.

have a far-reaching effect on future operations. Foremost among the negotiators were George Woods Humphery, General Manager of Imperial Airways, and Juan Trippe, founder of Pan American Airways, who in 1929 had begun to explore the possibilities of setting up a joint company to operate between New York and Bermuda. Although progress was slow because of the failure of Britain and Bermuda to agree on the building of an airfield on the island, the two men exchanged much valuable information — short of company secrets — which was to be of later benefit to both airlines.

One of the schemes they discussed was the setting up of a jointly-operated air mail service across the Atlantic, the idea being that Pan American would fly the mail to Bermuda, where it would be picked up by Imperial Airways and flown to London via the Azores. This scheme, however received a setback before the end of 1930, when the USA Post Office suddenly announced that bidders for the mail service must be citizens of the United States. This raised considerable fears among European governments that the Americans were attempting to exlude everyone else from the transatlantic field, and led to considerable manoeuvring by the nations who were interested in a stake.

Among these, the leaders were Great Britain, France and the United States, who controlled the Atlantic's facilities between them. The Americans controlled much of the transatlantic mail traffic — although not as much as they claimed at the time — while the British controlled the vital staging points of Newfoundland and Bermuda. The French had rights to landing facilities in the Azores, which they had acquired from Portugal; the Germans did not, hence their eventual dependence on airships and steamer/aircraft combinations, and Italy was nowhere in the running, even though in 1931 General Balbo of the Italian Air Force convened a Conference of Trans-Atlantic Fliers in Rome, which was seen by some rivals as a desperate Italian measure designed to give them some sort of standing in the business.

In 1930, then, it looked as though the Atlantic air routes would shortly be 'sewn up' by a tripartite agreement between Britain, France and the United States, with Canada and Ireland — both of them commanding excellent territorial positions on either side of the Atlantic — to come in at a later date. The Germans objected to being left out, and were told politely that the others had been thrown together by circumstances, and that nothing could be done about it. Smarting, the Germans therefore decided to concentrate on building up their mail services on the South Atlantic route, where their only real competitor was the French Compagnie Aéropostale. But while the Germans were discussing ways and means, the French, as though forewarned of their plans, pulled off a coup; on 11 May 1930, Aéropostale flew a cargo of mail to St. Louis-du-Senegal, where it was picked up the next day by a Latécoère 28 seaplane crewed by Jean Mermoz, Dabry and Gimié, who flew non-stop across the South Atlantic to land at Pernambuco at 8.10 am on the 13th after a flight time of 21 hours 10 minutes. From there, the mail was taken on to Buenos Aires and Chile. It was the first time that mail had been flown over the entire route; previously, it had been flown to Dakar and then taken on to Pernambuco by fast ship. Five years earlier, French pilots had inaugurated the Paris-Dakar air mail service, and the man who had founded Aéropostale, Pierre Latécoère, had always looked upon this as just a first step towards a full air service to South America (see Chapter Five). Now his dream had become reality.

Meanwhile, German aircraft designers were putting forward proposals for new types of aircraft for service on the South Atlantic route. At the close of the 1920s constructors such as Dornier,

Dornier Wal D-2069 being loaded on to the ramp of the support ship 'Westfalen' in readiness for a Lufthansa flight to Natal, 6 June 1933.

Junkers and Rumpler were all working on multi-engined flying boat designs, but only Dornier produced one which was aimed at carrying passengers over long distances. This was the Dornier Do X, a twelve-engined monster which, when it made its first flight on 25 July 1929, was by far the largest aircraft in the world, with a wingspan of 157 feet 5 inches and a length of 131 feet 4 inches. In October 1929 it made a one-hour flight with 169 people on board (including nine stowaways — probably a record!) and its standard passenger accommodation was 62-72.

On 2 November 1930, the Do X left Friedrichshafen for a world-wide demonstration tour that took it via Amsterdam, Calshot, Bordeaux, Lisbon, the Canary Islands, Boloma, the Cape Verde Islands, Fernando de Noronha, Natal, Rio de Janeiro. Antigua, Miami and New York, where it arrived on 27 August 1931. The design, however, was too unwieldy, and the huge machine ended its days in the Aircraft Museum in Berlin, where it was destroyed by Allied bombs a few years later.

However, other Dornier flying-boat designs were to become the workhorses of Lufthansa on the South Atlantic run, and elsewhere. Foremost among them was the Dornier Wal, a design that had proved itself time and again both on exploratory flights and regular services; Lufthansa had used these aircraft to fly over the Baltic to Scandinavia without mishap since the airline's foundation in 1926.

A Lufthansa Dornier Wal taxi-ing on to the drag-sail towed behind the 'Westfalen' prior to being winched on board.

Otto Bertram, the head of Lufthansa's Regional Directorate (Sea), summed up the airline's thinking when he wrote: "We must get our aircraft into the thick of the commercial battle, and that means out over the ocean." By the beginning of 1930, Lufthansa pilot training had already been geared to maritime air operations for some time, and an airmail service across the South Atlantic started that year, although it was sporadic and depended on an ocean rendezvous between Dornier Wal flying-boats and mail packets. In fact, the service provided by the *Gaf Zeppelin* was far more reliable.

The situation did not improve until the summer of 1932, when Lufthansa chartered the steamer *Westfalen* from the Norddeutscher Lloyd shipping line for conversion as a floating base for the transatlantic mail service. The conversion, which was undertaken by a shipyard on the River Weser, was a slow process, the 5,400-ton ship being fitted with a heavy stern crane for hoisting flying-boats aboard, while a catapult, designed and built by Heinkel, occupied the whole of the forward deck area between funnel and bow. Heinkel already had some experience of catapult design, having developed catapults for the German luxury liners *Europa* and *Bremen* for the launching of single-engined mail aircraft off the coasts of North America and Europe, but the 138-foot device fitted to the *Westfalen* was required to launch twin-engined machines of up to 14 tons and had to be four times more powerful than the earlier models. The recovery crane, too, which weighed fifteen tons, incorporated some untried design features; it was to be used in conjunction with a so-called dragsail, a

When Lufthansa began its regular airmail service between Germany and South America on 3 February, 1934, the world's first trans-ocean airline route was opened. From Germany, a Heinkel He 70 flew to Seville or Larache, North Africa, where a Junkers Ju 52 took over (photo) and transported the mail to a waiting Dornier Wal seaplane in Bathurst, West Africa. It carried the mail, with one stop-over at the base-ship, to Natal, Brazil, from where an aircraft of "Syndicato Condor Ltda" took it to Rio de Janeiro.

length of strengthened canvas which was trailed in the water behind the ship. The flying-boat taxied forward onto this sail, and when it was in position the ship increased speed, causing the sail and flying-boat to ride over the surface of the water in a fairly stable condition. The flying-boat could then safely be hoisted aboard, even if the swell was considerable.

After trials in Germany, the *Westfalen* sailed for a point in the Atlantic some 940 miles west of Bathurst, in the Gambia. On 6 June 1933, a Dornier Wal piloted by Captain Blankenburg took off from the Gambia Estuary, located the ship with its radio direction finder, landed alongside and was hoisted aboard. After refuelling, the Wal was catapulted off the ship at 93 mph and the pilot set course for Natal, where it landed the following day. The *Westfalen* returned to Germany, where she was fitted with a maintenance workshop and spare parts store, and in October 1933 she put to sea

A Dornier Wal on the catapult of the 'Westfalen' just before launch in the South Atlantic.

again for a second operational trial. On this occasion, a Dornier Wal took off from Bathurst, landed by the ship and her mail was transferred to a second Wal, which was already in position on the catapult waiting to take off for Brazil. The time for the transatlantic crossing was 14 hours and 5 minutes.

The first scheduled Lufthansa mail flight to South America took place on February 3, 1934, when a Heinkel He 70 took off from Berlin/Tempelhof carrying 107 pounds of mail and flew to Seville via Stuttgart and Marseille. The mail was then transferred to a Junkers Ju52, which flew on to Bathurst with one stop at Las Palmas. The *Westfalen*, with a Dornier Wal named *Taifun* in position on the catapult, picked up the mail and sailed for a point in the Atlantic, launching the aircraft thirty-six hours later. The Wal arrived in Natal at 5.05 pm and the mail was transferred to a Junkers W34 floatplane, which flew on to Rio Janeiro and a connecting flight to Buenos Aires.

Lufthansa made forty-seven scheduled flights to and from South America in 1934. The service was not without its problems; it demanded the utmost from both aircraft and crews, who often came down with malaria and yellow fever. There were inevitable delays in replenishing stocks of supplies and spares at both ends of the line, as well as frequent trouble with the radio D/F equipment. Before the landing strip at Bathurst was strengthened with steel mats, it was impossible for Ju52s to land there during the rainy season, and flying-boats had to operate the Las Palmas-Bathurst sector. Bathurst in the mid-1930s was summed up admirably by one Lufthansa captain, who wrote: "Groundnut bushes galore, but no hotel. We had to try and find accommodation in a factory."

Nevertheless, despite all the obstacles the mail got through. In that first year, the Lufthansa crews carried 8,600 pounds from east to west, and 6,000 pounds in the opposite direction.

Before the end of the year, Lufthansa had introduced an updated version of the Wal, the Do R Super Wal, which weighed ten tons and was powered by two 650 hp Rolls-Royce *Condor* engines, on

Dornier Wal D-2069 at the moment of launch from the 'Westfalen'.

the South Atlantic mail route, and a second catapult ship, the *Schwabenland,* was also brought into service. On 30 March 1935 a night service began, reducing the flying time between Germany and Rio to three days, and in July the German airline and Air France joined forces to a limited extent with the introduction of a twice-weekly pooled airmail service. A third support ship, the *Ostmark,* was also ordered.

The faithful Wals remained in service on the South Atlantic mail route until 1936, when they were replaced by five Dornier Do 18E aircraft. Powered by two tandem-mounted Junkers Jumo 205C diesel engines, these were D-AHIS *Monsun,* D-ANNE *Zyklon,* D-ABYM *Aeolus,* D-AROZ *Pampero* and D-ARUN *Zephir.* The Do 18s continued in service — with the exception of D-AROZ, which was lost in October 1938 — on the Africa-Brazil route until the outbreak of the Second World War, by which time they had been joined in service by the still more advanced Dornier Do 26. Two of these machines — D-AGNT *Seeadler* and D-AWDS *Seefalke* were used on the South Atlantic route during 1938-9, and on one occasion the latter aircraft flew from Warnemunde to Rio, a distance of 6,680 miles, in thirty-six hours carrying 1,300 pounds of medical supplies for earthquake victims in Chile.

Meanwhile, in the early 1930s, Lufthansa's French competitor, Aéropostale, had been having its problems. Despite the success of the non-stop flight across the South Atlantic by Jean Mermoz and his crew in 1930, two years later Aéropostale's airmail service still went only as far as Dakar, the mail being carried across the Atlantic by fast packet. Yet in 1928, the French Air Ministry had issued a specification for an aircraft capable of undertaking a non-stop service between Dakar and Natal, this specification emphasizing that such an aircraft must have four engines that could be serviced in flight, that it must be able to fly with one engine out of action, that it should be capable of carrying 2,200 pounds of mail as well as a crew of four over a range of 1,680 miles, and that finally it must be capable of landing and taking off on the water, even with a heavy sea running.

Three designs were submitted, by Latécoère, Bleriot and Farman, the Latécoère machine being the first to fly. Designated Laté 300 and registered F-AKCU, the prototype flew for the first time in December 1931, but on its first test flight it stalled and crashed in the Etang de Berre, near Marseille. It was salvaged in 1932, repaired, and flew again on 7 October that year, after which it was given the name *Croix du Sud* (Southern Cross) and re-registered as F-AKGF. Flight testing continued through most of 1933, and the programme by no means went smoothly; the aircraft repeatedly refused to take off with anything like an adequate payload. After weeks of head-scratching, the French engineers suddenly discovered the reason; the flying-boat's hull under the cabin floor was full of water, which had leaked in when some rivets had become corroded by the salt water of the Etang de Berre. The damage was repaired, steps were taken to see that it did not occur again, and this time the aircraft flew perfectly.

On 31 December, 1933, the aircraft took off from the Etang de Berre, piloted by Capitaine de Corvette Bonnot, and flew non-stop to St. Louis-du-Senegal — a distance of 2,286 miles — in 23 hours 6 minutes. Then, on 3 January 1934, it made the flight that was so eagerly awaited by Aéropostale — the crossing of the South Atlantic. This was successfully carried out in a flight time of 18 hours 50 minutes, the majority of the flight (13 hours 5 minutes) being made in darkness. Altogether, the flight from Berre to Natal had been made in 3 days 19 hours and 14 minutes, and that included a stopover of 51 hours 30 minutes at St. Louis. There were few who could dispute that the aircraft was worth every franc of the million that had been allocated to its constructor to cover the first of its five proving flights.

Meanwhile, in 1933, Aéropostale had got into severe financial difficulties; pleas for government aid fell on deaf ears, mainly because the French Government was about to merge all the French air transport companies under the single national banner of a new enterprise, Air France, and so the air mail organization founded on a shoestring by Pierre Latécoère fifteen years earlier, and subsequently carried through with such skill and determination by a valiant band of pioneer pilots, ended its days in sad liquidation. For French civil aviation, this had one immediate and unfortunate consequence: all the international agreements set up by Aéropostale over the years had now to be re-negotiated by Air France, creating a hiatus which, predictably, the astute operators of Lufthansa quickly jumped in to fill.

Air France's hopes of regaining some advantage on the South Atlantic route were therefore pinned on the new generation of big flying-boats, of which the Laté 300 *Croix du Sud* was the first. This machine made the Atlantic crossing six more times in 1934, and underwent some modifications that included increases in the wing dihedral and vertical tail area. These were incorporated in a developed version, the Laté 301, three examples of which were ordered by Air France. The first of these aircraft flew on 23 August 1935; this was F-AOIK *Orion*, the other two being F-AOIL *Eridan* and F-AOIM *Nadir*. Before entering service with Air France early in 1936, their names were changed to *Ville de Buenos Aires, Ville de Rio de Janeiro* and *Ville de Santiago du Chile.*

At the beginning of 1936, the Air France service across the South Atlantic was undertaken by four aircraft: the *Croix du Sud,* a Farman F.220 (F-ANLG *Centaure*), a Bleriot 5190 (F-ANLE *Santos Dumont*) and the Laté 301 prototype, F-AOIK. The Farman 220, in fact, had started life as the prototype of a four-engined bomber for the French Air Force before being handed over to Air France for use on the mail service. Unfortunately, the career of F-AOIK *Ville de Buenos Aires* was destined to be tragically short. On 10 February, 1936, it took off from Natal, bound for Dakar, and was never seen again, although the Blériot *Santos Dumont* followed its route as precisely as possible and ships searched for it for a long time.

Despite this tragic loss, the Air France machines made eighty-six non-stop crossings of the South Atlantic in 1936. Then, just before the end of the year, came a second tragic blow. At 4 am in the morning of 7 December, F-AKGF *Croix du Sud* took off from Dakar to make its twenty-fifth Atlantic crossing. At the controls was Jean Mermoz, the celebrated pilot who had done perhaps more than any other to pioneer long-range mail flights; the other crew members were Pichodou, Ezan, Cruveilher and Lavidalie.

Routine radio messages were received from the aircraft until, at 10.43 am — just after the wireless operator had given its position as 11°8′ North, 22°40′ West — a radio station picked up the broken message "... Cutting starboard rear engine ..." It was the last that was heard from it, and the whole of the aviation world was left to mourn Mermoz and his crew.

The Short-Mayo Composite Aircraft made long-range proving flights in 1938 and was used briefly to carry Imperial Airways mail in December of that year.

In 1937, the Air France mail line between Africa and South America came perilously close to foundering. In the early parts of the year the two surviving Laté 301s were awaiting new engines, and the only aircraft available to carry on the service were a couple of elderly Farmans *(Centaure* and a sister aircraft, *Ville de Mendoza),* as well as the Blériot *Santos Dumont.* F-AOLI returned to service in June 1937, but was withdrawn in February 1938. F-AOMI *Ville de Santiago* continued in service for a further month, when it was taken on to the inventory of Aéronavale, the French Naval Air Service and used for patrol duties with Escadrille E.4 at Biscarosse. It was still there in May 1940, when it was captured by the Germans. Its eventual fate is unknown.

Meanwhile, the race for ascendency in the North Atlantic area had been gathering momentum, and in 1935 there still seemed to be a good chance of an agreement between Imperial Airways and Pan American Airways reaching fruition. Two years earlier, in the summer of 1933, Charles Lindbergh — who was now Juan Trippe's Technical Adviser in Pan American — had carried out an extensive aerial survey of both the northern and southern Atlantic routes, not only to consolidate American interests but also to investigate the possibility of linking an Atlantic route with older routes to Asia, opened up by the Germans in the late 1920s but since abandoned after the rise to power of Adolf Hitler. Lindbergh's northern reconnaissance had taken him to Greenland, Iceland, the Faroes, the Shetlands, then across the Baltic to the Soviet Union, where he stayed for a short time before setting off homeward via the Gulf of Finland and Sweden and the southern Atlantic route, which he flew via Lisbon, the Azores, Punta Delgada on San Miguel Island, the Cape Verde Islands, Bathurst, Natal, Port of Spain, Puerto Rico, Santo Domingo, Miami, Charleston and Long Island. His conclusion at the close of this odyssey, which lasted from 9 July until 19 September, was that regular air services on both northern and southern routes were perfectly feasible.

A Pan American-Imperial Airways Agreement was signed against fierce opposition from the French, Germans and Dutch (and from some American companies as well) on 25 January 1936, but action was very slow to follow, even though both airlines were about to introduce flying-boats that could safely ply the Atlantic routes. The American machine was the Sikorsky S-42, which was powered by four 750 hp Pratt and Whitney Hornet radial engines, had a span of 118 feet, a maximum speed of 188 mph and a range of 1,200 miles. Ten of these machines had been ordered by Pan American and they began to enter service from April 1935, operating first on the San Francisco-Hawaii and later on the New York-Bermuda, Miami-South America and Manila-Hong Kong routes. However, the standard S-42's range was not sufficient for transatlantic flying, so three aircraft were fitted with extra fuel tanks and given the designation S-42B and preparations made to undertake a series of long-range proving flights. Another and more impressive flying-boat design was also on the horizon; this was the Boeing 314, powered by four 1,500 hp Wright Double Cyclone engines. It was planned to carry a crew of ten and up to forty passengers over a range of 3,600 miles at a cruising speed of 188 mph, and six were ordered by Pan American in July 1936.

Imperial Airways' aspirations centred on the Short 'C' Class flying-boat, designed in 1935 to meet the requirements of the Empire Air Mail Scheme. With Britain now lagging behind the United States in long-range flying-boat development there was no time to be wasted, so Imperial Airways took a gamble and ordered twenty-eight aircraft straight off the drawing board at a total cost of £1¾ million; as things turned out, the gamble was to be justified.

The 'C' Class boats had a two-deck hull, the upper deck designed to house 3,000 pounds of mail and the lower to accommodate 24 daytime passengers or 19 'sleepers'. The version intended for transatlantic operation was the S.30, nine of which were eventually built; it was powered by four 890 hp Bristol Perseus XIIC engines, giving it a maximum speed of 200 mph.

The other 'C' Class variant, the S.23, although highly successful on the England-Australia mail service (see Chapter Four), did not have sufficient range for transatlantic operations, but in December 1936 one example of the type, G-ADUU *Cavalier,* was fitted with extra fuel tankage and then crated and shipped to Bermuda, where, in May 1937, it began proving flights to New York alongside Pan American's S-42 *Bermuda Clipper.* Scheduled services began on 16 June, and by the end of November 405 passengers had been carried over the six-hour journey at a single fare of £20. *Cavalier* remained in service on the Bermuda-New York route until 21 January 1939, when severe engine icing forced it down in a heavy sea; the impact tore a hole in the hull and the aircraft sank in minutes, ten survivors later being picked up by a tanker.

Another S-23, G-ADHM *Caledonia,* was used to survey the first leg of the proposed transatlantic

In autumn, 1937, Lufthansa made several flights between the Azores and New York with this four-engined Blohm & Voss Ha 139 floatplane. The photo shows the aircraft on the catapult of the base-ship "Schwabenland".

route, flying from Hythe to the Azores via Lisbon on 5 July 1937. The next day she was joined on the same route by G-ADUV *Cambria* and these two aircraft made several survey flights during August and September. The first of these flights, on 5 July, coincided with the first transatlantic flight by a Pan American Sikorsky S.42B, NC16736 *Clipper III*, piloted by Captain Gray, which flew from Botwood in Newfoundland to Foynes in Ireland. This aircraft went on to make three out-and-back survey flights during the summer of 1937, and the Foynes-Botwood route was also surveyed by *Cambria* and *Caledonia* in August.

The first of the Short *Empire Boats* designed for the Bermuda run, G-AFCT *Champion,* flew for the first time on 28 September 1938 and was followed by four more, G-AFCU *Cabot,* G-AFCV *Caribou,* G-AFCW *Connemara* and G-AFCX *Clyde.* These aircraft were equipped with flight refuelling gear — trials having taken place earlier in the year, with *Cambria* being successfully refuelled in flight by an Armstrong Whitworth A.W.23 — and in 1939 three Handley Page Harrow bombers were equipped as tankers, two being stationed at Hattie's Camp (later Gander) in Newfoundland and the third in Ireland at Rineanna, which was later to become Shannon Airport. The Short S.30s *Cabot* and *Caribou* both underwent refuelling trials in conjunction with these aircraft in May and July, as a preliminary to starting a scheduled transatlantic service from Southampton to New York via Foynes, Botwood and Montreal.

Meanwhile, the preceding months had witnessed considerable technological developments in the transatlantic commercial race. The boldest of these was British: the Short-Mayo Composite Aircraft. This was the brainchild of Major R. H. Mayo, Technical Adviser to Imperial Airways, and was a revolutionary attempt to solve the problem of increasing range and payload without sacrificing performance by mounting one aircraft pick-a-back on top of another, the lower aircraft carrying most of the fuel and providing the power for take-off and climb. Both components were designed and built by Short Brothers under the designations S.20 and S.21, the latter — G-ADHK *Maia* — being similar in design to the Short 'C' Class flying-boat, although with modifications that included a broader hull beam and increased wing and vertical tail areas.

The second component, a much smaller four-engined twin-float seaplane, G-ADHJ *Mercury,* was attached to the larger aircraft by a trapeze-like structure mounted above the latter's wing centre section. The two aircraft were test-flown separately, *Maia* flying on 27 July 1937 and *Mercury* on 5 September, and the two flew as a composite on 20 January 1938. The first commercial flight was made on 21 July that year, *Mercury* separating from *Maia* over Foynes on the Shannon and heading for Montreal with a payload of 600 pounds of newspapers, press photographs and newsreels. The flight took 20 hours 20 minutes, the aircraft covering a distance of 2,930 miles; the pilot was Captain D. C. T. Bennett, who was later to command RAF Bomber Command's Pathfinder Force, and his radio operator (and Air Ministry observer) was A. J. Coster. The pilot of *Maia* was Captain A. S. Wilcockson, one of Imperial Airways' senior officers, who had also commanded the 'C' Class boat *Caledonia* during its first Atlantic flights in July that previous year.

On 6 October 1938, *Maia* launched *Mercury* on a record-breaking non-stop flight to South Africa. With Bennett once again at the controls and Ian Harvey as his radio operator, the aircraft flew a straight-line distance of 5,997.5 miles in just over 42 hours, landing on the Orange River near the Alexander Bay diamond-mine settlement. It flew on to Cape Town after refuelling. Further non-stop flights — to Alexandria from Southampton carrying Christmas mail — were made in December

The long-range Fw200 Kondor, the airliner that would have opened the first non-stop transatlantic mail service by a landplane had it not been for the outbreak of war. The aircraft shown is D-AMHC 'Nordmark'.

Boeing's famous Model 314 'Yankee Clipper', the aircraft that made transatlantic flying a commercial possibility in the late 1930s.

1938, and the success of operations so far encouraged Imperial Airways to plan a regular transatlantic service in the summer of 1939. This however was frustrated by the approach of war and the preoccupation with flight refuelling trials, and the Short-Mayo Composite never flew commercially again. *Maia* was used for a time to carry passengers between Southampton and Foynes and was taken over by the British Overseas Airways Corporation, which replaced the older companies in April 1940; it was destroyed by German bombs in Poole Harbour on the night of 11 May, 1941. *Mercury* was allocated to No.320 (Netherlands) Squadron in June 1940 and used as a trainer until it was withdrawn from service and broken up in August 1941.

The Germans, too, had been making considerable strides in the development of their catapult-launched Atlantic air mail service, although in the lighter-than-air field they had received a fearsome setback with the destruction of the airship *Hindenburg* at Lakehurst on 6 May 1937. The LZ129 *Hindenburg* had first flown just over a year earlier, in March 1936, and after trials had joined the *Graf Zeppelin* on regular services over both North and South Atlantic, carrying over a thousand passengers in ten round trips across the North Atlantic alone during her first ten months of operations. On 6 May 1937, however, she exploded in flames while mooring at Lakehurst, New Jersey, and thirty-five of the ninety-seven people on board were killed. This tragedy sounded the death-knell for another airship which was then under construction, the LZ130 *Graf Zeppelin II;* it had been intended to fill this craft's gas tanks with helium instead of the highly explosive hydrogen, but when German troops marched into Austria in March 1938 the United States placed an embargo on deliveries of the expensive and scarce helium gas to Germany, and although the LZ130 was completed and made a few test flights — using hydrogen — in 1939, she was broken up in 1940 and her aluminium framework used to build aeroplanes.

Later in 1937, however, the Germans greatly increased their capability in the catapult-launched aircraft arena with the introduction of a new type, the Blohm und Voss HA139 floatplane, into Lufthansa service. This large, four-engined, gull-winged machine was delivered in March 1937 and the first two examples, D-AMIE *Nordmeer* and D-AJEY *Nordwind,* carried out a series of successful catapult trials from the support ships *Schwabenland* and *Friesenland* between August and November, flying from Horta in the Azores to New York and back. A third HA139, D-ASTA *Nordstern,* was delivered in 1938, and by June 1939 the three floatplanes had made one hundred Atlantic crossings. This promising mail service was cut short by the war, the three aircraft being impressed into Luftwaffe service for use in the reconnaissance and transport roles.

It was the Germans, too, who achieved perhaps the most significant breakthrough of all on the North Atlantic air routes in the later 1930s. On 10 August, 1938, a new four-engined all-metal landplane, the Focke-Wulf Fw200 Kondor (D-ACON *Brandenburg)* made a non-stop flight from Berlin to New York in 24 hours 36 minutes, with Captains Henke and von Moreau at the controls. The Kondor had been developed to meet a Lufthansa requirement for a 26-passenger long-range airliner, and the flight would undoubtedly have heralded a regular landplane service across the Atlantic had it not been for the onset of war. As it was, the few civil-registered Kondors built before the summer of 1939 were acquired by the Luftwaffe as VIP transports, and the long-range maritime reconnaissance version subsequently developed for the Luftwaffe was to become infamous as the scourge of the Allied Atlantic convoys, guiding U-Boats to their prey.

Meanwhile, in 1938, hopes of achieving a workable bilateral agreement for operation on the North Atlantic route between Pan American and Imperial Airways had been steadily fizzling but, mainly because of pressure on Juan Trippe from Congress and rival American airline operations who did not wish to be excluded from a potentially lucrative service. Some Americans in positions of influence were particularly incensed by the 'gentleman's agreement' between Pan American and Imperial Airways, under which neither airline would start scheduled passenger services across the Atlantic before the other; they saw it as some sort of dastardly British plot to prevent Pan American and other airlines from capturing a slice of the transatlantic passenger traffic from fast luxury liners, especially the *Queen Mary,* which had just entered service.

The plain truth of the matter was that the British were nowhere near equipped to begin a regular transatlantic air passenger service, and would not be until a new class of flying-boat, the Short S.26 'G' Class, came into service. In fact they never did; the three examples produced were impressed by the RAF on the outbreak of war for use as armed VIP transports.

On the other hand, by the end of 1938 Pan American Airways already had a flying-boat that was quite capable of undertaking a safe and efficient transatlantic passenger service: the Boeing Model 314, the prototype of which had flown in June that year. With the entry of this aircraft into service with Pan American, pressure increased on Juan Trippe to start a regular passenger and mail run across the Atlantic, whether Imperial Airways was ready to do the same or not, and the lobby grew even stronger when the first Model 314, *Yankee Clipper,* flew from New York to Marseille via the Azores on 20 May 1939, carrying 1,800 pounds of mail, in a flight time of 26 hours 54 minutes.

The consequences were inevitable. On 17 June, *Yankee Clipper* made the first scheduled passenger-carrying run over the North Atlantic from New York to Southampton via Newfoundland, and on the 28th *Dixie Clipper* carried more passengers over the southern route to Marseille. The first aircraft carried 18 passengers, the second 22.

After that, Pan American's 'Clippers' carried out regular weekly services over the Atlantic and subsequently went on to have distinguished wartime careers, which is another story. Few in number though they were, they won the transatlantic commercial air race for the United States; it was a lead which would never be lost.

Chapter Two
The Pacific and the Islands

The aerial conquest of the Pacific Ocean, unlike that of the Atlantic, got away to a slow start. There was not the same sense of commercial urgency in the Pacific area; nor was there any real element of competition, for only the United States had cause to be interested in opening up air routes to the mid-Pacific islands. British and French island dependencies in the Pacific could eventually be served by using Australia and New Zealand as stepping-stones, but there was no such easy stages for a flight from the mainland USA to, say, Hawaii.

Prior to 1927, the only trans-Pacific flight from the USA to Asia had been made via Alaska, the Aleutian Islands, Kamchatka, the Kuriles and Japan; that had been early in 1924, when the American around-the-world team had made the trip in their Douglas DT-2 biplanes. Not until the advent of improved versions of the Fokker F.VII, the first aircraft with anything like a long-range capability, did long overwater flights become feasible; it should be remembered that the distance from North America to the Pacific's midway point was greater than that from Newfoundland to Ireland.

It was in an aircraft of this type — an F.VII-3m — that two Americans, Lieutenants Maitland (pilot) and Hagenberger (navigator) made the first Pacific crossing from San Francisco to Honolulu. Taking off at 4.09 pm on 28 June, they landed at Honolulu the following day after a flight of 25 hours 49 minutes 30 seconds, during which they covered a distance of 2,430 miles. Apart from radio failure in the early stages, the flight was completely uneventful, the airmen enjoying the advantage of fine weather and a strong tailwind.

The second crew attempting to fly the same route was less fortunate. At 10.10 am on 14 July, Ernie Smith and Emery Bronte took off from Oakland, San Francisco, in a Travel Air named *City of Oakland* and powered by a 200 hp Wright Whirlwind engine. The next day, after flying for 25 hours 36 minutes over a distance of 2,362 miles, the aircraft crash-landed on a beach seventy miles short of Honolulu and was completely wrecked, although the two men escaped unhurt.

Maitland and Hagenberger had already won a prize of 25,000 dollars for their earlier exploit, but now an American millionaire named John Dole went one better by offering a total of 35,000 dollars, to be divided between the first two crews who made the San Francisco-Honolulu flight in a properly organized contest. It was a laudable enough enterprise, but it turned out to be a disaster. Out of ten crews who applied to take part, three killed themselves during test flights, one was eliminated because the judges decided their aircraft could not carry enough fuel, and two aborted because of mechanical trouble. Of the four that did take part, two were lost at sea; these were J. Frost and G. Scott in a Lockheed Vega named *Golden Eagle,* and Pedlar, Knorpe and Miss Doran flying a Buhl Airsedan named after the lady. This was not the end of the tragedy; on 20 August another crew, Captain Erwin and his navigator, Eichwalt — who had not been able to take part in the race — took off in their Swallow *Spirit of Dallas* to look for the missing crews and never came back. The prize of 25,000 dollars went to Goebel and Davis in their Travel Air *Woolaroc,* which arrived in Honolulu after a flight of 26 hours 17 minutes 33 seconds; the runners-up with 10,000 dollars were pilot Martin Jensen and navigator Schulter in a Breese named *Aloha,* which made the journey in 28 hours 16 minutes.

The first complete crossing of the Pacific, made in the following year, was a joint Australian-American venture. The aircraft was a Fokker F.VIIB-3m named *Southern Cross;* the pilot and commander was Charles Kingsford Smith, his second pilot was C. T. P. Ulm, his wireless operator James Warner — both Australians — and his supremely skilled navigator was an American, Harry Lyon.

The *Southern Cross,* in fact, was a hybrid, built from the components of two Fokker monoplanes which had been used on various expeditions conducted by the Arctic explorer Sir Hubert Wilkins. Both machines had been wrecked, but Wilkins had salvaged the bits and pieces and had them shipped to the Boeing factory at Seattle, where they were made into one aircraft. After further service in the

A Lockheed Vega monoplane, the type in which Wiley Post and Harold Gatty made an around-the-world flight in less than nine days in 1931.

Arctic, the machine was sold to Kingsford Smith — minus engines — for £3,000 in 1927. Three 225 hp Wright J-5C Whirlwind engines were bought from the US Navy, and fuel tankage was increased to 1,080 gallons, giving a still-air range of 3,679 milies at a cruising speed of 100 mph.

After a long and careful preparation — involving an unsuccessful attempt on the world endurance record of 52 hours 22 minutes on 17 January 1928 (during which *Southern Cross* was airborne over San Francisco for 50 hours and 4 minutes, with Kingsford Smith and Lieutenant G. R. Pond at the controls) — the former felt confident that he could achieve a flight from California to Brisbane via Honolulu and Suva, Fiji, given the right weather conditions. The most difficult part of the crossing would be the leg from Honolulu to Fiji — a distance of 3,183 miles, which would take the aircraft an estimated $34\frac{1}{2}$ hours.

Southern Cross took off from Oakland in fine weather conditions on 31 May, 1928, heading for Honolulu. The Fokker had a good range of navigational aids, and in case of ditching the fuselage fuel tank could be quickly emptied to provide buoyancy. Two radio sets — one short-wave, one long-wave — were carried, and if the aircraft had to come down in the sea a 500-foot aerial could be raised by means of a small gas-filled balloon so that the wireless operator could continue to send out distress calls while the machine floated.

Fortunately, none of these refinements was to prove necessary. On the first leg of the flight, Harry Lyon was able to navigate with the help of the San Francisco radio beacon for 400 miles or so, after which he relied on his earth inductor and magnetic compasses and on 'fixes' obtained from ships. The *Southern Cross* arrived at Honolulu without incident on 1 June, after a flight lasting 27 hours and 27 minutes.

Taking off from Honolulu the next day presented a problem. With a full load of fuel the *Southern Cross* weighed 15,807 pounds, and take-off from Honolulu's strip would be dangerously marginal. Kingsford Smith therefore decided to fly to Kaoui Island, 110 miles from Honolulu, where there was a rudimentary airstrip 2,500 feet long, and he made a skilful take-off from there on 2 June, heading out on the second leg of the flight to Fiji.

This was the most difficult part of the flight, for the aircraft encountered violent rainstorms as it crossed the Equator, and before reaching Fiji it ran into a dense cloud layer that forced the pilot to climb to 7,500 feet. It was a supreme tribute to Harry Lyon's navigation that they reached their destination at Suva on 4 June after covering a distance of 3,183 miles in 34 hours 33 minutes; *Southern Cross* had achieved by far the longest over-water crossing up to that time, and it would be three years before anyone bettered its record.

The aircraft left Suva on 8 June, taking off from an airstrip at Nasalai. Because of violent electrical storms en route and also a strong headwind the aircraft made slow progress, taking 21 hours 35 minutes to cover the 1,800-mile leg, and matters were further complicated by the failure of Lyon's earth inductor compass and the wildly erratic behaviour of his two magnetic compasses during much of the flight; nevertheless, landfall was made at Eagle Farm, Brisbane, some ninety miles off the intended track, the *Southern Cross* having covered a total distance of 7,389 miles in an elapsed time of 83 hours 38 minutes.

Following this record-breaking voyage, Kingsford Smith (with different crews) took *Southern Cross* — now re-registered G-AUSU and later VH-USU — on more pioneering flights, beginning with a 2,090-mile trip from Melbourne to Perth on 8 August 1928. This was the preliminary to the first crossing of the Tasman sea from Australia to New Zealand, which was made from Richmond to Christchurch on 10-11 September in 14 hours 21 minutes. The return flight, from Blenheim to Richmond, took 22 hours 51 minutes. Kingsford Smith's crew on this round trip consisted of Ulm as second pilot, H. A. Litchfield as navigator and T. H. McWilliam as wireless operator.

Juan Trippe (right), President of Pan American Airways, and the famous aviator who had become his technical adviser – Charles Lindbergh.

The same crew left Richmond on the first stage of a flight to England on 31 March 1929, heading initially for Wyndham in Western Australia, but after a flight of 28 hours 30 minutes Kingsford Smith — unable to find his desination in bad visibility — had to make a forced landing on a mud flat of the Glenelg River when his fuel ran out. It was twelve days before the stranded aircraft was found and refuelled for the last 300-mile hop to Wyndham, from which airfield it continued its flight on 25 June, eventually reaching Croydon on 10 July after an elapsed time of 12 days 18 hours — a new record. The object of the flight to England was to negotiate the purchase of five Avro Ten aircraft (later increased to seven) for Australian National Airways, recently founded by Kingsford Smith and Ulm; while these talks were in progress *Southern Cross* went to Schiphol for a complete overhaul at the Fokker Company's factory in readiness for stage two of its around-the-world flight, which was accomplished in 1930. The aircraft was then shipped from Oakland to Australia and was used for a time on mail services for Australian National Airways, after which it made a 'joy-riding' tour of Australia and New Zealand, carrying some 70,000 passengers over the next three years.

The Lockheed Sirius monoplane, the aircraft used by Lindbergh to make his Pacific reconnaissance on behalf of Pan American in 1933.

Flying back to Australia in March 1935, it resumed mail services across the Tasman Sea, and during one of these flights on 15 May that year it almost came to grief when a propeller shattered 650 miles out from the coast. With great courage, the co-pilot, Captain P. G. (later Sir Gordon) Taylor collected oil from the dead engine and fed it to the reservoir of the ailing port motor, enabling *Southern Cross* to limp home. Afterwards, the aircraft was donated to the Australian nation, and is today preserved at Eagle Farm Airport, the scene of its landfall at the close of the trans-Pacific flight.

Meanwhile, in 1931, Pan American Airways had initiated a survey of the Pacific Ocean's northern perimeter, the object being to establish a link with China by way of Alaska, Siberia and the Kurile Islands. The survey flight, which began on 27 July from College Point, Long Island, was undertaken by Charles Lindbergh and his wife Anne — who had received training as a wireless operator — flying a Lockheed Sirius, a single-engined, low-winged twin-float monoplane. Their voyage — often a hair-raising enterprise — took them north to Baker Lake, then west to Alkavik and Point Barrow in Alaska. Then they turned south to Nome, jumping the Bering Sea to Karaginski and Petropavlovsk, Kamchatka, afterwards following the line of the Kurile Islands to Japan. Then it was westwards again, across the Yellow Sea from Osaka to the Yangtze River. Here, they volunteered to airlift doctors and medical supplies to communities isolated by severe floods — an operation during which they were almost overwhelmed by starving and desperate people who besieged their aircraft in search of food or a flight to safety. Escaping by a hair's-breadth, the Sirius threatened by the turbulent river as well as by the mob, they managed to take off and flew towards the estuary, where they made contact with the British aircraft carrier *Hermes.* They landed alongside and an attempt was made to winch the aircraft on board by derrick, but the machine overturned and the Lindberghs were forced to swim for their lives. They were hauled on to the ship, as was the ruined Sirius. It was an inglorious conclusion to a very gallant expedition, and in the end it was all for nothing, for in due course (for reasons made clear in Chapter Eight) the idea of pioneering a Great Circle route to Peking along the northern fringe of the Pacific and through Siberia was abandoned.

In 1931, however, this decision was still in the future, and Pan American was busily ordering new types of aircraft capable of carrying passengers and freight across the northern route to China, as well as the services close to home in the Caribbean. The first of a new generation of flying-boats, the

Sikorsky S.40, was already in operation in the Caribbean, and two even larger machines were on the way: the Sikorsky S.42 and the Martin M.130, both evolved to the same specification. But it was the Martin design that possessed the long-range overwater capability required by the airline, having a range of 3,200 miles. It was powered by four 830 hp Pratt and Whitney Twin Wasp radials, had a wing span of 130 feet and a cruising speed of 163 mph, and was of all-metal construction. Three were on order and they would be in service by 1936, about two years after the S.42.

By the beginning of 1934 it was clear that neither the northern Great Circle route nor the Atlantic-Siberia route to China was feasible, and this left only one other possible route; straight across the middle of the Pacific, using the widely-spaced islands as stepping-stones. The problem was that the water jump from San Francisco to Hawaii was the longest in the world, and even if Pan American's new aircraft had sufficient range to make it safely they would then have to fly via Wake Island, a tiny speck in the Pacific, which would require very precise navigation indeed — and so far, no landing facilities existed there. Wake was the real key, for if it was usable the rest of the trans-Pacific flight via Guam and the Philippines would be relatively easy, for there were US Naval bases at both these points. Also, between Wake and Guam the flying-boats could conceivably use Midway Island, for it possessed a big lagoon sheltered by coral reefs from the Pacific swell.

A preliminary survey of Wake and Midway Islands was carried out by a team of Pan American engineers in 1934, and in January the following year the airline chartered a freighter, the *North Haven* for use as a depot ship by the teams that would sail out to set up bases at the staging posts. The ship was loaded with every conceivable item, from tractors and generators to books, playing cards, and

The Sikorsky S-42, with which Pan American pioneered its trans-Pacific routes ....

.... and the Martin M-130, which helped them to become a commercial success.

ice-making machines. Meanwhile, in New York, Pan American's President, Juan Trippe sought and obtained approval for Wake Island to be brought under the control of the US Navy, with whom he had good relations, and he also engineered contracts for the development of Wake, Midway and Guam as air bases. This was a very shrewd move, for other aviation companies were showing an interest in the trans-Pacific route too; these were Inter-Island, whose small fleet of aircraft plied between the islands of the Hawaiian Group, and South Seas Commercial, a new venture which presented a still bigger threat as a competitor, for it was backed by Donald Douglas — manufacturer of Douglas Aircraft —in collaboration with an Australian navigator named Harold Gatty.

Trippe's real fear was that one of these potential competitors might be awarded a contract to carry US Mail across the Pacific. He needed to show that his aircraft alone could do it; there was no time to be lost. So, as soon as preliminary flight testing of the Sikorsky S.42B was completed in March 1935, he ordered the *North Haven* to sail for Midway island with her complement of engineers, her mission to deposit half of them there and then forge on to Wake.

Then, on 16 April 1935, came the trial on which everything depended: a flight to Honolulu and back by an S.42B. The aircraft, named *Oriental Clipper* and commanded by Captain Edwin C. Musick, made the journey in 18 hours 37 minutes. There was only one crisis during the flight, when the small externally-mounted propeller that operated the wind-driven fuel pump broke away, some fragments piercing the skin of the fuselage. The *Oriental Clipper* stayed at Pearl Harbour for four days before taking off the return flight. This proved to be far more tricky, for the aircraft encountered strong headwinds during the entire crossing, reducing its ground speed to only 96 mph, and when it finally landed at Alameda, California, after a flight of 23 hours 41 minutes there was not even enough fuel left to carry out a circuit of the bay.

However, neither the press nor the US Government knew this; the word was put out that the flight had been delayed to make survey detours on either side of the route. Work on the island bases continued, and meanwhile Pan American eagerly awaited the delivery of the first Martin M.130 — the machine that would carry the first mail, and later the first passengers, all the way to China. In the meantime, the S.42 *Oriental Clipper* made more proving flights to Honolulu, extending the fourth such flight as far as Midway in October. On this trip the aircraft achieved the best time yet — 17 hours 5 minutes — between San Francisco and Honolulu.

The first M.130 flying-boat for Pan American was commissioned and handed over at Baltimore on 9 October, 1935, and a fortnight later Trippe was awarded the coveted US Mail contract. It was hardly surprising, for Pan American was the only airline with equipment capable of making the Pacific crossing; in fact, it was the only bidder.

On 22 November, 1935, this first Martin M.130 — serialled NC14716 and appropriately named *China Clipper* — took off from San Francisco Bay with Captain Musick once again at the controls and set course for Honolulu, carrying 1,837 pounds of mail. Four days later it reached Manila in the Philippines to a tumultuous welcome after a flying time of 59 hours 47 minutes, and on 1 December it set off on the long journey home, arriving at San Francisco on the 6th after 63 hours 28 minutes in the air.

Two more M.130s — *Philippine Clipper* and *Hawaii Clipper* — were soon delivered, and by December these aircraft were making a weekly mail run through the islands between San Francisco and the Philippines and return. For the men on the Wake and Midway staging posts, life was far from easy; there were none of the home comforts or distractions of Honolulu, and tempers often became frayed. Among the less pleasant tasks that had to be performed by the men on Midway, for example, was dealing with dead gooney birds; when these were newly hatched they scrambled down to the water, where about half learned to fly and the other half drowned or were eaten by sharks. The men had to clear the pathetic corpses from the beaches before they began to stink. On other occasions, thousands of sooty terns appeared over the island, then alighted and started laying eggs everywhere. Movement along the Midway Station's newly-built road and pathways became a nightmare of squawking, aggressive birds.

Nevertheless, despite all the hardships the men on the island stations never failed in their duty. They were always there to receive the flying-boats, and their weather reports reached San Francisco on the dot each day. Things began to look up a little in January 1936, when the *North Haven* paid a return visit to the islands carrying, in addition to supplies, the components of three 45-bedroom hotels for erection on Wake, Midway and Guam; the accommodation was not exactly four-star, but it was a step towards turning the island route into a commercial venture fit for passenger traffic. There was one small drawback, as far as the island base personnel were concerned; the edict went forth that, if they wished to dine in the new hotels, they must wear jackets and ties at all times.

Although Pan American now had the beginnings of a successful trans-Pacific service, they still had no Chinese terminal for it. Juan Trippe really wanted Hong Kong, where his aircraft could connect with those of the Chinese National Aviation Corporation, but the British Government steadfastly blocked his approaches, being reluctant to give the Americans a firm foothold in such an important corner of their Empire — even though they themselves as yet had no means of serving Hong Kong by air. Trippe cleverly circumvented the British refusal by obtaining landings rights in Macao, which was administered by the Portuguese and which he had no intention of using; instead, he was content to bide his time while Macao businessmen spread the news among their Hong Kong colleagues that Pan American preferred to use their facilities rather than the British, an impression Trippe fostered by making no further approach to obtain Hong Kong rights. The propaganda had the desired effect; before long, the British came to Trippe and offered him their base.

With the Hong Kong landing rights theirs, there was nothing now to stop Pan American from starting a scheduled passenger service across the Pacific to the mainland of Asia. This was officially inaugurated on 21 October 1936, the trip taking five days and involving an elapsed time of sixty hours. In fact, early passenger flights only went as far as Manila; it was not until April 1937 that the route was extended to Hong Kong to link up with Chinese internal routes.

Meanwhile, Juan Trippe had been exploring the possibility of opening a new route from Hawaii to Australia and New Zealand. However, this too was blocked by the British, because the Imperial Airways had visions of extending their London-Australia route across the Pacific to the United States and Canada, and to do this they needed landing rights in Hawaii. The British Government made approaches to obtain such rights, but they were not forthcoming. Pan American had no power to grant them — this was the privilege of the U.S. Government — and in any case, Britain's earlier intransigent attitude over the Hong Kong rights still rankled in some influential American circles.

However, Trippe shrewdly reasoned that if he opened a new route to New Zealand in the first instance — which Britain could do nothing to prevent — the result would be the same as when he played off Macao against Hong Kong; in other words, Australian businessmen would soon bring pressure to bear on the Australian Government to agree to a terminal for Pan American. The British got to know about Trippe's approaches and called an Imperial Air Conference in New Zealand, at which they urged that both the latter and Australia should resist the American moves until the landing rights had been obtained for Imperial Airways in Hawaii — but they had underestimated the wily Trippe. His countermove was to despatch an agent — Harold Gatty, formerly of South Seas Commercial, which had been bought out by Pan American — to New Zealand with a tempting carrot. Pan American, he said, was offering New Zealand a chance to elevate itself from a second-class country in Australia's back yard to one which would stand astride one of the most important commercial air routes in the world. If people wanted to fly to Australia by that route, they would have to come to New Zealand first. On the other hand, if Pan American's Pacific terminal ended in Australia, New Zealand was likely to become even more of a backwater.

The New Zealanders took the bait and, on 11 March 1937, they granted full commercial traffic rights to Pan American. Six days later, Captain Musick took off from San Francisco in a Sikorsky S.42B to make a survey flight over the route — something which amazed the New Zealanders, who had not realised that all but the last leg of the route had been prepared weeks before. After Hawaii, the Clippers would make two stops on the 6,000 miles flight; one at Kingman Reef Atoll, 1,100 miles further on, and the other at Pago Pago in American Samoa. Kingman Reef was uninhabited and tiny — smaller even than Wake — but there was a large sheltered lagoon on which flying-boats could land. Trippe chartered a tanker, the *North Wind,* had it loaded with fuel and radio direction-finding equipment, and sent it out there to act as a support vessel.

Pago Pago was larger and already had a harbour, but it was not very large and was almost entirely surrounded by sheer 1,500-foot cliffs, which meant that flying-boats landing there would have to make a steep descent, likely resulting in quite a heavy landing, and also a steep climb out. Nevertheless, it was the best place available on that sector of the route, and a base was quickly set up there.

The first Pan American flight to New Zealand was not without its problems. They started when the port outer engine began to overheat halfway between San Francisco and Hawaii, forcing Musick to shut it down and dump fuel in order to maintain height and normal cruising speed; however, some of the dumped petrol drifted into the aircraft, and since the slightest spark might cause an explosion the crew closed all non-essential electrical circuits and then worked their way through the aircraft with fire extinguishers, spraying every corner where petrol vapour might be lurking. They continued the flight to Hawaii with every port wide open, sitting uncomfortably at their stations in a miniature gale.

At Hawaii, Musick sent a signal to San Francisco, advising Trippe that modifications to the S.42's fuel-dumping ducts would be necessary to prevent a similar occurrence in the future, and then continued the flight to Kingman Reef. By early afternoon the aircraft was flying through driving rainstorms, which made accurate navigation extremely difficult, and if the D/F transmissions from the *North Wind* had not been received it is doubtful whether the crew would have found the tiny atoll at all. As it was, Musick dropped down out of the overcast to find the lagoon and the tanker directly below him.

The weather was kinder the next day, for the 1,600-mile leg to Pago Pago, and the S.42 reached its destination in mid-afternoon. Predictably, the landing was tricky. Musick made one trial approach, decided that he was using up too much of the lagoon, and went round for a second attempt. This time he dived in steeply, rounding out at the last moment and smacking the aircraft down hard on the water. Taking off was even more of a problem, and Musick waited four days before he judged the wind conditions to be right for lifting the aircraft off the lagoon with enough fuel on board to reach Auckland, 1,800 miles away, in safety. Even then, he made two dummy runs before he was satisfied that he had picked the best line for take-off.

The last leg of the flight was trouble-free, and the S.42 reached Auckland — where 30,000 people were waiting to welcome it — without further incident. The New Zealanders were unaware of the troubles Musick and his crew had faced; nor would they be aware that, on the return flight, the S.42 would not have succeeded in taking off from Pago Pago if the captain had not ordered every surplus item — from spare parts to the trifling souvenirs picked up by his crew — to be placed ashore in order to lighten it.

It was clear that much work would have to be done on improving the route before it could be cleared for passenger flying, and clear also that the S.42B was inadequate for the task. Even the M.130s, excellent machines that they were, had severe payload limitations over long oceanic routes; the San Francisco-New Zealand service would never be a workable proposition until Pan American's big Boeing 314s were brought into service. Nevertheless, survey flights continued; Captain Musick made a second trip to New Zealand in December 1937, and set out on a third in the S.42B *Samoa Clipper* early in January. By this time, Musick was making no secret of his hatred for the tiny, cramped harbour at Pago Pago, which he considered to be downright dangerous and a serious obstacle to the success of future operations.

On this occasion, however, he had no trouble landing there, and at dawn on 11 January 1938 he and his crew of six filed on board to make the flight to Auckland. The weather was good, with a fair wind, and it looked like being a simple trip.

Then, ninety minutes later, a radio message from Musick reached Pago Pago: number four engine had developed an oil leak, and he was returning to the atoll. Some time later, Musick radioed again to say that he was dumping fuel, for it would be impossible to land at Pago Pago with a full load on board.

It was the last that was heard of him. When the *Samoa Clipper* became seriously overdue, worried officials on Pago Pago asked the Navy to organize a search. Some time later, a minesweeper came upon an oil slick some twelve miles south-west of the island, with fragments of the flying-boat and some of the crew's effects floating in it. An examination of these established beyond doubt that the flying-boat had exploded in mid-air, probably as a result of fuel vapour building up after dumping. It was a tragic irony that Musick, who had reported that this could happen — resulting in an order from the Department of Commerce that all fuel dumping valves on commercial aircraft should be sealed — should have met his death while flying an aircraft on which this modification had not been carried out.

Soon after this tragedy, the Department of Commerce withdrew its approval for Pan American to use Pago Pago, which meant that flights to New Zealand had to be suspended while a new route was set up via Canton Island and Fiji. At Canton Island, engineers spent months blasting coral before the lagoon could be made usable for flying-boats, and still more months elapsed before buildings were completed — all at enormous cost to Pan American

Then, six months after the S.42 disaster, came another blow to the airline's trans-Pacific aspirations. The Martin M.130 *Hawaii Clipper,* en route from Guam to Manila with six passengers and nine crew on board, disappeared. There had been no hint of trouble; the crew had been in routine radio contact throughout the flight. But the Clipper and its occupants simply vanished, and no trace of them was ever found. All sorts of wild rumours — most of them accusing the Japanese of sabotage — to account for the aircraft's disappearance circulated in the United States, but whatever the reason behind the loss the immediate consequence for Pan American's Pacific route was catastrophic; the two remaining flying-boats simply could not maintain the San Francisco-Hong Kong service. This, together with the fact that the Pacific services had been losing money at an increasing rate ever since they began, was a contributory factor in ousting Juan Tripe from his position as President and General Manager of Pan American — although his fall from power was destined to be short. In January 1940 he was voted back for one main reason: no-one else had the necessary drive to run the Company.

In the meantime, the Pacific routes had been reinstated following the entry into Pan American service of three Boeing 314 Clippers, which operated alongside the two surviving Martin M.130s. (The latter, incidentally, went on to accumulate some 10,000 flying hours each by 1940, which was equivalent to an average daily utilisation of $5\frac{1}{2}$ hours, and flew 12,718,200 passenger miles, as well as mail flights. They were eventually impressed for transport duties by the US Navy in 1942). With the advent of the Boeings, passenger services to Hong Kong were once more placed on a sound footing from 22 February 1939, when a Boeing 314 named *Clipper 18* and piloted by Captain Bill Cluthe made the westbound trip, returning on 14 March.

On 12 July, 1940, one of these aircraft also reinstated the southern Pacific route, flying from San Francisco to Auckland via Canton Island and New Caledonia; when a new British base was completed on Fiji later in the year, the route was switched from New Caledonia to pass through this new location. A year later, a Boeing 314 named *Anzac Clipper,* homeward bound from Auckland to the United States, had a very lucky escape; its pilot, Captain H. Lanier Turner, was approaching Hawaii on 7 December, 1941, when he was warned that Japanese aircraft were attacking Pearl Harbour and that he was flying right into them. He diverted to Hilo Bay, on the big island of Hawaii, and landed safely, continuing the flight to San Francisco the following day. At Wake, another Pan American aircraft, Martin M.130 *Philippine Clipper,* was floating on the lagoon ready to take off for Guam when the island was bombed and strafed by Japanese aircraft; the Clipper collected a few bullet holes but did not suffer serious damage, and no-one was on board. The captain, John Hamilton, loaded sixty people on to the aircraft — some of them wounded — and flew to Midway, which had also been heavily attacked. Then he went on to Hawaii, visible from a great distance away by the columns of thick smoke that rose from the devastated Pearl Harbour base. After refuelling there, the *Philippine Clipper* reached San Francisco safely.

Hong Kong Clipper, an elderly S.42B that flew the shuttle service over the last sector of the Pacific route from Manila to Hong Kong, was not so fortunate. Known affectionately as 'Myrtle' by her crew, she was repeatedly machine-gunned by Japanese fighters and set ablaze at her moorings.

Boeing 314 *Pacific Clipper* was in the air between New Caledonia and Auckland, with Captain Robert Ford in command, when news of the Japanese attacks came through. After landing in New Zealand, Ford went to the U.S. consulate and cabled New York for instructions. It was several days before he received a reply, which instructed him to fly home the long way around. On 15 December, Ford took off on an amazing 23,000-miles journey during which he had to pick his own route, land at unknown harbours, find his own fuel, and service the aircraft with whatever tools were on board. He had the benefit neither of navigational aids nor weather forecasts.

The first leg of the flight took *Pacific Clipper* back to Noumea, New Caledonia, where it picked up twenty-two Company employees and their families and flew them to Gladstone, Queensland. Then Ford made the long eleven-hour haul across the Australian continent to Darwin, never seeing a major lake or waterway along the whole route; if something had gone wrong he would have had to belly-land, wrecking the aircraft. But Darwin was reached without incident, and at 2 am on 17 December the flying-boat, carrying a full load of fuel, took off for Surabaya in the Dutch East Indies. A hair-raising experience awaited the crew of *Pacific Clipper* as the aircraft approached Surabaya. Back in Auckland, during his lengthy wait for orders, Ford had got his men to slap a coat of camouflage paint on the flying-boat's upper surfaces; now it almost proved to be his undoing, for the aircraft — looking not a bit like a civil airliner — was intercepted by a flight of RAF Hawker Hurricane fighters. The American crew picked up the fighters' radio transmissions, and heard the pilots discussing whether or not to attack. There was relief all around when one of the Hurricanes closed right in and the pilot spotted part of an American flag, showing between the camouflage on the flying-boat's wing. The fighters escorted the big machine down to a safe landing at Surabaya, and everyone had a good laugh — but from then on, Ford made sure that wherever possible, messages of warning of the Clipper's approach were flashed ahead of him along the route.

On 21 December, *Pacific Clipper* left Surabaya and flew west across the Java Sea and the Bay of Bengal. At one point in the flight, as the aircraft stayed low to keep under the cloud base, it flew right over the top of a Japanese submarine; as the enemy crew ran for their deck gun, Ford applied full power and climbed into the clouds to safety. A few hours later, he made landfall at Trincomalee, in Ceylon, where he and his crew rested for a day. They needed the respite, for the trip from Surabaya had taken twenty-one hours.

On Christmas Eve they took off for Karachi, but half an hour later a cylinder in the starboard inner engine blew and they were forced to return to Ceylon. It was two days before repairs were completed and the flight was able to continue, *Pacific Clipper* crossing India to land at Karachi in the afternoon of 26 December. Two days later the aircraft went on to Bahrain, the flight from Karachi taking 8 hours 9 minutes. At this point Ford had several worries to concern him, not the least of which was that ever since Ceylon the aircraft had been flying on ordinary petrol, supplies of high-octane fuel having proved impossible to obtain. Another worry was that permission had been refused for the Clipper to fly directly across Arabia, which — if Ford had complied — would have meant a detour of hundreds of miles around the southern edge of the peninsula. Instead, he chose to ignore the order and flew straight across, keeping just above a solid undercast which fortunately broke up just as the aircraft reached the Red Sea. The pilot followed the Nile and landed at Khartoum in the Sudan.

Soon after take-off on the next leg the port outer engine started to give trouble, but Ford pressed on and landed safely at Leopoldville in the Congo on 1 January, 1942. Take-off the next day, with a full load of fuel, was a nightmare; the flying-boat churned its way down the river for a full minute and a half before it lifted into the air, just managing to clear some cataracts and a gorge beyond. The aircraft was now in a sorry state, its wings warped from the strain of lifting the full load, and the ailerons would not move; Ford had to make all his turns using rudder only. But there was no turning back now: ahead lay the vast expanse of the South Atlantic, and Brazil.

On 3 January, *Pacific Clipper* touched down at Natal after a flight of 3,500 miles that had lasted 23 hours and 35 minutes. The aircraft stayed there only long enough to refuel, taking off four hours later for Trinidad, where Ford touched down in the early hours of 4 January after 13 hours 52 minutes in the air. Only one sixteen-hour leg now lay before the weary crew.

At 5.54 on the morning of 6 January, 1942, the Clipper droned towards New York, shrouded in winter ice and snow, a world away from the balmy climes of the Pacific. The flight it had just made was an epic of aviation history, but there was no sense of drama in the laconic words with which Captain Ford announced his approach.

"*Pacific Clipper,* inbound from Auckland, New Zealand, Captain Ford reporting. Due arrive Pan American Marine Terminal, La Guardia, seven minutes."

There was, after all, nothing more to say. He was an airline captain, and he had brought his aircraft safely back. That was what he was paid to do.

Chapter Three
Ring Around the World

On 17 March, 1924, four Douglas DT-2 biplanes left Santa Monica, California, on the first leg of a flight designed to circumnavigate the world from east to west. The DT-2s were externally similar to those in service as torpedo-bombers with the U.S. Navy, although they had been stripped of all non-essential equipment, fitted with dual controls and extra fuel tankage, and provided with radio direction-finding facilities. The DT-2 was powered by a 420 hp Liberty 12A Vee-type engine that gave it a top speed of 100 mph at sea level; the aircraft was of mixed construction and was very robust, a very necessary requirement for a flight that would take an estimated six months and follow a route over some of the most hostile parts of the globe, and its undercarriage was interchangeable, provision being made for twin floats. Range was 1,650 miles for the landplane version, and 1,262 for the floatplane.

Designated DWC (Douglas World Cruiser), the four DT-2s that embarked on the around-the-word tour had been specially procured by the U.S. Army and were named after American cities: *Seattle, Chicago, Boston* and *New Orleans.* Head of the expedition was Major F. L. Martin, who flew in *Seattle* with his co-pilot and navigator Alva Harvey; the crew of *Chicago* was Lowell H. Smith and Leslie P. Arnold, while *Boston* was flown by Leigh Wade and Henry H. Ogden and *New Orleans* by Erick H. Nelson and John Harding.

The east-west route and the time of departure had been selected so that the aircraft would cross the northern Pacific at a time when it was relatively fog-free and Asia before the rainy season set in. Then, if all went well, they would reach the Atlantic before the September fogs.

On 17 March, the four aircraft reached Sacramento after a flight of 350 miles lasting 4 hours 30 minutes, then the following day they flew on to Seattle, their real departure point. There, the start of the next stage was delayed for several days because of technical trouble with Martin's aircraft, and it was not until 6 April that the aircraft — with floats now fitted — were able to leave for Prince Rupert in British Columbia, 650 miles away. This stage was flown in times varying from 7 hours 15 minutes to eight hours, but there were further delays when Martin's aircraft sustained damage to one of its floats on landing.

After that the journey went well for five days, following its resumption on 10 April when the aircraft flew from Prince Rupert to Sitka in Alaska (300 miles in four hours) and from there to Seward (600 miles in 7 hours 37 minutes). It was on the next leg, from Seward to Chignik on 15 April, that things began to go wrong when *Seattle* began to leak oil from a cracked engine casing, forcing Martin to make an emergency landing at Kanotak. The three other aircraft continued their flight to Chignik, and on 17 April, without waiting for the expedition leader, they continued to Dutch Harbor in the Aleutian Islands, covering the 400-mile distance in 6 hours 10 minutes. This was the start of the Pacific crossing, and a thorough examination was made of the three machines which resulted in an engine change for Wade's *Boston*.

The three crews decided to wait for Martin and Harvey, who — having also changed their aircraft's engine — flew from Kanotak to Chignik on 25 April. Bad weather delayed their progress for the best part of a week, but on 30 April they took off to join the others at Dutch Harbor. A couple of hours into their flight, they found themselves lost in fog and their aircraft crashed into a mountain slope. Both Martin and Harvey escaped unhurt, and after ten days walking in the wilderness reached the settlement at Port Moller.

Lowell Smith now assumed command of the expedition, and the three remaining aircraft flew on from Dutch Harbor to Nazan (Atka Island) on 3 May, covering the 350-mile stretch in 4 hours 15 minutes. The next two legs were long ones: first a 530-mile jump from Nazan to Chicagoff, on Attu Island, followed by one of 900 miles from Chicagoff to Kashiwadara Bay. Flying times for the two legs, which were completed on 16 May, were 10 hours 50 and 12 hours 5 minutes respectively. The aircraft had now reached the southern tip of Kamchatka, and on 22 May they arrived in northern Japan, having completed the first-ever crossing of the Pacific by air.

The engines of all three aircraft were now changed before the expedition flew on south-westwards across Japan, making three stops before reaching Kagoshima, in the south of Kyushu, on 2 June. On the last Japanese leg, from Kiushimoto to Kagoshima, Lowell Smith had engine trouble and was forced to land and carry out repairs; the other two aircraft flew across the East China Sea to Shanghai, completing the 600-mile leg in 7 hours 32 minutes on 3 June, and Smith joined them the next day.

The crossing of Asia took all of June, the aircraft flying from Shanghai to Calcutta by way of Amoy, Hong Kong, Haiphong, Tourane, Saigon, Bangkok, Tavoy, Rangoon and Akyab. After reaching Calcutta on 26 June the three machines underwent another change and also had their wings replaced. Then, with their undercarriages switched from floats to wheels, they left Calcutta on 1 July and flew across India to Karachi, arriving on the 4th. They stayed there for three days, then carried on along the RAF mail route through the Middle East and into Europe, eventually arriving at Paris on 14 July. Two days later they were in London, and the day after that they flew north to Brough in Yorkshire.

On 30 July, in fine summer weather, they continued their northward flight to the Orkneys, the starting point for the most difficult and dangerous part of their long flight: the Atlantic crossing. This was begun on 2 August, the three aircraft flying in formation, but they had not been airborne for long

Lufthansa undertook test flights to explore the airmail routes to Istanbul, Seville and Tenerife with the Arado V 1 in 1929. The picture shows the aircraft at the La Laguna airport near Santa Cruz de Tenerife.

Vickers Vulture amphibian G-EBHO, the aircraft in which Major A. S. MacLaren attempted to fly around the world in 1924, pictured at Abu Sueir, Egypt.

when they encountered thick fog. Nelson and Harding in *New Orleans* got into a spin and only just managed to pull out above the water; they flew on to land at Horna Fjord in Iceland, but their two companion aircraft turned back and tried again the next day.

This time the weather was better, but Lieutenant Wade in *Boston* had to land on the water when his oil pressure dropped to zero. Smith and Arnold in *Chicago* went to alert the cruiser USS *Richmond*, which was on station in the vicinity; the vessel quickly reached the scene, but during the subsequent salvage operation a line snapped and the stranded aircraft was wrecked as it was being hauled on board.

The two surviving machines flew on to Greenland on 21 August, and after an engine change they left Yvigtut, on Greenland's west coast, on the 520-mile leg to Indian Harbor in Labrador, arriving on 31 August after a flight of 6 hours 30 minutes. The journey was not without incident, for as the aircraft passed the point of no return the fuel pump on *Chicago* failed and fuel had to be hand-pumped from the main tank for the rest of the flight. After repairs the two aircraft flew on through Nova Scotia to Pictou, in Canada, where they were joined by Wade and Ogden, the crew of the ill-fated *Boston;* a replacement DT-2 was waiting for them, and the three aircraft continued their flight in company across the North American continent, arrving at Seattle on 28 September. Their flight around the world had taken 175 days and they had spent 351 hours in the air.

Apart from bringing well-deserved honour to the crews, and praise for their flying and navigational skills, this epic voyage brought home a number of lessons which were to make their mark on the design of future aircraft and equipment. One such lesson was that wood and fabric were far from suitable materials for use in wing and float structures under hot and humid conditions; another was that the flight would not have been possible without massive support and organization, with US warships carrying spares, fuel and technicians positioned all along the route. Logistical support of long-range air operations was something in which the Americans, over the next decade and a half, would come to excel.

The development of strong mobile support, in fact, was to some extent forced on the Americans because of a lack of overseas bases world-wide. The British, on the other hand, had no such problems, and when they launched their own around-the-world attempt the route was planned to take full advantage of bases dotted around the Empire.

The British attempt, which started at Calshot on 25 March 1924, was made by a Vickers Vulture amphibian (G-EBHO), powered by a 450 hp Napier Lion II engine. The flight was commanded by Squadron Leader A. S. C. MacLaren, with Flying Officer W. N. Plenderleith as pilot and Sergeant R. Andrews as mechanic. The flight progressed along a well-worn mail route, the aircraft passing through Le Havre, Lyon, Civitta Vecchia and Rome to Corfu, where it underwent an engine change before flying on to Athens and Cairo, where it arrived on 17 April. Subsequent staging posts along the route were Ziza, Baghdad, Bushire, Bandar Abbas, Karachi and Parlu, where the engine was changed once again. On 13 May the Vulture flew on to Calcutta via Nasirabad and Allahabad, and on 21 May it reached Akyab Island off the coast of Burma.

So far, all had gone well; but by now the extremes of climate had seriously affected the Vulture's wooden structure, and when the pilot tried to take off from the sea at Akyab water came pouring into the hull through cracks which had developed and it proved impossible to maintain flying speed. The amphibian smacked back down on the water with such force that it broke up; fortunately, the crew escaped unhurt.

A replacement Vulture, G-EBGO, was shipped out to Akyab, and with this machine the flight resumed on 25 June, the aircraft now following roughly the same route as that taken by the Douglas World Cruisers, but in the opposite sense. After Akyab, MacLaren and his crew flew on through Rangoon, Bangkok, Haiphong, Hong Kong and Shanghai to Kagoshima in Japan. The expedition spent several days in Tokyo, then left on 13 July for Minato, 375 miles to the north.

After leaving Japan progress was slow, for as they flew on in stages to the desolate Kurile Islands the crew were hampered by fog and heavy seas, which made navigation difficult and landings dangerous. The aircraft reached Petropavlovsk, Kamchatka, at the end of July and that was the last that was heard of it for some days. Then it was learned that G-EBGO had been forced down by impenetrable fog soon after leaving Petropavlovsk, and had been damaged beyond repair in landing on a heavy sea at Nikolski on 2 August. The crew were safe and waiting to picked up from Paramoshir Island. They had covered 13,000 miles, halfway around the world, but no other replacement aircraft was available and the attempt had to be abandoned.

Several other around-the-world attempts during the 1920s also ended in failure, either because the aircraft and engines involved were not up to the stresses imposed upon them, or because adverse weather conditions resulted in mishap. Other attempts were not true around-the-globe flights, because the aircraft were carried part of the way on ships. In fact, it was not until 1929 that the world was truly circumnavigated by air, and then it was done by that remarkable airship the *Graf Zeppelin*.

The German airship L.59. The forerunner of commercial types such as the Graf Zeppelin, this made a long-range flight to East Africa in October 1917, when it was in the air for 95 hours 35 minutes, covering a distance of 4,200 miles.

The Graf Zeppelin at its mooring mast.

She set out from Lakehurst on 8 August and, after crossing the Atlantic from west to east, arrived at Friedrichshafen on the 10th. Setting out once more five days later, she flew over Berlin, Stettin and Danzig, heading out over the Baltic towards Russia. Early on the 16th she passed over the city of Vologda and cruised on towards the Ural Mountains, which she crossed north of Perm. On 16 and 17 August she was over the vast wastes of Siberia, the crew eventually picking up the Yenisei River; as they passed over the village of Verkne Imbatskoe they saw the terrified inhabitants hurl themselves to the ground in terror at the sight of the gigantic silver cigar nosing through the sky.

The worst part of the *Graf Zeppelin's* voyage across Siberia was the flight over the uncharted Stanovoi Mountains, running parellel to the east coast and plunging into the Sea of Okhotsk. Hugo Eckener, the airship's commander, negotiated them by flying through a narrow valley in gusty wind conditions that threatened to hurl the craft against the jagged rocks on several occasions. But Eckener's skill brought her through safely, and she scraped over the ridge that ran along the crest of the mountains with only feet to spare. Ahead of her now lay the glittering Sea of Okhostsk, and beyond it Japan; the great airship had just completed the first non-stop flight across the length of Russia.

She had enough fuel and supplies to take her direct to Los Angeles, but for political reasons she was scheduled to make a call at Tokyo. She reached the Japanese capital on 19 August, having covered 7,000 miles in 101 hours 44 minutes. Apart from running through severe turbulence in cloud over Siberia, and skirting the outer fringes of a typhoon off Sakhalin, she had encountered kindly weather.

The *Graf Zeppelin* left Tokyo on 23 August and set course east-south-east over the Pacific, using winds that raced across the sky in the wake of a typhoon to help her along. Later, she had to nose her way through dense fog for twenty-four hours, but on the third day of her Pacific crossing she emerged into clear weather again and at sunset on 25 August she cruised over San Francisco, welcomed by dozens of aircraft. Then she flew on to Los Angeles for a dawn landing that proved extremely tricky because of a temperature inversion; as the airship descended into the cooler layers of air she became lighter, and the crew had to valve off a large amount of gas before she could be safely moored. When she took off again the following evening the opposite applied; quantities of gas had been automatically valved off during the day when the sun heated the airship's envelope and she was dangerously heavy, and as there were no more supplies of hydrogen to top up her gas cells Eckener had to make a long, slow take-off, nosing up gradually into the warmer layers of air. She bounced several times as her tail struck the ground and only just cleared some high tension cables, but she gained height safely and flew on to Lakehurst, where she moored on 29 August after an around-the-world voyage of 21 days, 7 hours and 34 minutes, of which a week had been spent on the ground at her ports of call. From Lakehurst, she flew home across the Atlantic.

The *Graf Zeppelin* had circumnavigated the world with only three stops — a remarkable achievement, for this had been much more than a prestige flight: the airship had carried freight and mail as well as a small group of passengers. As an achievement, it far overshadowed the flight of Charles Kingsford Smith's *Southern Cross,* which flew across the Atlantic on 25 June 1930 and from there on to Oakland, California, completing the world tour which it had begun two and a half years earlier. A much more significant flight was made a year later, when the Americans Wiley Post and Harold Gatty left New York in a Lockheed Vega monoplane named *Winnie Mae of Oklahoma* on 23 June 1931 in an attempt to fly around the world in less than ten days. They got off to a fine start by crossing the North Atlantic from Harbour Grace, Newfoundland, to Chester, England, in 16 hours 17 minutes. They were back in New York on 1 July, having successfully made the first around-the-world flight by a commercial aircraft (as distinct from an airship) in 8 days 15 hours 51 minutes, which earned them a prize of 10,000 dollars. Their total flying time was 107 hours 2 minutes.

In 1933, Wiley Post broke his own record with a solo flight around the world in the same aircraft, albeit with some modifications that included enlarged tail surfaces and conversion to a Wasp C1 engine. Setting out on 15 July, he flew from New York to Berlin in 25 hours 45 minutes, and from there his route took him through Königsberg, Moscow, Novosibirsk, Irkutsk, Khabarovsk, Flat (in Alaska), Fairbanks and Edmonton back to his start point. He made the journey in 7 days 18 hours 50 minutes, including 115 hours 54 minutes' flying time.

So it could be done commercially and quickly — and three years later, for the first time, a fare-paying passenger proved that it was possible to fly all the way around the world for anybody who had the time and money. He was H. R. Ekins of the *Scripps Howard Journal,* and he began his journey by flying from New York to Frankfurt aboard the airship *Hindenburg* on 30 September 1936. From Frankfurt, he flew to Athens with KLM, and took the same airline to Batavia; then he went on to Manila with KNILM, KLM's East Indies subsidiary, and from there caught Pan American's *Hawaii Clipper* to San Francisco. The last stage to New York, with one change en route, was flown via United Airlines and TWA.

Men had flown around the world, both solo and in crews; so had a woman (Lady Drummond Hay, aboard the *Graf Zeppelin* in 1929). But a woman had yet to make an around-the-world flight as pilot in command of an aircraft, and in 1937 Amelia Earhart determined that she would be the first. An initial attempt, in March 1937, ended in disaster when her Lockheed Electra ground-looped on take-off from Honolulu, shearing off the right mainwheel and damaging a wing.

The aircraft was repaired, and she tried again three months later. With Fred Noonan as her navigator, she planned to follow a route around the equator — the first time this would have been done — flying from west to east. Taking off from Miami on 1 June she flew to San Juan in Puerto Rico and then on to Caripito in Venezuela, Paramaribo in Dutch Guiana and Natal, the jumping-off point for transatlantic flight to Dakar. Haze over the coast of West Africa caused some navigational problems for Noonan and in fact they landed at St. Louis-du-Senegal on 8 June, flying on to Dakar the next day.

From Dakar they went on via Gao and Fort Lamy to El Fasher, in the Anglo-Egyptian Sudan, and then on through Khartoum to Massawa on the Red Sea. From there they flew to Assab on the coast of Eritrea, the last staging-point before a non-stop flight to Karachi that took 13 hours and 10 minutes. At Karachi, Imperial Airways and Royal Air Force mechanics checked the Electra thoroughly while Amelia and Noonan enjoyed a two-day rest; they resumed their flight on 17 June, following the Imperial Airways route to Calcutta, 1,390 miles away. They landed at Calcutta's Dum Dum Airport to find the field waterlogged; weather was now giving them cause for concern, for the monsoon was about to break and it was essential to press on as quickly as possible. The next leg of the flight from Calcutta to Akyab in Burma, was uneventful, but between Akyab and Rangoon the Electra was battered by storm-force winds and monsoon rain, lashing head-on from the south-east with such force that it stripped paint from the leading edges of the aircraft's wings. It was impossible to find a way through the massive clouds, so they turned around and flew back to Akyab.

They managed to reach Rangoon on 19 June, and the following day they flew on to Bangkok and Singapore, hoping to make up some lost time. They seemed to have left the bad weather behind them, and they flew the next leg from Singapore to Bandung, Java, in excellent visibility over some of the most beautiful scenery in the world. At Bandung, KLM technicians checked over the aircraft; then, on 27 June, the flight continued to Port Darwin, Australia, with one stop en route at Timor.

The next stretch, over 1,200 miles of water between Port Darwin and Lae, New Guinea, was difficult. The trip took eight hours, the aircraft having to fight its way through strong headwinds and turbulence, and by this time both Amelia and Noonan were feeling the strain of having flown 22,000 miles. The two days of rest they enjoyed at Lae were not only welcome; they were essential.

Then, on 2 July 1937, they took off from Lae on the 2,556-mile jump to Howland Island in the central Pacific — the last port of call before Oakland, California. They would actually land on 1 July, gaining a day when they crossed the International Dateline.

But they never reached Howland. Apart from a few fragmentary radio messages, nothing was seen or heard of them again. Despite a massive search that encompassed half the Pacific and a dozen nations, their disappearance remained one of aviation's great unsolved mysteries.

In his book *Winged Legend,* Amelia Earhart's biography, author John Burke points out that she and Noonan disappeared just when Pan American and Imperial Airways were establishing a routine around-the-world service. "One plane missing," as a newspaper editorial on her disappearance remarked, "far out on the lonely Pacific. Another plane heading into the dawn, half a world away. And the day of the ocean pioneers is closed."

But not quite. On 10 July, 1938, a Lockheed 14 — an improved version of the Electra — took off from New York and flew around the world in just under four days; to be exact, 91 hours and 24 minutes. It also made the fastest New York-Paris crossing so far, in 16 hours 31 minutes. It was a record that would stand until April 1947, when a Douglas A-26 Invader flew around the world in 78 hours 56 minutes.

The man who captained the Lockheed 14 was one of the wealthiest and most controversial figures of all time; he was also one whose contribution to aviation was immense. His name was Howard Hughes.

The Graf Zeppelin taking off.

Chapter Four
The Empire Routes

1. The Middle East and India

On 28 July, 1918 — with the end of the First World War still more than three months away — a Handley Page 0/400 bomber took off from Manston in Kent and set course over the Channel. There was outwardly nothing unusual in this, for 0/400s were used by the Royal Air Force's bombing arm in France, and replacement aircraft were constantly flying out to join their squadrons.

This flight, however, was different. The 0/400, bearing the serial number C9681 and captained by Major A. S. C. MacLaren, was heading out on the first leg of a route which, on 7 August, was to end in Cairo. To the 0/400 and MacLaren fell the honour of completing the first ever flight from England to Egypt, and consequently laying the foundations of RAF long-range route flying.

On 29 November, the same aircraft, now flown by Captain Ross Smith, took off from Cairo and, the following evening, arrived at Baghdad, having staged through Damascus on this flight, C9681 carried a VIP passenger: Major General Geoffrey Salmond, Commander-in-Chief of the Royal Air Force in the Middle East, who was on his way to make an inspection tour of RAF units in Mesopotamia. Subsequently, on 4 December, the 0/400 flew on from Iraq to India, arriving at Delhi on the 12th and then continuing as far as Calcutta, its crew's task being to survey a potential air route.

The next logical step was to make a through flight from England to India, and the machine chosen for this was a Handley Page V/1500. Powered by two pairs of Rolls-Royce Eagle VIII engines, mounted in tandem, the V/1500 had been designed and built to bomb Berlin from bases in East Anglia, but the end of the war had come before the type became operational. Although it was a very new type and consequently untried, its long range made it theoretically ideal for route pioneering work.

The V/1500 chosen for the flight to India was serialled J1936, and the man picked to fly it was Major MacLaren, who since his Cairo flight had delivered another 0/400 to Egypt. His second pilot was Captain Robert Halley, who had some experience on the new type; he was a member of No. 166 Squadron at RAF Bircham Newton, which had received three V/1500s just before the Armistice. The aircraft was to carry three other crew members: two fitters, Flight Sergeant A. E. Smith and Sergeant W. Crockett, and a rigger, Sergeant W. Brown. In addition, Brigadier General Norman McEwen, who had just been appointed to command the Royal Air Force in India, was to make the trip as a passenger.

Named H.M.A. (His Majesty's Airliner) *Old Carthusian* — a tribute to Charterhouse, where both pilots had been educated — the V/1500 took off from Martlesham Heath at 9.42 am on 7 December 1918, but was forced to return soon afterwards with engine trouble. The next start was made on Friday, 13 December, and as though Superstition was proving a point they ran into dense cloud over France, narrowly missing some high ground in the murk. Shortly afterwards MacLaren became disorientated and decided to turn north in search of somewhere to land, and at 12.50 the V/1500 touched down at Bergues, near Dunkirk, where the crew spent the night.

The next morning they flew on to Le Bourget, where MacLaren collected another passenger: his Maltese terrier *Tiny,* placed in quarantine at the French airfield when the pilot was returning to Britain from Egypt a few weeks earlier.

They left Le Bourget on 15 December and, after precautionary landings because of the weather at Beaune and Pisa, flew down the Italian coast towards Sicily. It had originally been planned to fly from Rome to Athens, but then it was found that the ceiling of the heavily-laden V/1500 was not sufficient to enable it to clear the Apennines safely. The weather was still bad, and over the Straits of Messina the turbulence was so severe that it took the combined efforts of both pilots to keep the aircraft — unstable at the best of times — in level flight. They thankfully landed at Catania, Sicily, at dusk, and the aircraft immediately became bogged down in soft ground. Italian soldiers were recruited to help pull it clear, and on the 21st it resumed its flight to Malta.

Non-mechanical transport, circa 1926; bringing back the engine of a wrecked DH9 mail aircraft from the desert.

The Mediterranean weather was near-perfect, and the V/1500 left Marsa airfield on Malta — narrowly missing a stone wall at the far end — and climbed away on the 1,150-mile leg to Cairo. Landfall was made on the North African coast near Benghazi at 06.50 on 22 December, only two miles off track, but shortly afterwards rear engine failed and so MacLaren decided to make for Alexandria. Then the other starboard engine failed too, compelling Halley, who was at the controls, to make an emergency landing on flat scrub some fifty miles west of Mersa Matruh. An inspection showed that broken reduction gears had caused the engine failures, and to complicate matters further two tyres had been punctured in the landing.

Fortunately, after only a few minutes some Arabs appeared, and on promise of payment in gold they went off to get help. This duly arrived the following morning, and on 29 December a party of RAF ground crew arrived from Aboukir, bearing the necessary spare parts. Repairs were carried out within forty-eight hours, and at 1 pm on 31 December the aircraft took off and flew to Heliopolis, where it was thoroughly overhauled. So far, it had covered a distance of 3,085 miles in a flying time of 35 hours 8 minutes, at an average speed of 88 mph.

Old Carthusian left Heliopolis at 3.30 am on 8 January, 1919, the crew intending to fly non-stop to Ahwaz in Persia, but after passing Damascus two of the engines began to run roughly. Fuel was pumped from the main tank and the fitters cleaned the filters, which were choked with dirt, but they were unable to reach the carburettor filters, and at 12.45 the port front engine stopped. MacLaren, fixing his position by the River Euphrates, headed for Abu Kemal aerodrome, where he landed at 2 pm. The filters were thoroughly cleaned, and in the last remaining light MacLaren took off again to make the 220-mile run to Baghdad. However, strong headwinds and an approaching storm made another emergency landing necessary a hundred miles short of the objective, so after spending the night camped by the aircraft the crew made the last hop to Baghdad the next morning.

The next leg of the flight, from Baghdad to Ahwaz, was made on 11 January in the teeth of a strong headwind. From Ahwaz, they flew on to Bushire at low level, racing across the desert at less than 100 feet, much to the consternation of occasional tribesmen who saw the massive aircraft bearing down on them. The 400-mile stage from Bushire to Bandar Abbas was flown on 12 January in 6 hours 20 minutes, progress once again being delayed by headwinds.

With so much time lost already they decided to press straight on from Bandar Abbas, although some of the crew felt that it would have been prudent to give the engines another overhaul at this stage. They were right. Six hours after leaving Bandar, the port rear engine seized with a terrific bang, leaving the pilot with no alternative once again but to make an emergency landing. At this point the V/1500 was a few miles out over the Arabian Sea, so MacLaren quickly turned inland and brought the aircraft down safely on the shore near Ormara, a fishing village 170 miles west of Karachi.

They were now faced with a problem of considerable proportions, for it would take a long time to obtain spares and the aircraft's wooden structure would almost certainly warp in the heat and humidity. MacLaren briefly considered attempting to fly out on three engines, but dismissed the idea. The only course seemed to be to dismantle *Old Carthusian* and ship her out, writing finis to any hope of reaching India by air.

However, among the people — mostly natives — who turned up at the scene of the forced landing was one who was to prove of inestimable service: an Indian official of the Eastern Telegraph Company, who spoke impeccable English and who, as well as sending out messages for assistance, organized accommodation for the crew. Provided with good quarters and feeling a little happier, the crew set about stripping the aircraft of every surplus item, for MacLaren had revived the idea that it might be possible to take off if the weight were reduced considerably. They also drained the tanks, leaving only just enough fuel to get them to Karachi.

On the morning of 15 January an old gunboat, HMS *Britomart,* arrived from Karachi and the crew loaded their baggage on to her. She also took on board Brigadier General McEwan, who had been suffering badly from heat exhaustion and who was anxious to get to his new HQ. Meanwhile, the fitters worked hard on the three good engines, and by mid-afternoon all three were running satisfactorily at 1,600 rpm.

MacLaren and Halley held a brief conference and decided to risk a take-off, although as an extra weight-saving measure only one other crew member — Flight Sergeant Smith — was to travel with them. Smith, in fact, was needed to sit in the tail as human ballast to provide the correct trim for take-off.

By late afternoon the tide was out, giving the V/1500 a take-off run of about two miles over wet but firm sand, and a stiff breeze was blowing along it. Aided by this, MacLaren took off successfully at 5.45 pm in just over a mile and climbed thankfully away. It took them twenty minutes to reach 1,000 feet, but the two pilots were confident that they could reach Karachi on three engines.

The scene at Abu Sueir, Egypt, in the mid-1920s. This airfield was an important staging post for the Empire mail in the Middle East; the aircraft are DH9As and Vickers Vimy bombers, and the occasion is the Air Officer Commanding's inspection.

Then, suddenly, two of the engines stopped, leaving only the front port motor still developing power. At once, MacLaren and Halley knew what had happened. the pump that fed petrol from the main tanks to the starboard gravity tank was wind-driven by small vane cups, and these had come adrift. Halley dashed back to the engineer's position and began to operate the emergency hand pump; to his relief the engine re-started, and then Flight Sergeant Smith came forward from the rear turret and took over.

The aircraft lumbered on, with Halley and Smith taking turns at the pump. By 6.45 pm it was dark, and with thirty-five miles still left to run there came a fresh crisis: the rpm of the starboard rear engine dropped abruptly and it began to overheat, so it had to be shut down. An oil pipe had fractured, and since nothing could be done about it in flight the crew had to struggle on with the two remaining engines, hoping that these would hold out.

For thirty minutes the V/1500 wallowed along at 52 mph, her two engines at full throttle, losing height steadily. MacLaren scraped her in over the high ground to the west of Karachi and made a straight-in approach to the airfield, where Royal Engineers — forewarned of the aircraft's arrival by telegraph — had made an improvised flarepath from petrol-soaked rags. At 9.15 pm, *Old Carthusian's* wheels touched the ground at the end of her epic flight of 5,560 miles, accomplished in a flying time of 72 hours 41 minutes at an average speed of 77 mph.

For their respective parts in the flight, MacLaren was awarded the OBE, and Halley the AFC; the NCOs each received the Air Force Medal. Yet there was no escaping the fact that, although the aircraft had managed to arrive in India, she had only once landed at one of the aerodromes designated on her flight plan, and reports on her technical troubles were to fill pages. She had, quite simply, proved to be the wrong aircraft for the task.

However, *Old Carthusian's* story was not quite over. Repaired and overhauled, she went into action on 24 May, when Halley flew her from Delhi to bomb Kabul in support of operations against dissident tribesmen.

In the rugged desert operating conditions, crashes were all too frequent. Photographs show two DH9As that came to grief.

In May 1919, the Air Ministry proposed that two squadrons of the well-tried Handley Page 0/400 bombers should be used to implement a regular weekly mail service between Cairo and India. New airfield facilities would have be to developed, at a cost of about £100,000, and it was stressed that the setting up of an air route would greatly facilitate air reinforcement in times of unrest, which were fairly frequent along India's turbulent North-West Frontier. However, the Treasury, eager to clip the RAF's wings now that the war was over, received this plan coldly, and their attitude became even more entrenched when, out of fifty-one 0/400s of Nos. 58, 214 and 216 Squadrons that were re-deployed from France to Egypt between April and October 1919, fifteen were destroyed by accidents en route, with the loss of eight crew members. An experimental mail service in India was in fact begun on 24 January 1920, with DH 10s of No. 97 Squadron flying regularly between Karachi and Bombay, but this was stopped after a few weeks on economic grounds.

Economic reasons were also given as the reason for abandoning an embryo air mail and passenger service started by the RAF between Cairo and Baghdad early in 1920 on the initiative of Lieutenant-Colonel A. T. Wilson, the Civil Commissioner in Mesopotamia. It was not until March 1921 that a Cairo-Baghdad air service was approved, and then only because the British forces in Mesopotamia (re-named Iraq in September 1921) were having difficulty in maintaining law and order. The new route's primary function, therefore, was to provide rapid air reinforcement to Mesopotamia; previously aircraft had had to be shipped through the Red Sea and Persian Gulf.

It would not be an easy route to fly. It was a little over 850 miles long, and 550 miles of it was over an arid desert plateau rising up to 2,000 feet above sea level. The first step, therefore, was for ground parties to mark out suitable emergency landing grounds at twenty-mile intervals, and a thorough survey of the whole route was started in May 1921. The operation was completed in July, the ground parties being supplied entirely by air.

Aircraft flew along the entire route for the first time on 30 June, 1921, when two DH9As of No. 47 Squadron left Baghdad at 4.30 am and reached Heliopolis at 7.45 that evening, and on 9 July another 47 Squadron DH9A flew in the opposite direction with Air Vice Marshal Sir Geoffrey Salmond as

A Vickers Victoria of No. 70 Squadron, RAF, which flew the Cairo-Baghdad mail from 1926.

passenger. On 28 July a consignment of air mail left Baghdad and reached London on 9 August; in the meantime, another batch of mail had left London on 4 August, and this arrived in Baghdad on the 17th. So far, all the mail carried had been of an official nature, but on 8 October 1921 the service was extended to the public at a charge of a shilling per ounce (later reduced to threepence). Aircraft left Baghdad and London every fortnight, on a Thursday.

The mail service was undertaken by three squadrons, Nos. 30, 47 and 216. Nos. 30 and 47 both operated DH9As, the former based at Baghdad West and the latter at Helwan, Egypt; No. 216, based at Kantara, exchanged its 0/400s for de Havilland DH10s in October 1921 and its crews found these aircraft much more manoeuvrable and fast, although they had an unpleasant tendency to swing on take-off and their 400 hp Liberty engines were not always reliable. (This, in fact, was due to a defect in the fuel system rather than the powerplant itself). Cruising at 110 mph, however, the DH10 could make the Cairo-Baghdad run in about ten hours, and could carry two passengers; the DH9, on the other hand, had to make two refuelling stops en route, and its cruising speed was reduced to less than 90 mph by the dozen or so four-gallon fuel drums that were lashed to its bomb racks. It could carry one passenger, but luggage had to be stowed externally, lashed to the upper surface of the lower mainplane.

Despite the shortcomings of their equipment, the three squadrons carried four and a quarter tons of mail and 140 passengers during their first year of operations on the Baghdad route. The volume of both mail and passengers carried increased considerably after January 1922, when No. 216 Squadron re-equipped with Vickers Vimy aircraft; by April of that year the DH9As of Nos. 30 and 47 Squadrons had also been withdrawn from regular route flying, their places taken by Nos. 45 and 70 Squadrons. Both these units were equipped with Vickers Vernons; the military version of the Vimy Commercial, the Vernon could carry up to eleven passengers and was the first aircraft to serve with the RAF specifically in the transport role. It suffered from being slow and underpowered — its cruising speed was a mere 70 mph — and, since it was of wooden construction, it suffered badly from warping in the hot desert climate. Nevertheless, the Vernon was the aircraft that really turned the Baghdad route into a viable proposition. Matters improved still further at a later date, when the Vernons were re-engined with 450 hp Napier Lions.

The crews who flew the Baghdad Mail were among the most experienced in the RAF, and included men who were later to rise to high command. Among them was Squadron Leader Arthur T. Harris, who was to become C-in-C of Bomber Command in the 1939-45 War, and Flight Lieutenants Ralph Cochrane and Robert Saundby, his flight commanders in No. 45 Squadron. Another 45 Squadron pilot during this period was the celebrated Flight Lieutenant Basil Embry.

Air and ground crews together formed a closely-knit team, the like of which was to be found nowhere else in the RAF of the 1920s. They were proud of their status, and the aircraft they flew and maintained were personalized with names such as *Valkyrie, Vagabond, Vesuvius, Morpheus* and *Aurora.* Every member of a Vernon's four-man crew — pilot, second pilot, fitter and wireless operator — had to be able to perform a variety of tasks, from changing a wheel to stripping down an engine. In an environment where a forced landing could signify slow death, either from thirst or at the hands of unfriendly tribesmen, skilled teamwork on everyone's part was an essential factor in rectifying trouble with the minimum delay.

Line-up of Vickers Vimy aircraft at Abu Sueir in the early 1920s. These aircraft were used by No. 216 Squadron to carry Empire mail until they were replaced by Vernons.

In 1923, the RAF suddenly found itself with a serious competitor on the Baghdad route when the Nairn Motor Company started a weekly service across the desert between Egypt and Iraq. This enabled mail to reach England just as quickly as by the RAF's fortnightly service, and it was also cheaper. The Air Ministry reacted by reducing the air mail surcharge, but in 1924 loads fell by fifty per cent. The RAF did not appear to be unduly perturbed; on 18 February 1925, Sir Philip Sasson, the Under Secretary of State for Air, replying to criticism that the RAF was not using faster aircraft and generally operating the Baghdad route on a more efficient basis, said that the primary object of the operation of the desert air route was not the carriage of mails, but the affording of a training exercise to pilots and ground personnel of the RAF in long-distance flying under conditions similar to those of active service. And, a few months later, the Air Ministry had the chance to laugh up its sleeve when the land service had to be suspended because of activity by hostile tribes in Syria. In fact, the RAF Vernons sometimes had to go to the aid of Nairn Company drivers who had broken the rules about travelling in convoy, and who found themselves stranded in the desert.

The Vickers Vernon, military version of the Vimy Commercial. This was the aircraft that really made a success of the RAF's Middle East mail services.

In the summer of 1926, Nos. 70 and 216 Squadrons re-equipped with Vickers Victoria aircraft. Developed from the Virginia bomber, the Victoria could carry up to twenty passengers and was powered by two 450 hp Lion engines. No. 70 Squadron was the first to receive the new type, and used four of them on the Cairo-Baghdad route until the end of the year, when the mail service was taken over by Imperial Airways.

The Cairo-Baghdad section, in fact, was to form part of Imperial Airways' mail and passenger route from the United Kingdom to India, and was to represent a further step towards the airline's objective of carrying all Empire mail by air. The decision that the responsibility for the carriage of mail to the Middle East and India by Imperial Airways had been taken in 1925, a year after the airline's foundation, but the scheme had been slow to start because of a lack of suitable equipment; the aircraft types which then formed the fleet of Imperial Airways would not stand up to the rigours of continual operation over long distances in tropical climates.

What was needed was an entirely new type, specifically designed for long-range operations, and the machine that fulfilled Imperial Airways' needs in this respect was the de Havilland DH66 Hercules. Five were ordered initially, and the first of these, G-EBMW, flew for the first time on 30 September 1926, powered by three 420 hp Bristol Jupiter VI radial engines.

The Hercules carried a three-man crew — two pilots and a wireless operator — and there was accommodation for seven passengers, with two separate cargo compartments measuring a total of 620 cubic feet. The aircraft's wingspan was 79 feet 6 inches and its length 55 feet 6 inches; it cruised at 110 mph and had an operational ceiling of 13,000 feet, sufficient to clear any of the high terrain it was likely to encounter on the route to India.

On 18 December, 1926, G-EBMW left Croydon en route for the Middle East; on arrival in Egypt she was named *City of Cairo,* and on 12 January 1927 she made the first scheduled civilian mail flight to Baghdad. Meanwhile, the second Hercules, G-EMBX, had left Croydon on 27 December, carrying the Secretary of State for Air, Sir Samuel Hoare, and his wife. The aircraft staged through Dijon, Marseille, Pisa, Naples, Homs, Benghazi, Sollum, Aboukir, Bushire, Lingeh, Djask, Pasni,

The Empire mail routes crossed some of the most rugged and beautiful scenery in the world – such as the River Indus, pictured here. The aircraft are Westland Wapitis, probably of No. 11 Squadron.

Karachi and Jodhpur, finally arriving at Delhi on 8 January 1927 after a flying time of 65 hours. The flight marked the official handover of the mail service from the RAF to Imperial Airways. G-EBMX was named *City of Delhi* on her arrival in India; the other three Hercules, all of which had been delivered by the spring of 1927, were respectively named *City of Baghdad* (G-EBMY), *City of Jerusalem* (G-EBMZ) and *City of Teheran* (G-EBNA).

Significant though these inaugural flights were, it was to be another two years before the London-India run became a regular fortnightly occurrence; in the meantime, Imperial Airways flights from Cairo went only as far as Baghdad and Basra. One of the reasons for this delay was the lack of suitable air transport to ply the middle section of the route, across the Mediterranean, and also because the French had refused to allow Imperial Airways to fly across France to Genoa, mainly because the British airline had refused, soon after its formation in 1924, to participate in a joint Anglo-French flying-boat service from Marseille to Alexandretta (Iskenderun) — despite the fact that the Air Ministry had stated, in 1923, that such co-operation would be desirable. The result was that, although through passengers for Baghdad (and later India) were flown to Paris from Croydon on board Imperial Airways Armstrong Whitworth Argosy aircraft, they then had to travel by rail and steamer from Paris to Cairo in order to join the next stage of the air link.

The situation was alleviated when, on 31 March 1929, Imperial Airways began a new service across the Mediterranean from Genoa to Alexandria with three Short Calcutta flying-boats, developed from the Singapore I. Passengers were now flown from Croydon to Basle by Argosy; they then travelled by train to Genoa, where they boarded the Calcuttas, which flew to Alexandria via Ostia, Naples, Corfu, Athens, Suda Bay and Tobruk. Then it was the train again, as far as Cairo.

In 1931, some mail services in India were flown by two Handley Page Clive aircraft, versions of the Hinaidi bomber, which were based at the RAF's Heavy Transport Flight, Lahore. One of them is pictured here, surrounded by a crowd of interested onlookers.

The Short Calcutta flying-boat was used on the Mediterranean sectors of Imperial Airways' mail routes.

The three Calcuttas were named *City of Alexandria* (G-EBVG), *City of Athens* (G-EBVH) and *City of Rome* (G-AADN). The aircraft, which was powered by three 540 hp Bristol Jupiter XIF engines and had a top speed of 118 mph, could accommodate fifteen passengers and was the first flying-boat with a metal-skinned hull to go into commercial operation. It was luxuriously furnished, the passenger seats being fitted with pneumatic cushions upholstered in royal blue leather; these could be detached quickly for use as lifejackets in an emergency. The seat backs incorporated padded head rests and folding tables, and aft of the seating there was a well-appointed galley adjacent to a separate water closet and washroom. The crew consisted of two pilots, a radio operator and a steward.

In the late 1920s, some internal mail services in India were flown by aircraft whose primary role was policing the turbulent North-West Frontier, such as these Westland Wapitis. The photographs give an excellent idea of the kind of terrain over which crews had to operate.

The early success and popularity of the flying-boat service received a severe setback when, in the middle of 1929, the Italian government inaugurated a parallel service from Genoa to Alexandria, using Dornier Super Wal flying-boats, and demanded that all receipts over this sector be pooled and shared. Imperial Airways refused to agree to this arrangement, and so the Italians withdrew British rights to stage through Italian ports with effect from 31 October 1929. This blow went hand-in-hand with a tragedy; on 26 October, G-AADN, having left Ostia in a gale, had to make a forced landing with engine trouble at Spezia. She was taken in tow by an Italian tug, but in the darkness and the storm her towlines parted and she capsized and sank, with the loss of her three crew, four passengers and all the mail she was carrying. Then, on 30 October, the two remaining Calcuttas were put out of action following heavy landings in rough seas off Mersa Matruh. They were repaired and returned to service several weeks later, forced now to operate from Athens because of the Italian embargo, and in 1930 they were joined by two more aircraft of the same type, G-AASJ *City of Khartoum,* and G-AATZ *City of Salonika,* the first entering service in January and the second in June.

Meanwhile, in June 1929, a sixth DH66 Hercules, G-AAJH *City of Basra,* had joined the Imperial Airways fleet at Cairo. Unlike its sister aircraft, this example was fitted with an enclosed cockpit; the others were so modified at a later date. By this time, all the original five machines were beginning to show signs of fatigue, and this culminated in the loss of G-EBMZ in a crash in September 1929. The aircraft was replaced by a seventh DH66, G-AARY *City of Karachi,* but in February 1930 G-EBNA was also lost, and this was followed by the crash of G-EMBW in April of the following year. The latter crashed en route from Karachi to Darwin while it was carrying air mail on an inaugural service between Croydon and Melbourne; although the crew were killed, the mail was recovered and flown to Darwin by Charles Kingsford Smith in his Fokker Tri-motor *Southern Cross.*

To make good these losses, Imperial Airways purchased two more Hercules from West Australian Airways, which had received four machines of this type in the spring of 1929. These aircraft also had enclosed flight decks, and other modifications that included seating capacity for fourteen passengers. The two machines were named *City of Cape Town* (G-ABMT) and *City of Jodhpur* (G-ABCP). The latter, too, was lost in a crash in November 1935, but by the end of that year the Hercules had been withdrawn from Imperial Airways service.

Calcutta flying-boats continued to operate on the Mediterranean sector until 1936. The idea was that they were to be replaced by a larger version, the Short Kent, early in 1931, permitting the Calcuttas to be transferred to operations on the Khartoum-Kisimu sector of the Cairo-Cape Town route, but the Kents did not become operational until May, and so for several months the older boats struggled to maintain services in both areas. Fresh agreement with the Italians had resulted in the opening of a new route from Brindisi to Corfu, Phaleron and Mirabella, and the Calcuttas also operated between Castelrosso, Cyprus and Haifa in 1931-2. Then, on 31 December 1935, G-AASJ, with twelve passengers on board, ran out of fuel on a night flight between Mirabella and Alexandria, crashing just short of the latter airfield and killing everyone but the pilot. On the same night, G-EBVH just scraped into Alexandria with about ten minutes' fuel remaining in its tanks. It was a clear warning that the Calcuttas did not have the range to undertake the new route sectors with adequate safety margins; they were withdrawn soon afterwards, ending their careers as crew trainers.

The first of three Short Kent flying boats, designed to augment the Calcuttas, entered service with Imperial Airways in April 1931, and enabled the non-stop flight from Mirabella to Alexandria to be made in safety. The Kent was basically a scaled-up version of the Calcutta, fitted with four 555 hp Jupiter X FMB radial engines, and could carry fifteen passengers.

The first Kent to enter service with Imperial Airways was G-ABFA *Scipio,* and this was followed by G-ABFB *Sylvanus* and G-ABFC *Satyrus.* On 16 May, *Satyrus* inaugurated a new route from Genoa to Alexandria, while *Scipio* took off in the opposite direction carrying mail from India. Unfortunately, the latter damaged a float in heavy seas at Candia, and was out of commission for several weeks; she had scarcely been repaired when her sister ship, *Sylvanus,* collided with a Dornier Wal in Genoa harbour, damaging two engines.

All three Kents were back in service by the end of August, and in October they were operating a mail service from Alexandria to Cyprus via Haifa, a twice-weekly run that involved each aircraft in flying some 4,000 miles every seven days. They continued in service until the end of 1935 with an excellent record of trouble-free operation; then, on 9 November that year, *Sylvanus* was set on fire at Brindisi by an Italian arsonist and totally destroyed. On 22 August 1936 *Scipio* was severely damaged in a heavy landing at Mirabella and sank in deep water; the sole surviving Kent, *Satyrus,* was used to survey proposed Empire mail routes to Singapore in 1937, one via Rangoon and the other via Bangkok, before being withdrawn and scrapped the following year.

The second Short Kent, G-ABFB 'Sylvanus', taking off from the Medway on 31 March, 1931, flown by Major H. G. Brackley.

Imperial Airways H.P.42 at Khartoum, en route for South Africa, during 1930.

Meanwhile, a new type of aircraft had been brought into operation at both ends of the Imperial Airways London to India route. This was the Handley Page HP42, the first four-engined airliner to see regular service anywhere in the world. Powered by four 555 hp Bristol Jupiter XFBM nine-cylinder radial engines, arranged two on the upper and two on the lower mainplane, it had a wingspan of 130 feet and cruised at just over 100 mph over a range of 250 miles. It was, at first sight, a far from attractive aircraft, and yet its very ugliness gave it a grace all of its own, together with a fully justified impression of reliability and sturdiness.

The HP42 prototype, G-AAGX *Hannibal,* flew for the first time on 17 November 1930, and production aircraft came in two basic models: the HP42E, destined for the Cairo-Delhi run, and the HP42W, for service in Europe. The aircraft carried a crew of five — captain, first officer, radio officer and two stewards — and there was accommodation for six passengers in the forward cabin and twelve in the cabin aft of the wings. Later, the number of passengers carried was increased to twenty-four. They travelled in considerable comfort, and the positioning of the engines, illogical though it might have seemed to a layman, was in fact designed to reduce noise in the passenger cabins to an absolute minimum.

Apart from the prototype, G-AAGX, three other HP42Es were built for service on the eastern route sector: G-AAUC *Horsa,* G-AAUD *Hanno* and G-AAUE *Hadrian.* The four destined for the European route were G-AAXC *Heracles,* G-AAXD *Horatius,* G-AAXE *Hengist* and G-AAXF *Helena.*

It was G-AAGX *Hannibal* that made the type's first proving flight from London to Paris on 9 June 1931, and it operated on this route until August, when it left for Cairo to take up the eastern route sector. It was joined by the other three HP42Es before the end of the year.

In 1932, Imperial Airways showed an interest in operating flying boats along the whole of the route from Cairo to Karachi, and in fact consulted No. 203 Squadron RAF, which was then based at Basra and equipped with Short Rangoon flying boats, about the feasibility of such operations. However, since there were only two possible places where a flying-boat harbour could be set up along the coastline of the Trucial Oman, and since neither of these was really suitable, the idea was abandoned. Instead, the HP42s were fitted with extra fuel tanks, containing 125 gallons, and this increased their range to 620 miles, which gave a suitable safety margin over this crucial part of the journey.

From Basra, the HP42s' route took them across the Shatt al Arab (the delta of the Tigris and Euphrates) and out over the Gulf of Kuwait, their next port of call being Bahrain. The aircraft's arrival was timed to give passengers the opportunity to have dinner in Manamah, the island's capital. After dinner, the flight continued along the Trucial coast, the route passing over Yas Island, where there was an emergency landing strip (in fact, emergency strips had been set up at various points along this sector, following negotiations with the local sheikhs). Next stop was Sharjah, where passengers and crew stayed the night in a hotel a mile or so outside the town, everything being organised by a British political representative.

The following morning, the aircraft crossed the mountainous peninsula that juts out into the Strait of Hormuz and headed out over the Gulf of Oman towards Jask, turning eastwards and remaining three miles clear of the coast so as not to infringe Persian territory. From here the flight was straightforward, the pilot keeping the coastline off his port wingtip before heading in to land at Gwadar, in Baluchistan, after a flight of 340 miles from Sharjah. Gwadar was the last stop before Karachi.

On 7 July, 1933, Imperial Airways passed another important milestone with the inauguration of a service from Karachi to Singapore, passengers being taken from there to Australia by a Qantas service. (Qantas, it should be recalled, was one of the world's oldest airlines, having been founded in 1920 as Queensland and Northern Territory Aerial Services Ltd by Lieutenant Hudson Fysh and four partners. Equipped originally with one war-surplus BE2E and one Avro 504K, the company had pioneered air taxi and mail services across the Australian continent. It safety record was — and, in the 1980s still is — without parallel). Following a series of historic pioneer flights from England to Australia (the first by Ross and Keith Smith in a Vickers Vimy in 1919) a proper commercial survey flight had been made by Alan Cobham in 1926, flying a DH50J, G-EBFO, which was specially fitted with floats for the trip.

Cobham left England on 30 June, 1926, accompanied by his engineer, A. B. Elliott, and the flight went more or less according to plan until 6 July, when — flying between Baghdad and Basra — hostile tribesmen fired on the aircraft, shooting the petrol feed through and mortally wounding Elliott, who died that night. Cobham, although saddened, decided to continue the journey with another mechanic, Sergeant A. H. Ward of No. 84 Squadron RAF, who joined the flight at Shaibah (Basra). The two reached Darwin on 8 August 1926, and after wheels had been fitted the aircraft flew on to Melbourne, which was reached on 15 August. Cobham and Ward — and C. J. S. Capel of Armstrong Siddeley, who had helped Ward to overhaul G-EBFO's Jaguar engine — returned home on 1 October, having completed a round trip of 28,000 miles in 78 days.

Some experimental mail services had been flown between England and Australia in April and May 1931, but it was quickly found that these were not economical unless passengers were carried too, just as the Dutch airline KLM was doing on its own route from Amsterdam to Batavia. Arrangements were made with the Australian Government for the latter to operate the Singapore-Brisbane sector, and a new company, Qantas Empire Airways, was formed for that purpose; the Government of India also founded a new company, Indian Trans-Continental Airways, to operate a sector from Karachi to Rangoon.

The aircraft selected to operate the Karachi-Singapore sector was the Armstrong Whitworth AW15 Atalanta, which in fact was specifically developed to meet the requirements of the airline's African and Far Eastern routes. Powered by four Armstrong Siddeley Serval III ten-cylinder radial engines that gave it a cruising speed of 130 mph, the Atalanta had sufficient reserves of power for satisfactory operation in hot and high conditions, and particular attention was also paid to interior design for maximum passenger and crew comfort. The aircraft carried a crew of three and up to seventeen passengers, or various combinations of passengers and freight.

The prototype Atalanta, G-ABPI, flew for the first time on 20 June 1932, and was given the name *Arethusa.* A second aircraft, G-ABTI, piloted by H. G. Brackley, made a proving flight to Cape Town in December; it left England on 31 December and arrived at the Cape on 14 February 1933. Eight Atalantas were in service with Imperial Airways by the end of April 1933, and on 29 May the last aircraft to be delivered, G-ABTL *Astraea,* fitted with extra fuel tanks, made a proving flight to Australia. The machine, piloted by Captain J. V. Prendergast and Major Brackley, reached Darwin on 20 June and Melbourne on the 29th. The return flight was much faster, G-ABTL leaving Melbourne on 2 July and landing at Croydon on the 24th.

Scion Senior floatplane VT-AGU was one of the four delivered to the Irrawaddy Flotilla Company in Burma from 1936 to carry out survey and river transport duties.

The Karachi-Singapore service was opened by G-ABPI on 7 July 1933, and it ran until 1 March 1938, when it terminated at Calcutta. Four Atalantas were used by Imperial Airways on the route, and one of these, G-ABTK *Athena,* was destroyed in a hangar fire at Delhi in September 1936. Of the others, one, G-ABTH *Andromeda,* flew in Imperial Airways colours until June 1939, when it was withdrawn from service; the remaining two, G-ABPI and G-ABTM *Aurora,* were re-registered VT-AEF and VT-AEG, and operated under the flag of Indian Transcontinental Airways until April 1941, when they were taken over by the Indian Air Force for transport duties.

Imperial Airways flights to Singapore in the mid-1930s were undertaken in fierce competition with KLM, and in 1935, when the Dutch airline introduced fast Douglas DC-2s to replace its Fokkers, there was no doubt that the British were losing the battle. Many of the airfields used by landplanes along the route were regularly unserviceable because of heavy rain, and so the decision was made to re-equip Imperial Airways with flying-boats to serve its long-range routes.

Short Brothers, the Belfast-based flying-boat specialists, were invited to tender a design that would meet the new requirement; their answer was the 'C' class flying boat, the prototype of which, G-ADHL *Canopus,* flew for the first time on 4 July 1936 (see Chapter One).

The first eastbound proving flight by an Empire Boat was made on 22 October, when *Canopus* flew from Rochester to Alexandria via Caudebec, Bordeaux, Marseille and Rome. The return trip was started on the 30th, the aircraft flying via Athens, Mirabella and Brindisi. On 13 December, G-ADHM *Caledonia* set out for India with five and a half tons of Christmas mail on board, carrying a similar load on the return trip. On the homeward flight, the pilot, Captain Cumming, left Alexandria on 21 December and flew the 1,700 miles to Marseille non-stop in $11\frac{1}{4}$ hours; the following day, he flew direct across France to land at Southampton after $4\frac{1}{4}$ hours.

Regular flights from Marseille to Alexandria via Rome were started on 4 January 1937, using G-ADUW *Castor,* and on 12 January a through service was started between Alexandria and Southampton with G-ADUT *Centaurus.* G-ADUX *Cassiopeia* also joined the service on 26 January, and on 18 February G-ADHM *Caledonia* flew the whole 2,200-mile distance from Southampton to Alexandria non-stop in thirteen hours.

By the end of 1937 twenty-two Empire Boats were in service with Imperial Airways, and two more — VH-ABA *Carpentaria* and VH-ABB *Coolangatta* — were also supplied to Qantas for use on the Singapore-Brisbane sector. Early the following year the Australians received a third aircraft, VH-ABC *Coogee,* which was transferred from the British register.

Although the Empire Boats brought a new dimension of speed and efficiency to the Far Eastern route, there were three unfortunate casualties in 1937, the first on 24 March when G-ADVA

Capricornus (Captain Paterson) crashed in a snow-storm near Lyons. The aircraft had been carrying the first through mail to Australia, but had turned back when the pilot encountered bad weather over the Alps. Then, on 1 October, G-ADVC *Courtier,* flew into the sea as a result of a misjudged landing at Phaleron Bay, three passengers being drowned when the hull split open; and finally, on 5 December, G-ADUZ *Cygnus* porpoised out of control at Brindisi when the pilot tried to take off with full flap and sank, drowning two passengers and injuring seven. The latter included Air Marshal Sir John Salmond, now a director of Imperial Airways.

Inevitably, the flying-boats suffered less serious mishaps too; on 23 June 1937, for example, one of *Canopus's* engines failed and the captain made an emergency landing in the Mediterranean. The aircraft taxied into Mirabella, the faulty engine was removed, the open engine nacelle blanked off and the flying-boat flown back to England on three engines.

In September 1937, G-AETX *Ceres* made a survey flight over a new route from Alexandria to Karachi, the aircraft flying via the Dead Sea, Habbaniyah and Sharjah, and a regular service was started the following month by G-AEUA *Calypso.* On this occasion, mail was flown from Southampton to Alexandria by G-AETY *Clio,* the journey being continued by *Calypso,* but on the return service G-AEUB *Camilla* made the entire through trip from Karachi to Southampton.

On 15 November G-AEUD *Cordelia* left Karachi to make a survey flight to Singapore, where she arrived six days later, and on 3 December G-ADUT *Centaurus* left Hythe to carry out a survey flight all the way through to New Zealand, completing the last leg from Sydney to Auckland on 27 December. This sector of the route was to be operated by Tasman Empire Airways Ltd., formed jointly by the British, Australian and New Zealand Governments, and three Empire Boats were allocated for this purpose. Originally ordered by Qantas as G-AFCY *Captain Cook,* G-AFCZ *Canterbury* and G-AFDA *Cumberland,* they were renamed *Aotearoa, Australia* and *Awarua* before delivery to New Zealand; this in fact did not take place until 1940, so in the meantime Imperial Airways retained the three aircraft for service on the Southampton-Karachi service.

Meanwhile, in 1938, delivery of six Empire Boats to Qantas had been completed, and these were used on the Singapore-Darwin sector. One of them, VH-ABE *Coorong,* came to grief on 12 December, when she was driven ashore in a gale at Darwin. The engines and mail were salvaged, and the boat was later repaired. There had been a more serious casualty three weeks earlier, on 27 November, when G-AETW *Calpurnia* ran into an unexpected sandstorm and crashed in Lake Habbaniyah, killing two crew members and two passengers; the casualty figures may have been higher had it not been for the RAF, who mounted a rapid rescue operation and also salvaged the Christmas mail carried by the aircraft.

Meanwhile, on 24 January 1938, the prototype of a second aircraft — a landplane this time — ordered by Imperial Airways for service on the Empire Air Mail routes had made its first flight. This

Armstrong Whitworth AW27 Ensign.

was the Armstrong Whitworth AW27 Ensign, a cantilever monoplane powered by four 880 hp Armstrong Siddeley Tiger IX radials that gave it a cruising speed of 170 mph. The aircraft could carry up to forty passengers in great comfort over a range of 800 miles.

Flight-testing of the Ensign prototypes revealed some snags with the rudder controls and the fuel feed system, and the reliability of the Tiger engines left a lot to be desired, but Imperial Airways — which had ordered twelve machines off the drawing board in 1935, followed by two more in 1936 — began a series of route-proving flights with the type on October 1938, and two months later three were impressed into service as relief aircraft to carry Christmas mail to Australia. Their debut, however, was hardly inspiring; one, *Egeria,* was grounded at Athens with a faulty engine, a second, *Euterpe,* developed a serious landing gear fault and failed to reach India, and the third, *Elsinore,* although it got as far as Karachi, developed engine trouble there and could go no further. All three were withdrawn and returned to Armstrong Whitworth for major engine modifications. For the time being, the routes to Australia would have to be sustained by the flying-boats; and no-one could have envisaged the sterling work they would perform, or the terrible risks they would run, in the dark years that lay ahead.

2. The Nile and South Africa

Following a preliminary series of survey flights (see Chapter Five), the first through mail service from London to Cape Town was inaugurated by Imperial Airways on 20 January 1932, using a variety of aircraft that included HP42s, Short Kent flying-boats, Armstrong Whitworth Argosys, Short Calcuttas and a de Havilland Hercules. Between them, the aircraft transported 20,000 letters and 150 packages, and although no fare-paying passengers were carried two VIPs — Francis Bertram, the Deputy Director of Civil Aviation, and Air Vice Marshal Sir Vyell Vyvyan, the Government Director of Imperial Airways, made the trip.

The outward flight — made by HP42, Argosy, Kent and DH66 as far as Cairo — went well, but weather problems caused delays on the next leg of the journey and the aircraft involved, HP42 *City of Baghdad,* arrived at Nairobi eighteen hours late. A tropical rainstorm caused more delays the next day, forcing the machine to make an unscheduled stop, and when it eventually reached Cape Town it was two days behind its timetable. There were more problems on the homeward run, which was made by HP42 *City of Basra;* the aircraft was damaged when it struck a deep unmarked pothole at Salisbury, Rhodesia, and a relief aircraft had to be sent down from Cairo to collect the all-important mail. This machine was compelled to make a forced landing after flying only fifty miles, and nosed over when its undercarriage ploughed into boggy ground. The mail eventually reached England nine days late.

After this inauspicious start, the next scheduled flight on the South African route was made on 27 April, starting at Cape Town. The one-way ticket cost £130, including meals and hotel accommodation, and passengers had to travel by rail between Brindisi and Paris. The aircraft on the final Paris-London leg, HP42 *Heracles,* landed at Croydon on 8 May; of the twenty-five passengers who disembarked, only one had made the whole journey from the Cape. The next day, HP42 *Horatius* took off from Croydon on the first leg of the return flight, carrying thirteen passengers, but a lightning strike over Croydon burnt out the radio and caused some other damage, so the pilot — Captain O. P. Jones — elected to turn back. He set off again soon afterwards in HP42 *Helena* — minus five passengers who had received a bad scare.

The workload on the Cairo-Cape Town route was shared by Imperial Airways HP42s and Armstrong Whitworth Atalantas until 1937, when the first Empire Class flying-boats joined the service. A second route was also opened between Khartoum and Lagos, aircraft staging through El Obeid, El Fasher, Fort Lamy, Maiduguri and Kano; in 1938 this was extended to include Lagos, Accra and Takoradi, this western sector being operated by Short Scion Senior seaplanes of Elders Colonial Airways Ltd. A further extension came into being in January 1939, running via Freetown and Bathurst to Dakar, where it connected with the Deutsche Lufthansa air mail service to South America.

In the summer of 1937, the Empire Boats started an air mail service to Durban, and at the same time one of them — G-ADUV *Cambria,* commanded by Captain Egglesfield — made a 20,000 miles survey of the African routes that ended on 4 June. Generally, there were fewer accidents on the African mail run than on the India-Australia route, although on 14 March 1939 *Corsair* was driven off track by strong winds and ran out of fuel, compelling her captain to make a forced landing on the River Dangu in the Belgian Congo, 150 miles south-west of Juba. There were no injuries and the mail was salvaged, but the hull was holed and the aircraft sank in shallow water. A repair crew of Imperial Airways and Short Brothers engineers flew to Juba, and after travelling as far as they could by road literally hacked their way through the jungle to the stranded flying-boat. Enlisting the help of local tribesmen, they managed to beach the aircraft and completed their repair work by the end of June, labouring in sweltering conditions and tormented constantly by mosquitos and other savage insects.

By this time the rainy season was at its height and the river was in spate; nevertheless, the pilot, Captain Kelly Rogers, decided to attempt a take-off, even though there was a dangerous bend in the river some way ahead. This proved to be his undoing, because as he swerved the aircraft to negotiate the bend it lost speed and he could not get it airborne in a safe distance. As he turned to taxy back, *Corsair* struck a submerged rock, which tore another hole in the hull, and she immediately flooded.

This time, the repair crew had to remove the engines and lash petrol drums to the flying-boat to raise her, and repair work had to begin all over again. While it was in progress, teams of locally-recruited natives felled timber and built a dam to create an artificial lake. The work took months, and was completed just in time for the start of the new rains. At last, on 6 January 1940, Captain Rogers took off along a waterway fifty yards wide — only twelve yards more than *Corsair's* wingspan — and refuelled at Juba before flying on to Alexandria, where the aircraft was completely overhauled. The saga had lasted ten months from start to finish, and was commemorated in an unusual way; today, by the banks of the River Dangu, there stands a little village known as Corsairville. The lake built by the engineers and Africans is still there, and the village is served by the road they carved through the jungle to the site.

Short 'C' Class flying-boat G-ADUX Cassiopeia.

The growth of air mail services to the Cape gave impetus to the development of internal feeder airlines in South Africa. The first commercial air services in that country had been started in 1929 by a private company, Union Airways; based at Port Elizabeth, the Company had a small fleet of five de Havilland Gipsy Moths and these carried mail to Johannesburg, Durban and Cape Town, their services connecting with mail packets from Europe. Later, three Junkers F.13s, a Junkers W.34 and a Fokker Universal were also acquired. In 1932, a second company, South West African Airways, also began services between Windhoek and Kimberley with two Junkers A.50s and a Junkers F.13.

A year earlier, South African Railways had received government approval to operate aircraft for the transportation of passengers and freight, but it was not until 1934 that a new company, named South African Airways and financed by the Railways Administration, came into being and took control of Union Airways, which was hard put to keep pace with growing air traffic demands. South African Airways flew its first scheduled service on 1 February 1934, between Durban and Johannesburg, and in November that year the Company acquired three Junkers 52/3m transports for use on its main services. Twelve more aircraft of this type were bought later, followed by eighteen Junkers 86s, four Airspeed Envoys and a Miles Magister.

In 1935, South African Airways also absorbed South West African Airways, and in April a new service was started between Johannesburg and Cape Town via Kimberley, with connections to Windhoek. The airline moved its main base from Durban to Johannesburg later in the year, and in 1938 it began external flights to Bulawayo, Lourenco Marques and Kisumu in Uganda via Rhodesia and Tanganyika. From 1939, following the outbreak of war, services ceased with the transfer of the airline's main equipment to the South African Air Force.

Chapter Five
Wings Over Africa

In the spring of 1919, with the eyes of the aviation world focused on the race for the honour of making the first Atlantic crossing by air, a number of enterprising French airmen embarked on an mission which was to have far-reaching consequences: the first stage of an aerial survey of the African continent.

On 19 March 1919, two noted French aviators, Lemaître and Latécoère, took off from Toulouse in a Salmson biplane and crossed the Mediterranean to Casablanca, Morocco. In a visit that lasted just over five days they flew on to Rabat, then returned to France via Casablanca — carrying with them a contract, signed by Marshal Lyautey, to set up a postal air service between France and North Africa.

It was only a beginning. A month later, on 12 April, Lieutenant de Vaisseau Lefranc of the French Navy, accompanied by Second Mate Mechanic Rouhaud, carried out an air reconnaissance of the Senegal River in a Donnet-Denhaut seaplane fitted with a 200 hp Hispano-Suiza engine. The reconnaissance, which took place over five days and involved a total flying time of twelve hours, was made in three stages, the longest being 330 miles. The total air distance flown was 683 miles. The aircraft's main base for the operation was Dakar, with forward bases at Kayes and St Louis, and the whole mission was undertaken in conditions of intense heat and humidity. At the end of it, the seaplane's wings and wooden hull were found to have warped considerably, indicating just some of the problems that would have to be overcome on future African air operations.

In June, it was once again Lieutenant Lemaître's turn. On the 18th, accompanied by a mechanic named Guichard, he took off from Villacoublay, Paris, in a Breguet 14B-2 biplane powered by a 300 hp Renault engine, with Port Etienne in Mauritania as his eventual destination.

The flight was made in six stages, the second of which was Casablanca, and the total distance covered was 2,375 miles in a flying time of 25 hours 20 minutes. The last leg was the longest of all, representing a distance of 1,062 miles and an airborne time of ten hours; as it turned out, Lemaître had stretched the Breguet's capabilities too far, because it ran out of fuel short of its destination and, despite determined attempts by Guichard to start the engine again in flight, the pilot had to make a perilous forced landing in a desert of shifting sand.

Nevertheless, the flight was a considerable achievement, and it was the first time that an aircraft had flown over Mauritania. Subsequently, Lemaître emphasized the need for setting up adequate meteorological services as a prerequisite to future long-range flights over Africa, as well as a network of radio stations. He also stressed the need for adequate charts, and recommended that future flights over the desert should be undertaken by multi-engined aircraft.

In accordance with this recommendation, the next aircraft to attempt a flight to Mauritania was a twin-engined type, a Farman Goliath biplane powered by two 260 hp Salmson engines. It was already in use on several internal postal services, and was a well-proven design. Carrying a crew of eight — pilots Lucien Coupet and Bossoutrot, navigator Captain Bizard, observers Lieutenants Boussot and Guillemot, and mechanics Leon Coupet, Jousse and Mulot — the aircraft took off from Toussus-le-Noble, Paris, on 11 August 1919 and flew non-stop to Casablanca in 18 hours 23 minutes.

The aircraft reached Mogador, Morocco, on 14 August, and left the following day for Dakar in Senegal, its itinerary planned to take it across Mauritania. It never arrived, and a desperate search by land — no aircraft being available in this part of the world — only ended on 27 August, when French Naval HQ in Dakar received a telegram from Koufra. Sent by Bossoutrot, it said that the Goliath had been forced to make an emergency landing in the sea 100 miles north of Saint-Louis-du-Senegal after the propeller of the starboard engine had become detached in flight. The pilot had continued for as long as possible on one engine and had headed for the coast, bringing the machine down in the shallows. All the crew had got ashore safely with as much of the aircraft's provisions as they could rescue, and after an exhausting trek through the sand dunes in appalling heat they eventually reached safety. They were picked up by a naval party from Dakar six days later.

The Breguet XIV, workhorse of the Lignes Aériennes Latécoère in their early days of air mail operation.

There was one other African exploration flight in 1919, made by Henri Lefranc and Rouhaud on 28 November from St Raphael to Dakar in a GL 400 seaplane. The same crew and aircraft also flew from Agadir, Morocco, to Dakar via the Canary Islands early the following year.

In the closing months of 1919, however, it was Latécoère's newly-created airmail service to North Africa that was the real landmark in French commercial aviation. His company, named the Société des Lignes Aériennes Latécoère (the name would later be changed to Aéropostale) was based at Toulouse-Mautaudran, and the mail service was inaugurated by Didier Daurat, who flew to Morocco via Spain on 1 September 1919 carrying several bags of letters.

The early mail flights were made without serious snags, Daurat sharing the runs with three other pilots named Dombray, Delrieu and Beauté on a daily rota basis. With the end of the summer, however, the pilots began to run into trouble; the onset of autumn brought with it violent storms, particularly over Spain, caused by the meeting of cold and wet Atlantic air masses with the warmer sub-tropical air of the Mediterranean. Blinding rainstorms, accompanied by winds of up to 70 mph, were not infrequent over the Pyrenees and the Cordilleras.

In one memorable twenty-four hour period in October 1919, bad weather compelled four of Latécoère's mail aircraft to make emergency landings at various points of the compass; one at Perignan, two in Spain and one at Rabat, in Morocco. Both the machines which had landed in Spain had damaged propellers, so Didier Daurat took off in a Breguet 14, with two spare propellers lashed to its wings and the second seat occupied by a pilot named Raymond Vanier, to go to their aid. His own words describe the harrowing flight:

"As soon as we took off for Alicante (from Barcelona) the sky changed. Accompanied by gusts of wind, a storm built up ahead of us, and cumulo-nimbus clouds soon formed an impenetrable wall in our path. It was impossible to go either under or over them. The only solution was to fly out over the sea, where the clouds did not seem so dense.

"I took a last visual fix on Tarragona and headed out over the open sea. For a few minutes everything was normal and I thought I had made it, but then another storm surged up ahead. As I was over the Mediterranean and therefore not worried about colliding with anything, I dived as low as possible in order to fly visually. At low level, the sight of the churned-up sea was extraordinary. The waves seemed to climb toward us. My compass was haywire, and with no other means of holding my course I knew that I had to get back to the coast. The storm had swept me away from it, and to get back I had to fly right into the murk. I tried to fly as low as possible, but a sudden torrential downpour blinded me. The Breguet rose and fell without warning, and shuddered like a leaf. Soaked through and frozen, Vanier and I peered ahead for a glimpse of the coast; several times we thought we saw it, but each time it turned out to be only a mirage, created by the storm.

"An hour went by, and then I suddenly noticed something unusual. Although the engine was running perfectly, the aircraft was gradually losing speed. I was now thoroughly worried, because I had no means of knowing whether the storm that was now sweeping me along was the same as the one I had first encountered near Tarragona; if it was a different one, it might be taking me further out to sea. Then, purely by chance, I saw a fishing boat flash by underneath; despite a very tight turn I failed to locate it again, but the sight had renewed my confidence. I reasoned that the boat must not be operating very far from its home port in weather such as this.

"The Breguet continued to lose flying speed, and I was finding it increasingly difficult to keep firm control. Suddenly, a dark mass loomed in my windshield and I turned hard to avoid it; it was a great rock, lashed by the storm. Immediately afterwards, the engine missed a few times; I calculated that we had enough fuel left for a further hour's flying ... Thirty minutes later, there was no longer any doubt; there was land, right ahead of us. We were saved! The aircraft crossed the coast near Sagunto, thirty miles north of Valencia. By this time she was barely staggering along, and making a shallow dive to build up speed I set her down on a beach a mile and a half from Valencia. The beach was bordered by palm trees, stripped by the tempest, and cluttered with boats which had been torn from their moorings. We jumped from the aircraft. It was basically intact, but now I understood the reason for the progressive slowing down. The wooden propeller had been chewed up by the rain and was only a fraction of its normal size. It was nothing short of a miracle that the fragment that was left had propelled the Breguet this far."

There were now five of Latécoère's machines standing uselessly on the ground. As soon as he heard the news by telegraph, Latécoère himself set out in a Salmson biplane, with two pilots named Rodier and Massimi, to bring assistance. Arriving over Spain at noon the following day, they too ran into a violent storm and came down in a bog near Valencia, just a mile or two from where Daurat was stranded. The aircraft was badly damaged, and although the occupants were unhurt they had to claw their way out of the sodden morass. An hour later, the mud-caked trio were drinking brandy with Daurat and Vanier in a hotel in town. Latécoère, thoroughly disillusioned, was all for winding up the airmail service there and then, but the others managed to talk him out of it. The aircraft were duly repaired, and the mail continued to be flown to and from North Africa, week in, week out, summer and winter alike.

Early in 1920, the French Air Force, on the initiative of General Nivelle, organised an aerial expedition to the mountainous Ahaggar region of the southern Sahara and the valley of the Niger. The expedition had considerable financial backing, and was to consist of eight aircraft and crews supported by thirteen landing strips, six of which were to be equipped with radio and four more with meteorological facilities. In addition, four fuel depots and two radio stations were to be set up between Ahaggar and Timbuktu.

The eight aircraft, all Breguet 16 Bn2s, powered by 300 hp Renault engines, were split into two flights, one of three machines led by Commandant Vuillemin (who was later to become Chief of Air Staff) and the other of five aircraft under 'Captain Rolland. The expedition was doomed to failure from the outset; there were no adquate maps of the areas to be covered, flight planning was non-existent, the difficulties of refuelling and (if necessary) repairing aircraft in the desert had been badly under-estimated, and no-one seemed to have taken into account the blinding sandstorms which sweep across the Sahara early in the year.

Nevertheless, the expedition went ahead, Rolland's five Breguets leaving Algiers for Tamanrasset in the Sahara on 24 January 1920. Only three arrived, and of these only one was destined to return safely to Algiers. Of the other two, one was wrecked as the result of a bad landing; the other, carrying General Laperrine as an observer, set off for the Niger Valley on 18 February, but crash-landed in the desert. The general was badly injured, and died on 5 March before help could reach him. The two crew members, Bernard and Vaslin, were eventually rescued on 22 March, utterly exhausted, after a month in the wilderness.

Vuillemin's flight of three aircraft, meanwhile, had departed from Paris, leaving on 14 January. The two other pilots were Captain Mézergues and Lieutenant Dagneaux, and each aircraft carried a mechanic. The flight got off to a poor start when Mézergues fell ill and had to abandon his journey at Istres; Vuillemin and Dagneaux flew on to Algiers, arriving on 6 February. The flight was delayed by sandstorms, and it was not until 16 February that the two aircraft reached Tamanrasset — where Dagneaux smashed his undercarriage hopelessly in a bad landing.

Vuillemin and his mechanic, Challus, continued the expedition alone. On 23 February they made an emergency landing, out of fuel, at Menaka, forty miles from Gao; it was two weeks before a supply of petrol reached them overland and they were able to continue their flight on 7 March. Then, after landing at Gao, Vuillemin found that he had two flat tyres. Using his initiative, he stuffed the inner tubes with straw and managed a bumpy take-off. He eventually arrived at Dakar, his ultimate destination, on 31 March. It was just as well that this was the end of the line; the Breguet was so worn out that it had to be scrapped.

It had taken Vuillemin and Challus two months and twenty-one stages to cover the 4,143 miles from Paris to Dakar — an average of less than seventy miles a day. Despite the courage and endurance of the airmen, the expedition could hardly be called a success, as it represented no advancement in terms of time over other forms of transport. In the wake of this disappointment, it was to be more than two years before the French resumed their exploration and proving flights over Africa.

Meanwhile, the British had also begun to respond to the African challenge. The goal was to link Cairo and Cape Town by air, and the first aircraft to attempt it was the Vickers Vimy Commercial prototype G-EAAV, the civil version of the famous First World War bomber. The flight was organized by *The Times* under the sponsorship of Lord Northcliffe, and the crew consisted of Captains F. C. G. Broome and S. Cockerell (pilots), Sergeant-Major J. Wyatt (mechanic), C. Corby (rigger) and Dr. P. Chalmers Mitchell, a representative of *The Times* who was acting as observer.

The Vimy Commercial took off from Brooklands at 11.30 am on 20 January, 1920, and flew steadily southwards for four weeks, staging through Cairo as planned and crossing Egypt and the Sudan. Then, on 27 February, came disaster. G-EAAV crash-landed at Tabora, in Tanganyika, and was so badly damaged that the attempt had to be abandoned.

On 21 January, the day after G-EAAV's departure, another aircraft — Handley Page 0/400 G-EAMC, powered by two Rolls-Royce Eagle VIII engines, left Cricklewood Aerodrome on the start of a similar quest. Again, the incentive was a prize of £10,000, offered by the *Daily Mail,* for the first successful flight from Cairo to the Cape. The 0/400 and its crew — Major H. G. Brackley and Captain Frederick L. Tymms, navigator — was entered by the *Daily Telegraph.* It reached Cairo on 20 February, where it was joined by three passengers, one of whom was Major C. C. Turner, the *Daily Telegraph* correspondent and observer. Sadly, the attempt was to be short-lived; five days later, G-EAMC crashed in the Sudan and was damaged beyond repair.

The next aircraft to make the Cape Town attempt was a standard Vickers Vimy, carrying the civil registration G-UABA and the name *Silver Queen,* for it was painted silver overall. It had been purchased by the South African Government, and the two pilots were South Africans: Wing Commander Pierre van Ryneveld and Flight Lieutenant C. J. Quintin Brand. Accompanied by Flight Sergeant E. F. Newman and W. F. Sherratt, they took off from Brooklands at 7.30 am on 24 January, 1920, on the first leg of a trip that was to be beset by mishaps.

The Vimy reached Cairo without incident, but on the next leg, only 530 miles south of the Egyptian capital, radiator trouble was experienced and the aircraft had to make a forced landing at Korosko, near Heliopolis. The Vimy ran into some boulders and was badly damaged, but her engines were quickly transferred to a surplus RAF Vimy at Heliopolis, and this aircraft — named *Silver Queen II* — took off from that airfield at 6.45 am on 22 February. On 5 March it landed at Bulawayo, Southern Rhodesia, after nine stages totalling 2,687 miles, but crashed there while taking off the following day.

Undeterred, the South African Government offered the pilots the use of a DH 9 (serial number H5648 and named *Voortrekker),* in which to resume their flight. Using this aircraft, van Ryneveld and Brand finally reached Wynberg Aerodrome, Cape Town, on 20 March 1920. They had covered a distance of 7,500 miles in a total flying time of 4 days, 13 hours 30 minutes, the average daily distance flown being 168 miles.

The prize was theirs, but the achievement had been far less than expected. It had been estimated that the distance between Cairo and Cape Town could have been covered by a single aircraft in fourteen days; the two South Africans had taken six weeks and used three aircraft.

A third crew also attempted the London-Cape flight, leaving Hendon in a de Havilland DH 14A, registration G-EAPY, on 4 February. This aircraft, flown by Flight Lieutenant F. S. Cotton and Lieutenant W. A. Townsend, got as far as La Marmilla, Messina, where it overturned in a forced landing and was badly damaged. It had to be shipped back to the United Kingdom for repairs; the crew had planned to have another try, but van Ryneveld and Brand reached Cape Town in the interval.

French airmen re-entered the African scene in the summer of 1922. The first significant flight, on 8 July, was to investigate the feasibility of setting up a direct commercial air link between North Africa and Paris, instead of having to use the roundabout Spanish route; the pilot was Pelletier d'Oisy, who left Tunis at 5.30 am with his mechanic, Bussard, in a Breguet 14 fitted with auxiliary fuel tanks and arrived at Paris — Le Bourget at 5.50 that day. The flight was remarkable mainly for the severe weather the crew encountered; from Lyon onwards, they were forced to fly through a blinding hailstorm, which became so violent that the pilot eventually decided to make a precautionary landing in a field seventy miles south of the French capital. A sudden lull in the storm, lasting barely ten minutes, allowed him to take off once more and reach his destination.

On 6 September, Lieutenant Battelier, a pilot who had set up a recent speed record and was something of a celebrity in France, attempted to fly non-stop from Paris to Casablanca, but technical trouble compelled him to abandon the flight at Rabat. The following month, Pelletier d'Oisy made the same trip in several stages, and on 16 October he flew non-stop from Casablanca to Tunis — a distance of 1,093 miles — in ten hours.

On 3 May, 1923, pilots and aircraft of the Société des Lignes Aériennes Latécoère, still going strong despite its earlier reverses, carried out an extensive reconnaissance of the African coastline between Casablanca and Dakar as a preliminary to establishing a regular mail service. Three Breguet 14s were used, and the mission was completed in three days. The only incident came when one pilot's tropical helmet flew off and jammed the controls for a few unpleasant moments!

The next significant exploration flight began on 2 November 1923, when three Breguet 14s flown by Commandant Vuillemin, Captain Dagneaux and Captain Papin left Perpignan to make an aerial tour of North Africa. This was completed in many stages, the longest of which did not exceed 500 miles, and after a round trip covering some 6,250 miles the aircraft flew back to France (Metz) on 8 January 1924.

This flight was overshadowed by an expedition, consisting of three Breguet 14s fitted with supplementary fuel tanks, that set out from Dakar to make a journey to Colomb-Bechar and back on 2 December 1924. The pilots on this flight, which involved the first double crossing of the Sahara, were Lieutenant-Colonel Tulasne, Captain Gama, and Lieutenant Michel, with Adjutant-Chef Cadoux as reserve. The expedition's goal was to examine the possibility of setting up airstrips across the Sahara, and to plot landmarks which would be of use to cartographers in drawing maps for an air route between French West Africa and Algeria.

Two of the pilots experienced gastric troubles early in the flight, and a halt was made at Bamako between 5 and 13 December. The two sick pilots made a quick recovery, but on the next leg they came upon an unexpected obstacle: the River Niger had flooded, inundating the countryside for miles around, and it was extremely difficult to follow an accurate course by map-reading.

The three aircraft followed the Niger from Timbuktu to Gao, having staged through Sama. After Gao they were over the desert, and on this leg — as far as Tessalit — the Breguets flew in 'vee' formation, with 200 yards between each machine, for reasons of safety in case one of them had to make a forced landing. Engine repairs to one machine made a night stop necessary beside the Tilemsi Valley, a dried-up tributary of the Niger, and more trouble led to another unscheduled landing fifteen miles north-west of Adrar Tashdai, where the troublesome aircraft was finally abandoned. The two remaining aircraft reached Tessalit, then, after refuelling, flew back with mechanics on board to repair the stranded machine's engine.

The aircraft stayed at Tessalit from 30 December until 15 January, 1925, on the orders of higher authority, and during this period the crews carried out an extensive reconnaissance of the surrounding desert terrain. They continued their journey into the Sahara on the 15th still flying in formation, and despite encountering strong headwinds reached Colomb-Bechar without further incident. The return flight, which ended at Dakar on 20 February, was much more hazardous, for the crews had to contend with sandstorms en route.

During the flight, the crews navigated visually by following a track across the desert pioneered by employees of the Citroen automobile company, checking their position by reference to the Adrar and Ahaggar Mountains. The importance of these mountain massifs in visual navigation over the Sahara was one of the main conclusions reached as a result of this flight; another was the sheer folly of trying to fly in a sandstorm. Desert flying was something that had to be achieved in good weather conditions.

Nineteen twenty-five was to become what the French later called the 'Year of Africa', when the lessons learned during the early explorations of the first half of the decade were put to good use. From now on, expeditions would be far better equipped and planned, with as little as possible left to chance. At last, aviation was beginning to face up realistically to the rigours of the African climate.

On 19 January, 1925, an expedition set out from Paris with Bangui, on the border between Chad and the Belgian Congo, as its ultimate destination. Equipped with two four-engined Bleriot 115 aircraft, the expedition was led by Colonel de Goys. With the latter, in the Bleriot named *Roland Garros* after the French air ace of 1914-18 War, flew Lieutenant Pelletier d'Oisy, Adjutant-Mechanic Besin and a photographer named Dely; the crew of the second aircraft, the *Jean Casale,* comprised Colonel Vuillemin, Captain Dagnaux, Sergeant Knecht and Sergeant Wendel, the radio operator.

The plan was to carry out a series of proving flights in North Africa; then, if the equipment proved satisfactory, the expedition was to fly across the Sahara to the River Niger, from there to Lake Chad, and finally — if aircraft and crews were still in reasonable shape and the expedition's logistics were still functioning — to Bangui. Afterwards, the return flight would be made via the Sudan, Senegal, Dakar, Morocco and Spain.

In December 1931, a Fokker F.VII of SABENA flew from Brussels to the Congo to inaugurate a regular Belgium - Africa service. Mr Tony Orta, managing director of SABENA (Africa) - seen here third from right - flew as a passenger. On his right is Paul Cocquyt, SABENA's chief pilot at the time.

The expedition's task was fourfold. First, to examine the possibility of creating a regular air link between France and her principal African colonies; second, to pioneer the use of heavy aircraft, of the kind that would be used commercially, over long distances and in vastly differing climatic conditions; thirdly, to carry out meteorological observations, with particular reference to high-altitude operations; and finally, to gather information that would lead to the improvement of long-range air navigation techniques over difficult terrain.

There was no doubt that the Bleriots were well equipped for their task. Their 180 hp Hispano-Suiza engines were among the most reliable of their day, and each aircraft was fitted with dual (sometimes triple) instrumentation. In addition, the *Jean Casale's* radio equipment would enable the expedition to communicate with ground stations at ranges of up to 250 miles in flight, or 60 miles on the ground.

Bad weather delayed the expedition's start from Paris on 19 January, and weather conditions on the flight across Spain were appalling. By the time they reached Morocco, the crews of the two aircraft were practically exhausted. The proving flights, however, proved satisfactory and the two aircraft continued their journey, reaching Gao early in February. Here, additional supplies were taken on board, the heaviest load being carried by the *Jean Casale.* In addition to a full load of fuel, this machine was also laden with 360 pounds of spares, 320 pounds of clothing and accessories, 118 pounds of armaments, 112 pounds of camping equipment and 120 pounds of miscellaneous gear. This all contributed to a loaded weight 12,199 pounds, which was nearly a thousand pounds higher than normal.

It was too much. On 7 February, the heavily-laden Bleriot, piloted by Vuillemin, failed to attain safe flying speed and crashed only seconds after taking off from Gao. It was a miracle that only one crew member, Sergeant Wendel, was killed. The loss of the *Jean Casale,* with its all-important radio equipment, meant that Colonel de Goys had no alternative but to abandon the expedition. It was small comfort to know that, had it not been for this tragic accident, the mission would almost certainly have been an unqualified success.

On 3 February, while the ill-fated de Goys expedition was provisioning at Gao, two more French Air Force pilots, Captain Lemaître and Captain Arrachart, left Etampes-Mondesir airfield in a

The Westland Wessex was used by SABENA on the Brussels-Croydon run in the early 1930s, and also on internal services in the Congo.

The Handley Page W.8e enabled SABENA to undertake long-range services to the African colonies.

single-engined series production Breguet XIX on a long-range penetration flight into French West Africa. The aircraft was fitted with dual controls and supplementary fuel tanks, one of which contained benzole. Mixed with ordinary petrol, this boosted the engine to 550 hp on take-off. Loaded weight of the aircraft was 7,616 pounds, 2,460 greater than normal, and even though the Breguet had been stripped of all non-essential equipment it needed two attempts before it finally wallowed into the air and climbed precariously away from Etampes.

The aircraft took off at 11.30 am and, circumnavigating the higher summits of the Pyrenees in order to conserve fuel, flew over Madrid just as the sun was setting. It headed out over the Straits of Gibraltar and made landfall at Tangier, following the coast until it reached Casablanca at 1.30 am on 4 February. The Breguet overflew Cape Juby at 7.30 that morning and landed at Villa Cisneros, Rio de Oro, at noon. The engine had been running roughly for some time, and although the aircraft still had sufficient fuel in its tanks to fly on to Port Etienne the crew judged it prudent to land in Spanish territory rather than risk an accident. Despite the interruption, they had flown 1,978 miles non-stop, setting up a new world distance record.

They continued their journey to Dakar the following day, and on 18 February they reached Timbuktu, having flown via Kayes and Bamako. They stayed at Timbuktu for two days and then took off with the itention of flying to Adrar, in Algeria, via Tessalit. On this leg they carried less than a full load of fuel, because of the restricted take-off area available at Timbuktu, and this, combined with a navigational error and a sudden strong wind that blew them badly off track, was to prove their undoing. At 11.45 on 20 February, they ran out of fuel and had to make a forced landing in the open desert ten miles west of Ain-Mezzer. The landing was rough, resulting in a burst tyre and some damage to one of the Breguet's lower mainplanes.

Taking as much water as they could handle, Lemaître and Arrachart set out to trek across the desert to find help. Just after noon the following day, they had the good fortune to encounter some Arabs, who provided them with two camels. Using this unaccustomed and temperamental means of transport, the two airmen reached El Golea, sore and weary, on 26 February.

They rested for ten days, and then, using vehicles provided by a local Foreign Legion detachment, returned to the scene of the forced landing with fuel and a spare tyre. They then flew the Breguet to El Golea, where they carried out repairs to the damaged wing before flying on to Algiers on 10 March. On 24 March they finally landed at Villacoublay, Paris, having returned home via Oran, Fez, Casablanca, Alicante, Barcelona and Lyon.

The crew of Handley Page W.8E 'Princesse Marie-Jose' on arrival in the Congo, February 1925, with Belgian colonial representatives.

Three days after their homecoming, another aerial expedition set out for Africa, this time from Lisbon. The Portuguese crew comprised Commandant Pinheiro Correa, Lieutenant da Silva and Miguel Antonio, a mechanic; their aircraft was French, a series-production Breguet XIVA-2, seven years old and fitted with an extra fuel tank that increased its endurance to seven and a half hours. In seven days, the aircraft covered the 2,875 miles between Lisbon and Boloma, Portuguese Guinea, in eight stages, the longest of which was a 612-miles leg between Villa Cisneros and Saint-Louis du Senegal. For several days after its arrival at Boloma, the Breguet took part in military exercises, which included bombing a small island offshore.

By this time, the Belgians had also begun to exploit the aircraft's potential as a means of communication in Africa. As early as July 1920, in fact, Belgian aviators had started a regular air link between Kinshasa and N'Gombe, in the Belgian Congo, and in 1921 this had been extended to Lisala, although who these airmen were and what aircraft they used does not appear to be on record. Nevertheless, there is little doubt that Belgian interest in furthering aviation in Africa was stimulated by King Albert, who — after visiting Marshal Lyautey in Rabat in October 1921 — was flown home in a Breguet of the Latécoère Line, piloted by Jean Dombray.

On 12 February, 1925, a Belgian expedition left Brussels for Leopoldville, its purpose being to pave the way for the establishment of a regular air service between Belgium and the Congo. The aircraft used was a Handley Page W.8e Hamilton tri-motor, one of a number supplied for use by

Sabena, the Belgian airline; it was powered by one 360 hp Rolls-Royce Eagle in the nose and two 240 hp Armstrong Siddeley Pumas on wing struts.

The aircraft's crew comprised Edmond Thieffry, pilot, with Leopold Roger as second pilot and Josef de Bruycker as flight mechanic. The flight of 5,077 miles was accomplished in fifty-one days and involved a flying time of 75 hours 25 minutes, the Handley Page — named *Princesse Marie-Jose* — flying nineteen legs (Brussels-Dijon-Lyon-Perpignan-Alicante-Oran-Colomb-Bechar-Quallen-Gao-Niamey-Tessoua-Zinder Rive-Ogoué-Bouyae-m'Bassa-Fort Archambault-Bangui-Irebu-Leopoldville). The flight was relatively trouble-free, the aircraft having to make only one emergency landing near Ouallen because of an approaching sandstorm. The use of two different types of aero-engines proved to be a snag, for the Handley Page had to carry spare parts for both, which cut down the amount of fuel it could carry.

On 2 June, pilots of the Latécoère Line — now renamed Aéropostale — finally inaugurated a regular mail service between Casablanca and Dakar, the route they had pioneered two years earlier, and so opened up French West Africa to commercial aviation. This was the real milestone of French aerial work in Africa during 1925, and the culmination of five years of work.

There was another milestone later in the year, when the Royal Air Force carried out the first of a series of exploration flights over East Africa. On 27 October, three de Havilland DH 9s, led by Squadron Leader A. Coningham, made the first flight from Helwan, Egypt, to Kano in Nigeria and back, covering a total distance of 5,000 miles. Their route took them through Cairo, Aswan, Wadi Halfa, Khartoum, El Obeid and El Fasher, ending at Kano on 1 November. The DH 9s, all of 1918 vintage, were fitted with extra tanks, and modifications included tropical radiators and a new oleo-type undercarriage. Before flying back to Egypt they visited Fort Lamy and Abeshr, in French Equatorial Africa; they eventually returned to Cairo on 19 November.

Before the end of 1925, British interest switched back to the London-Cape Town route. This route, full of perils, had yet to be flown by a single-engined machine from start to finish, but on 16 November 1925 a de Havilland DH 50J, powered by a 380 hp Armstrong Siddeley Jaguar III engine and bearing the civil registration G-EBFO, took off from Croydon to make the attempt. Its pilot was Alan Cobham, who was accompanied by A. B. Elliott as flight engineer and B. W. G. Emmott, a Gaumont cinematographer. Flying by way of Paris, Lyon and Marseille, Cobham and his crew reached Cairo, their first staging point on the African continent, and then flew on to Khartoum, where they landed on 22 December. They continued their journey on 6 January 1926, flying over tropical forest for 400 miles between Kisumu on Lake Victoria and Tabora, then navigating over more forest and swamps for 280 miles to Abercon.

They arrived at Broken Hill, Northern Rhodesia, on 18 January, and Emmott expressed a wish to take some aerial film of the famous Zambezi falls. Cobham obliged by flying as close to them as possible — so close, in fact, that at one stage spray saturated his carburettor to the point where the engine suffered a serious power loss and for a few unpleasant minutes it was touch and go whether he would be able to climb out of the Zambezi Valley at the foot of the falls. His skill, however, saved the situation, and the flight continued. From Broken Hill the aircraft went on to Livingstone, which was reached on 30 January; three days later it was at Pretoria, and on 5 February it arrived at Johannesburg. After a south-westerly flight across South Africa, it reached its destination — Wynberg Aerodrome, Cape Town — in the evening of 17 February 1926. On its journey from England, it had covered a distance of 8,115 miles. G-EBFO stayed in South Africa for nine days before flying home via the same route; the homeward flight took fifteen days, the aircraft landing at Croydon at 4.20 pm on 13 March 1926.

On the first day of March, while Cobham and his crew were homeward bound, four Fairey IIID aircraft of the Royal Air Force, under the command of Wing Commander C. W. H. Pulford, left Cairo and flew to Cape Town, pioneering the type of long-range navigation exercise that was to become routine for RAF squadrons in the Middle East over the years to come. Returning to Cairo on 27 May, the four aircraft were equipped with floats and then flew on to Lee-on-Solent, arriving on 21 June at the close of a 14,000-mile cruise.

The route down the Nile was also exploited in March 1926 by three Belgian pilots, Medaets, Verhaegen and Coppens, who left Brussels on 9 March and flew via Cairo to arrive at Leopoldville (Kinshasa) on the 30th. The flight from Brussels took twelve days and was accomplished in seven stages, the flying time being 47 hours 49 minutes. The aircraft, a Breguet XIX A2, returned by the same route, reaching Brussels in eighteen days. Total flying time for the round trip was 101 hours 31 minutes, and the distance flown 11,180 miles.

One of the most significant African flights of 1926, however, was made by two Frenchmen, Lieutenants Girardot and Cornillon, who took off from Le Bourget at 7.25 pm on 9 September in a Breguet XIX A2 and flew to Rabat, Morocco, at an average altitude of 10,000 feet. The remarkable thing about the flight was that it was made in darkness, the crew navigating with the aid of experimental radio direction-finding equipment. D/F fixes were successfully obtained along the route from ground stations at Viry-Châtillon, Bordeaux, Toulouse, Algiers and Casablanca. From now on, aircrews on the route to French West Africa would not have to rely solely on their eyesight and the evidence of maps whose accuracy still left a great deal to be desired.

Nevertheless, desert flying still held plenty of perils, and the pilots of Aéropostale experienced them all to frequently. On 21 May 1926, for example, a Breguet flown by one of the service's most experienced pilots, Mermoz, was compelled to make a forced landing in the Sahara. The pilot was extremely fortunate; captured by the Tuareg — the savage blue-veiled desert warriors — he was released, unharmed, on payment of a substantial ransom several days later.

Other Aéropostale pilots were not so lucky. On 11 November that year, two of them, each flying a Breguet and accompanied by a Spanish mechanic named Pintado and Ataf, an interpreter, came down in the desert and were immediately attacked by Tuareg. Pintado and one of the pilots, Erable, were shot dead and the other pilot, Gourp, mortally wounded. He was ransomed, dying, together with Ataf. Other pilots, forced down in the desert with engine trouble, managed to make temporary repairs and escape by the skin of their teeth.

Two more long-range exploratory flights over Africa were made by the French before the end of 1926. The first, organized by the Aeronautical Directorate of the French Admiralty, was designed to make a thorough reconnaissance of a potential route from France to Madagascar, crossing the African continent from north-west to south-east, and since it was envisaged that rivers would be an important feature of this route, two seaplanes were assigned to the expedition, a CAMS 37 G-4, powered by a 450 hp Lorraine-Dietrich engine, and a Lioré-et-Olivier, fitted with a 420 hp Gnome-Rhône Jupiter. The crew of the CAMS were Lieutenant de Vaisseau Guilbaud and First Mate Bougault, and that of the LeO Lieutenant de Vaissau Bernard, with First Mate Gara as his mechanic.

The two seaplanes left Berre on 12 October, 1926, with Tangier as their first port of call. From there they staged through Casablanca, Las Palmas, Port Etienne, Saint-Louis du Senegal, Kayes, Bamako, Timbuktu, Gao, Gaye, Djebba and Lokodja, reaching the last-named point on 3 November.

By this time the CAMS was suffering from constant engine trouble, and Guilbaud was reluctantly compelled to give up. Bernard's mechanic, Gara, had fallen sick, so Bougault replaced him and the LeO continued the flight alone, reaching Garoua in Cameroon on 5 November. It subsequently staged through Fort Archambault, Stanleyville, Lissala, Albertville, Fort Johnston (Nyasaland), Kitouta, Quilimane (Portugue East Africa) and Mozambique, which it reached on 20 November. The next day, it made the 300-mile hop over the Mozambique Channel to Madagascar, landing at Majunga on the north-west coast of the island. It had covered 9,680 miles in twenty stages, each one averaging 500 miles. The impact of the crew's achievement was underlined when the Governor of Madagascar held an open-air reception for them; eighty thousand people turned up.

In the course of its flight, the seaplane had made landings on the rivers Senegal, Niger, Benoué, Chari, Ubanghi, Congo, Zambezi and also on Lakes Nyasa and Tanganyika, proving conclusively that a seaplane was the right form of air transport for the trans-African Madagascar route. The LeO's homeward route took it through East Africa, reaching the Mediterranean via Lake Victoria and the Nile.

On 28 November 1926, a week after Bernard and Bougault arrived in Madagascar, a second French expedition left France for the same objective. This time, the aircraft was a landplane, a Breguet XIX; the pilot was the highly experienced Commandant Dagnaux, with Corporal Dufert as his mechanic. Leaving Le Bourget and staging through Morocco, the aircraft suffered a great deal of mechanical trouble, and was not fit to undertake a crossing of the Sahara until 6 December. The crossing was made non-stop between Adrar and Gao, a distance of 875 miles, in conditions of intense heat, which became so bad that the pilot was obliged to make an emergency landing at Niamey. On

10 December the aircraft ran into a sandstorm and had to make another forced landing east of Tessaoua, but no damage was done and it flew on to reach Lake Chad on the 16th. Three days later it reached Bangui, having flown via Fort Lamy and Fort Archambault, but there it suffered a delay of two days while the local populace was enlisted to cut down trees to make a longer take-off strip. A further delay — of eighteen days, this time — was caused by torrential rain at Luebo, the aircraft's undercarriage sinking into the mud whenever the crew tried to move it.

The flight got under way again on 15 January, 1927, and this time everything went smoothly. By the 20th the Breguet was at Mozambique, and the following day it made the final hop to Madagascar. Dagnaux and Dufert had proved that landplanes could make the long journey too; but the obstacles they had encountered had also shown that seaplanes could do it with much less trouble.

Dagnaux had less good fortune when, accompanied again by Dufert, he set out to make the Madagascar trip again on 26 November 1927. His Breguet XIX reached Tananarive in Madagascar on 10 February 1928, after covering 7,753 miles in twenty-four stages, but on the return flight — a mechanic named Treille having replaced Dufert — it was destroyed in a forced landing at Chicoa on 20 July.

By the end of 1928, sufficient data had been amassed by exploratory flights over the African continent for the nations concerned to set about the actual organisation of commercial air services between Europe and various points in Africa. A joint Franco-Belgian enterprise, Air Afrique, was created, and plans were laid to inaugurate a regular service between Brussels, Paris and Lake Chad, calling at various points en route. On 29 January, 1929, as a preliminary, a Farman F.190 set out from Le Bourget to make a flight to Lake Chad, the task of the three-man crew — Lalouette, Richard and Cordonnier — being to work out an itinerary for the commercial service. Although the flight involved a non-stop crossing of 750 miles of Sahara Desert between Reggane and Gao, it was completed without incident in both directions, apart from two precautionary landings that had to be made to clear oiled-up plugs.

The success of this flight encouraged the French Air Ministry to begin an experimental air mail service between Paris and Madagascar, using the same type of aircraft. The inaugural flight began on 17 October 1929, when a Farman 190 piloted by Warrant Officer Marchesseau, with Captain Goulette as navigator and Flight Sergeant Bourgeois as engineer, left Le Bourget on the first leg of the long journey to Tananarive. The flight was successfully completed in 10 days, 8 hours and 40 minutes, despite a number of unexpected setbacks; shortly after flying over Colomb-Bechar, for example, Goulette made a navigational error, so as the sun went down the pilot decided to land rather than risk flying on, lost, into the darkness. The crew spent the night in the desert, huddled together for warmth in the cockpit. The same thing happened all over again on the following night, but the only serious obstacle to navigation after that was a torrential rainstorm, encountered over the jungle of the Congo. The Farman reached Madagascar on 27 October and set off on the return flight on 3 December, having carried out a number of survey flights over the island in the meantime. The aircraft also made the first flight from Madagascar to Reunion Island, away to the east in the Indian Ocean.

The home run got off to a poor start when the Farman suffered a fractured fuel line shortly after taking off from Tananarive. The pilot quickly turned round and made an emergency landing on Juan de Nova Island, but the propeller was damaged when it sliced through some tree branches. Temporary repairs were carried out and the Farman limped back to Tananarive, where it was thoroughly overhauled.

It set off once more on 6 December, reaching Elisabethville in the Congo two days later. There, its wheels ran into a boggy patch on take-off and the Farman tipped on its nose, smashing the propeller. This could be repaired fairly easily, but Captain Goulette had been badly knocked about in the accident and he was not fit to resume the journey until several weeks had gone by. The Farman eventually left Elisabethville on 19 March, 1930, and arrived at Fort Lamy on the 23rd. Soon after landing, it was caught out in the open in a sandstorm, which meant that the engine had to be stripped down and cleaned thoroughly. It was perhaps hardly surprising that, on a subsequent leg of the flight between Gao and Reggane on 22 April, the engine failed completely and Marchesseau was forced to make an emergency landing in the desert. The aircraft was a write-off, but its three occupants were fortunately unhurt and were rescued by friendly tribesmen five days later.

The second Farman 190 to make the Madagascar mail run left Le Bourget on 28 October 1929, ten days after Marchesseau's aircraft. This machine was powered by a 240 hp Gnome-Rhône Titan engine (Marchesseau's had been fitted with a 230 hp Salmson) and its crew was Bailly, Reginensi and Marsot. In contrast to the previous effort, this flight was a complete success in every respect, the Farman reaching Madagascar in a flying time of 84 hours 25 minutes after 8 days, 6 hours and 27 minutes en route, beating by a handsome margin the best time of 44 days set up by Commandant Dagnaux in 1927. The return flight was made in 8 days 6 hours, representing an airborne time of 78 hours, and the round trip was made at an average speed of 95 mph. The journey was favoured by excellent weather, apart from a solitary storm on the outward trip near Broken Hill.

The third Farman 190 bound for Madagascar left Le Bourget on 13 December, carrying 78 pounds of mail. The names of the crew were Roux, Caillol and Dodement. The aircraft was delayed for a day on the outward journey by a sandstorm at Reggane, and further delays were experienced between Coquilhatville and Quilimane because of violent storms and strong headwinds, with the result that it took twenty days before the aircraft reached its destination. It took off for the return trip on 10 January 1930, and was seen to overfly Port-Franqui in the Belgian Congo on the 13th, battling its way through a tropical rainstorm. It was the last anyone saw of it until 14 March 1930, when its wreckage — with the bodies of the three crew still inside — was found in the jungle near Kasai, 200 miles from Brazzaville.

The lesson derived from these three missions was glaringly obvious. The first had been dogged by poor navigation; the third had failed tragically because the crew had tried to press on through storm clouds that extended from ground level to an altitude greater than the aircraft's ceiling. Only the second, executed by a crew which was generally more experienced and highly trained than the others, had been an unqualified success. France now had the equipment to make successful trans-African flights; what she now needed was more crews trained to meet the rigours of African flying.

Training and experience in long-range flights over Africa was something which the RAF, by the beginning of 1930, possessed to a considerable degree. On 11 January, four Fairey IIIF aircraft left Cairo for the Cape, arriving on 1 February after taking part in military exercises at Entebbe and Tabora en route. They returned to Cairo on 24 February, accompanied by four DH 9s of the South African Air Force. Joint air exercises between SAAF units and RAF squadrons from Egypt had in fact been taking place in East Africa since 1927, an indication of the high level of proficiency attained in long-range flying by the two Services.

Three important flights were also made from England to South Africa by civilian crews in 1930. On 20 March, Alan S. Butler, chairman of the de Havilland Company, left Heston in Gloster A.S.31 Survey G-AADO, accompanied by his wife Lois and an engineer named Millyard, and arrived in Cape Town on 15 April after a 27-day flight which was achieved in 16 stages. The Gloster Survey was later purchased by the South African Air Force and was used on mapping operations, remaining in service until 1943.

The second civilian flight to the Cape in 1930 set out from Lympne on 10 April. The aircraft involved was Fokker F.VIIa G-EBTS, named *The Spider* and owned by Mary, Duchess of Bedford, who at the age of sixty-four had just obtained her pilot's licence. She travelled as a passenger on this flight; the crew were C. D. Barnard and R. F. Little. The trip was made in ten stages over nine days, the aircraft arriving at Maitland Aerodrome, Cape Town, on 19 April after a flying time of 100 hours, and the flight back to England started two days later. This went well until 29 April, when choked-up oil filters compelled Barnard to make a forced landing in the Dragoman Pass at Fliunitza, Bulgaria. The aircraft took off safely the following morning after the trouble had been rectified, and it landed at 5.30 pm at Croydon, having made a round trip of 18,800 miles.

The next flight from England to the Cape was made by a South African pilot, Lieutenant R. F. Caspareuthus, who took off from Croydon on 5 October 1930 to make a delivery flight in de Havilland Puss Moth ZS-ACD, powered by a 120 hp Gipsy III engine. He reached Maitland Aerodrome eight and a half days later, on 13 October, setting up a new record with a flying time of 78 hours.

On 27 October 1930, three Italian pilots named Lombardi, Mazzotti and Rasini set out from Rome in three Fiat AS 2 aircraft to make a tour of Africa that was to last until 11 January 1931 and cover a total distance of 17,250 miles. The flight was made for tourist, rather than exploratory purposes, and therefore deserves its place in history, but a much more hazardous venture was undertaken in November 1930 by two French pilots, who set out to make the first ever flight from Paris to Madagascar in light aircraft.

The pilots were René Lefèvre, who had flown the Atlantic in 1929, and Desmazières, and their aircraft were Potez 36 high-wing monoplanes fitted with 100 hp Renault engines. Leaving Le Bourget on 16 November, they ran into bad weather almost immediately as they flew across France in short hops to Blois, Poitiers, Mansles, Montpont and Caracassonne. At Montpont, near Bergerac, the rain had reduced the landing ground to such a state tht Lefèvre's aircraft ploughed into some mud and overturned on take-off; fortunately the damage was restricted to some tears in the fabric, and after repairs had been affected the flight resumed.

The weather improved over Spain and the two pilots crossed the Straits of Gibraltar to reach Oran on 29 November. They left on 2 December after giving an air display at the request of the Oran Aero Club, and the next day found them at Colomb-Bechar, where they decided to overhaul their engines before crossing the Sahara. Their efforts were devoted mainly to ensuring that the oil cooling system was working as efficiently as possible, a task in which they received invaluable help from French Air Force mechanics. They left Colomb-Bechar on 9 December, and on the 11th they reached Reggane.

The Reggane-Gao leg was too long to be made in a single flight, so the two pilots decided to land and refuel at Bidon V, one of the chain of refuelling points set up in the desert for use by the vehicles of the Trans-Sahara Company. The Company's director, M. Estienne, arranged for some of his men to lay out some white-painted fuel drums in the form of a cross, to help the airmen find the site; then he gave them the key to the fuel pump and wished them good luck.

Lefèvre was the first to land at Bidon V, with only a gallon and a half of petrol remaining in his tank. He waited for Desmazières to arrive, but as the minutes went by and there was no sign of him Lefèvre grew increasingly worried, particularly since the other pilot had the key and there was no means of obtaining fuel until he showed up.

After a while, Lefèvre realised that his colleague must have come down in the desert, and decided to use what was left of his petrol in searching for him. He was lucky; only a few minutes after taking off, he spotted Desmazières' Potez sitting on the sand about three miles away, apparently undamaged. Landing alongside, Lefèvre found that not only had his friend run out of fuel, but that he had also experienced engine trouble.

There was nothing for it but to unpack their tool kits and set to work on the faulty motor. They worked all night, in brilliant moonlight, and finished the job by 6 am. Then, after a short rest, they set off for Bidon V with a couple of empty cans to get some petrol.

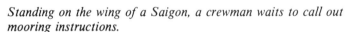

Standing on the wing of a Saigon, a crewman waits to call out mooring instructions.

The three-mile walk across the desert to the fuel dump presented no problems, but on the return trip the sun was well up and, burdened now with full cans, the two pilots were practically exhausted by the time they arrived back at their aircraft. Gasping for breath, they poured the fuel into the tanks of their machines and made the short hop as far as Bidon V, but the heat was by now so intense that they knew there was no question of continuing that day. They spent the sweltering daylight hours sheltering as best they could in the scant shade provided by the wings of their aircraft, then topped up their tanks after dark and flew on at dawn the following day.

On reaching Gao, they found it necessary to overhaul their engines again, for the oil temperature had risen to 102 degrees C during the crossing of the Sahara. From Gao they flew on towards Fort Lamy in eight stages, hampered by a constant strong wind from the east. During this part of the flight they made use of several unexplored landing strips, which were later expanded and turned into emergency landing grounds along the regular air route to Madagascar.

Two views of the Breguet 'Bizerte', from which the civil 'Saigon' was developed. Two Saigons, F-AMSV 'Algerie' and F-AMSX 'Tunisie', flew passenger services across the Mediterranean from 1935.

They overhauled their engines again at Fort Lamy before flying on to Bangui, in the Congo, where they were enthusiastically received by the Belgians on 17 January 1931. The subsequent flight across the Congo was the most nerve-racking of the whole journey, for the pilots knew that it would be fatal if one of them suffered an engine failure here, over the dense virgin forest. Also the flight was made at the height of the rainy season, which meant that some airstrips were in an appalling condition. Moreover, some takeoffs were made extremely hazardous by the altitude of the strips, some of which were over 5,000 feet above sea level; at those heights, the little Renault motors failed to develop adequate take-off power.

Sometimes, the pilots were lucky. On 7 February, as they were flying over Rhodesia, Lefèvre experienced engine trouble almost directly overhead the only flat piece of ground for miles around: a ranch. The other pilot landed too, and both were stuck for a fortnight until spare parts arrived from Elisabethville, 250 miles to the rear. They resumed their flight and on 1 March reached Umtali, on the border between Rhodesia and Portuguese East Africa, landing on a golf course. They completed their long journey on 8 April, when they reached Tananarive.

The achievement of Lefèvre and Desmazières did much to dispel lingering fears that long-range flying across Africa could not be achieved without an insupportable element of danger. Unlike crews who had made the flight to Madagascar before them, the two pilots had taken no risks; they had planned each stage of their journey with meticulous care, leaving nothing to chance. It may truthfully be said that they had ushered in the era of air tourism in Africa. And, as though to prove a point, the intrepid René Lefèvre made the same journey again in December 1931 — solo this time, in a tiny Mauboussin light aircraft powered by a 40 hp Salmson engine. Leaving Paris on 3 December, he returned on 1 June 1932, having demonstrated the aircraft to potential customers all along his route and covered a distance of some 18,000 miles in the process.

The exploits of aircrews over the past decade had shown that it was possible to traverse the African continent in every direction; from 1931 onwards the quest was for speed, to achieve the transcontinental links in the shortest time possible. On 28 October, 1931, two more French airmen, Moench and Burtin, showed that it was possible to fly from Paris to Madagascar in only 6 days, 9 hours and 45 minutes, using a Farman 190; they were back in France, at Le Bourget, on 25 November. This was by far the fastest time yet, but it was only a beginning; setting out on 23 November, another Farman 190 flown by Salel and Goulette made the journey in 4 days 8 hours, and also set up a record on the return flight by reaching Paris in 5 days 9 hours 45 minutes.

With flights to Madagascar now fairly routine, it was only a question of time before a woman pilot made the trip. It happened on 31 January 1932, when a Frenchwoman, Maryse Hilz, accompanied by a mechanic named Dronne, took off from Le Bourget in a Farman 291 powered by a 399 hp Gnome-Rhône Titan engine. She reached Tananarive on 31 March and set off on the return flight on 8 April, landing at Le Bourget on 7 May. She had to change her engine once on the way out, and on the homeward journey there was one serious incident when she had to make a forced landing on Juan de Nova Island, in the Mozambique Channel, but apart from that the flight was fairly uneventful.

Meanwhile, on 26 February 1932, a French pilot named Dieudonné Costes, employed by the Air Union Company, had set out to explore a possible new route to Madagascar. Flying a Breguet 27 powered by a 500-hp Hispano-Suiza engine, and accompanied by Jean Schneider and a mechanic named Veron, his route took him to Cairo via Marseille, Rome, Naples, Tunis, Tripoli and Benghazi. From Cairo he followed the Nile southwards through Wadi Halfa and Khartoum, then swung southwest to Fort Archambault and Bangui, in the Congo, picking up the original Madagascar route at this point. Costes then returned to Tunis, having covered a distance of 9,300 miles, and arrived back in France on 23 March. It was apparent that this route offered no real advantage over the existing one.

A new route across Africa, this time from east to west, was also pioneered in April 1932. Once again, the aircraft involved was a Farman 190, fitted on this occasion with a 240 hp Lorraine Mizar engine; a year earlier, this same machine, named *Paris,* had made a tour of Africa, visiting Morocco, the Ivory Coast, the Congo, South Africa, Zanzibar, French Somalia, Egypt and Tunisia, its voyage taking it over a distance of 23,000 miles.

Now, on 15 April 1932, the same pilot who had taken it on that cruise — Pierre d'Estailleur-Chanteraine — was also at the controls as the aircraft took off from Toussus-le-Noble on its new venture. He was accompanied by another pilot named Freton and a mechanic, Mistrot. The Farman

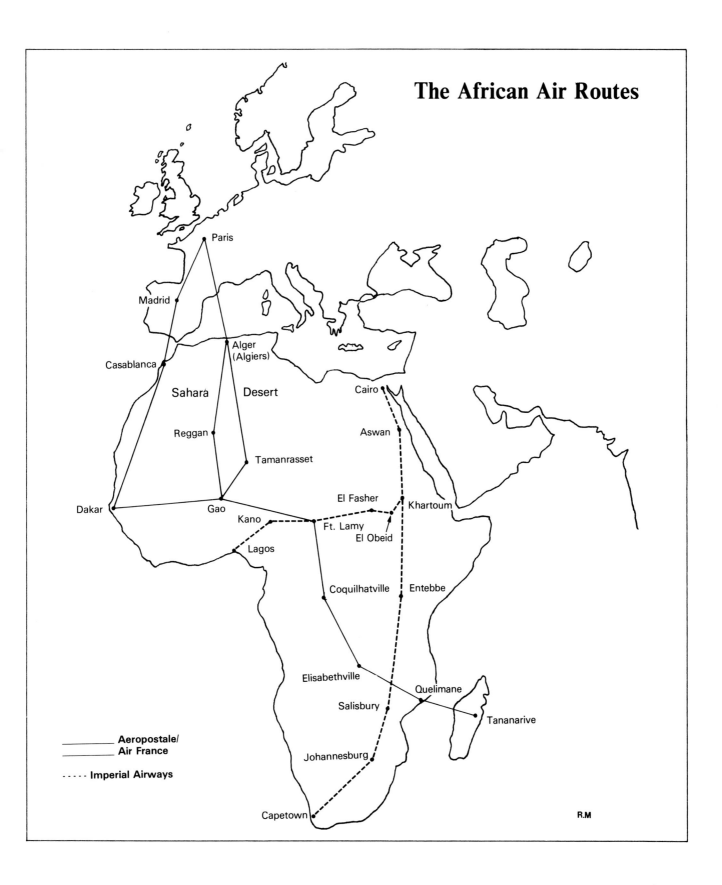

The African Air Routes

Paris

Madrid

Alger
(Algiers)

Casablanca

Sahara   Desert

Cairo

Reggan

Aswan

Tamanrasset

El Fasher

Dakar

Gao

Khartoum

Kano

Ft. Lamy

El Obeid

Lagos

Coquilhatville

Entebbe

Elisabethville

Quelimane

Salisbury

Tananarive

Johannesburg

Capetown

_____ Aeropostale/
_____ Air France

- - - - - Imperial Airways

R.M

flew to Perpignan and then on to Tunis with one stop en route; on 18 April it reached Cairo and two days later it arrived at Djibouti, in French Somalia, having covered a distance of 5,600 miles in 4 days 21 hours. On 23 April it went on to El Obeid via Khartoum, and from there via Fort Lamy and Niamey to Dakar. It returned to Paris on 30 April by way of Port Etienne and Rabat, having covered a distance of just over 14,000 miles in a flying time of 258 hours. A significant navigational point about this flight was that the trans-Africa crossing from east to west had been made along the same parallel of latitude, 15° North, which meant that the aircraft had been able to follow a constant rhumb line track during much of its flight. Also of significance was the fact that the Farman was putting in a second appearance at many of the places it visited, and was everywhere received with great enthusiasm by people who had seen it on its tour the previous year. It brought home, to many of them, that African air travel was moving fast out of the experimental stage.

This flight co-incided with another French success: a record-breaking flight from Paris to Cape Town by another Farman 190, crewed this time by Salel and Goulette. It left Paris on 17 April and arrived at the Cape on the 20th after 3 days, 18 hours and 25 minutes. The Farman, named *Marcel Lallouette,* left Cape Town on 24 April and reached Brazzaville (where, incidentally, the crew encountered Mlle. Maryse Hilz on her homeward run) on 1 May; its final leg, started on 7 May, was from Oran to Brussels, where it delivered mail picked up in the Belgian Congo before returning to Paris. The return flight from Cape Town to Paris was accomplished in 3 days and 18 hours of flying time.

This record-breaking flight to the Cape was a direct challenge to the British, who had planned to make a record attempt on the London-Cape Town route in February 1932 using the Fairey Long Range Monoplane II, K1991. This aircraft was now equipped with three altimeters, an auto-pilot which had been tested by various RAF units — particularly No. 7 Squadron, which operated Vickers Virginias in the long-range bombing role — and roller bearings on the wheels to assist take off at an all-up weight of 17,000 pounds. Extra 1,000-gallon fuel tanks had also been fitted into the wings.

However, the attempt was postponed because of bad weather, and it was not until 6 February 1933 that K1991 finally took off for Africa from Cranwell, Lincolnshire, with two pilots on board: Squadron Leader O. R. Gayford and Flight Lieutenant G. E. Nicholetts. On 8 February, the aircraft touched down at Walvis Bay, South-West Africa, after a non-stop flight of 57 hours 25 minutes. The distance covered was 5,309.24 miles, at an average speed of 93 mph. On 12 February the aircraft flew on to Cape Town, where a new Napier Lyon engine was installed before the flight back to England. Gayford and Nicholetts returned in triumph to Farnborough on 2 May, 1933.

By the mid-1930s, the dangers of trans-African flight had been mostly overcome. Only the crossing of the Sahara remained a real peril, and in March 1934 two pilots of the French Compagnie Transafricaine, Hirschauer and Poulin, were briefed to find a less hazardous route across the desert from Algiers to Brazzaville. Setting out in a Farman from Algiers on 18 March, they made a round trip of the Sahara and explored a more westerly route over the Tanezrouft, reaching the conclusion that although this was longer than the route used previously, it avoided the high ground of the Ahaggar region and was therefore a good deal safer.

This was the route adopted subsequently by aircraft flying to French West Africa and the Congo, and accidents decreased sharply as a result. Even the desert had yielded, at last, to the progress of flight.

Chapter Six:
The Polar Routes

On 11 July, 1897, a hydrogen-filled balloon named *Oernen* – Eagle – rose into the air from Danes Island, off the north-west coast of Spitzbergen. Ninety-seven feet high and sixty-eight feet in diameter, the balloon carried a crew of three: Salomon August Andrée, an experienced aeronaut, Knut Fraenkel, a civil engineer, and Nils Strindberg, a university professor turned photographer. All three were Swedish, and they were setting out on what was probably the most daring and ambitious undertaking in the history of flight to that time: a voyage to the North Pole.

As well as the three men, the balloon's double-deck basket carried a wide variety of equipment — photographic supplies, extra clothing, navigational instruments, maps, books, guns and ammunition — and food supplies sufficient for an estimated three and a half months. It also held thirty-six carrier pigeons, in small wicker cages.

The balloon, caught by the wind, receded slowly into the grey northern sky. It was never seen again.

Two days after its departure, a homing pigeon arrived on Danes Island. It bore the following message: "13 July, 12.30. Proceeding East 10° South. Latitude 82° 2′, Longitude 15° 5′. Third message despatched by carrier pigeon." There had been no sign of the other two birds.

After that, all contact with the balloon and its occupants was lost. It was not until August, 1930, that their fate became known to the world when the crew of the Norwegian sealer *Bratvaag,* going ashore briefly on White Island — between north-east Spitzbergen and Franz Josef Land — stumbled on the bones of Andrée and Strindberg. They also discovered the prow of a small boat, with lettering on it: "Andrée's Polar Expedition, 1897." A few weeks later, further searches turned up Fraenkel's body, too.

Most significantly of all, there was a diary. It had lain in the snow for thirty-three years, but Andrée had padded it with straw and wrapped it in oilskin; he appeared to have died with the little book clutched to his chest, under the protective clothing he wore. Its pages were still legible, and they told a story of tragic failure.

Even before the *Oernen* had taken off, the flight had been in jeopardy. The balloon leaked. Andrée knew this, but he had already postponed the flight once, in May, and received a great deal of adverse publicity as a result; he dared not postpone it again.

In fact, the balloon was losing a lift capacity of 99 pounds in every twenty-four hours. This was not immediately apparent in the hours after take-off, when the balloon rose to a comfortable height of 1,800 feet, but on the third day out a layer of ice began to form on the envelope. The weight of the ice, coupled with the steady loss of gas, caused the balloon to lose height gradually until, in the end, the bottom of the basket struck the ice hummocks below. The balloon bounced up 500 feet before slowly settling once more. For hour after hour, in the afternoon of that third day, the exhausting cycle continued, the balloon rising and falling, dragging the basket over the rugged ice for long stretches, then rising again as the men jettisoned ballast.

On 14 July the balloon suddenly rose, probably as a result of a temperature change, but this unexpected good fortune was not to last. The rough jolting over the ice had loosened an escape valve, the hydrogen was now venting from the envelope in large quantities. By 7 p.m. after a long, bruising drag across the ice hummocks, it was clear that the flight could not continue, and Andrée gave the order to open the ripvalves, deflating the envelope. By 7.30, the *Oernen* was down for good.

The balloon's final position was 82°55′7″ North, 29°52′ East. It was still a long way from the Pole; the explorer Nansen, using sleighs drawn by dog teams, had got much closer to the objective on his expedition of 1895, reaching 86°12′ North.

On 21 July, after resting and taking stock of their position, the three men struck out southwards. Their transport consisted of a small sledge and a collapsible canvas boat. They were heading for Seven Islands, off the north coast of Spitzbergen, but they never reached their destination. Badly off course, frustrated by contrary winds and currents and the unpredictable drift of the ice, they wandered through the Arctic wilderness for three months until they found their final resting place on White Island, where their remains were to lie undiscovered for more than thirty years.

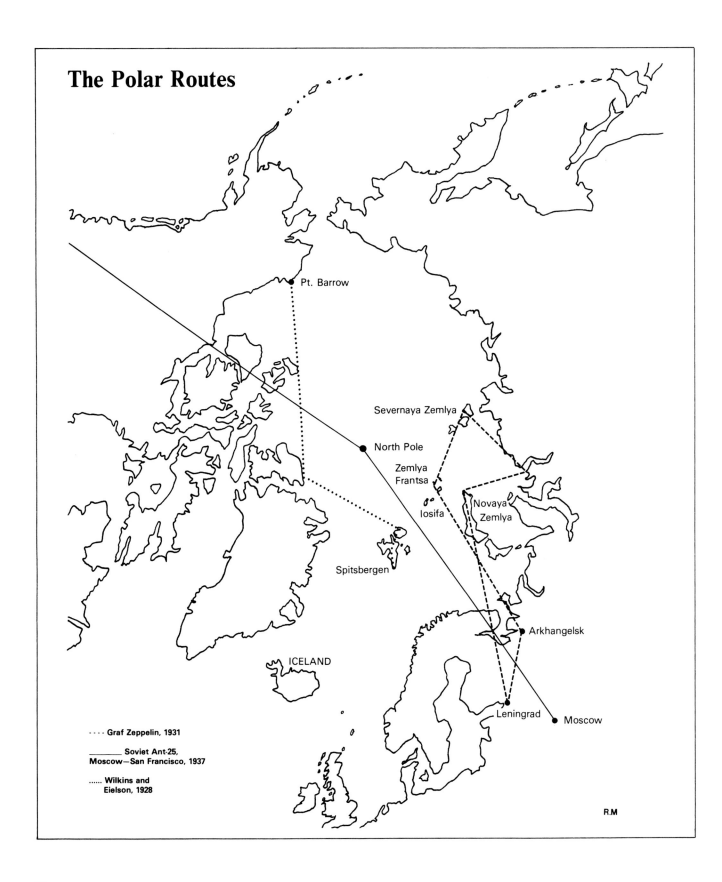

The Polar Routes

Pt. Barrow

Severnaya Zemlya

North Pole

Zemlya
Frantsa

Iosifa

Novaya
Zemlya

Spitsbergen

Arkhangelsk

ICELAND

Leningrad

Moscow

- - - - Graf Zeppelin, 1931

————— Soviet Ant-25,
Moscow—San Francisco, 1937

...... Wilkins and
 Eielson, 1928

R.M

80

The first man to reach the North Pole was the American explorer Robert Peary, on 6 April, 1909. Like Nansen before him, he used dogs and sleighs; it was to be a quarter of a century after the disappearance of Andrée and his companions before another attempt was made to reach the Pole by air.

At 5.10 p.m. on 21 May, 1925, two Dornier Wal flying boats took off from Ny Aalesund, Spitzbergen, and set course for the North Pole. The two aircraft, bearing the registration numbers N-24 and N-25, were powered by two 360-hp Rolls-Royce Eagle engines, modified to assure reliable operation under extremely low temperatures. Both aircraft had been licence-built in Italy by the Societa di Costruzione Mecaniche Aeronautiche, at Marina-di-Pisa.

Money for the expedition had been raised by the American financier Lincoln Ellsworth, and it was under the command of the celebrated Norwegian explorer Roald Amundsen. The latter had originally planned a polar flight for the summer of 1923, using a Junkers monoplane, but had been forced to postpone the attempt when the aircraft was written off during a test flight on 21 June that year.

Now, two years all but a month later, Amundsen was to have another determined try. Aircraft and personnel were ferried to Ny Aalesund via Tromsö, in Norway, and preparations ran exactly to schedule. Amundsen was to fly in Dornier N-25 as navigator and expedition leader; the aircraft's pilot was Lieutenant Rijser Larsen, a Norwegian naval officer, and the flight engineer was a man named Feucht. Dornier N-24's crew comprised Lieutenant Leif Dietrichsen as pilot, Lieutenant Omdal as second pilot and engineer, and Lincoln Ellsworth as observer.

The two aircraft flew on over the Arctic wastes for eight hours in sunny conditions and an agreeable outside air temperature of minus 10 degrees centigrade. Then, for the first time since leaving Spitzbergen, the crews sighted a patch of clear water, and Amundsen gave the signal to land. The pilots needed a rest, and it would be a good opportunity to top up the Dorniers' fuel tanks.

The two aircraft touched down on the water several miles apart. As they did so, N-24 struck some unseen floating obstacle, which caused damage to her hull, and to make matters more serious one of her engines refused to re-start. Lief Dietrichsen, the pilot, consequently decided to abandon her; after considerable difficulty the crew reached a nearby ice floe, and on 26 May, after a hazardous trek across the ice with as much food and survival equipment as they could manage, rejoined Amundsen and the other crew members of N-25.

The position reached by the two aircraft, with only a minor difference, was 87°43′ North, 10°30′ West. They had covered a distance of 687 statute miles, and were still 158 miles short of the Pole.

Reduced to one aircraft carrying a double crew, Amundsen knew that there could no longer be any question of reaching his objective. Moreover, there was also a possibility that the expedition might not be able to regain Spitzbergen; in the days that had elapsed between N-24 being abandoned and her crew reaching N-25, the ice had closed in, effectively blocking the narrow strip of water on which the flying boat lay.

With a superhuman effort, the two crews succeeded in dragging her ashore, and set about levelling a take-off strip on the ice; ice take-offs had been a successful feature of the Wal's trials prior to the expedition's departure. It was a long and arduous task, complicated by the fact that the food supply had to be strictly rationed and the strength of the men consequently fell to a low ebb. It was not until 10.30 a.m. on 15 June that Dornier N-25, carrying its unaccustomed load, was able to take-off from the improvised strip and set course for Spitzbergen. Much of the homeward flight, which took eight and a half hours, was made in dense fog, which obliged pilot Rijser Larsen to fly at low level and made accurate navigation extremely difficult.

The conclusion drawn by the bitterly disappointed Amundsen as a result of this abortive trip was that, because of the complete absence of firm ground in the polar regions and the scarcity of ice-free stretches of water, future expeditions would not be able to rely on neither landplanes nor seaplanes. The only other possibility was to make use of an airship, and Amundsen accordingly sought to acquire one for his next attempt.

Rijser Larsen was a qualified airship pilot; part of his training had been carried out in Italy, where he had become acquainted with one of that country's leading airship exponents, Umberto Nobile. The Norwegian made enquiries and, discovering that Nobile's latest semi-rigid airship, the N-1, was up for sale, suggested that she might be the ideal craft to use on the next try for the Pole. She was, after all, already a proven design; on 25 May 1925, together with the Italian airship *Esperia* (formerly the

German *Bodensee*) she had undertaken a two-day cruise over the Mediterranean with twenty-five passengers on board.

Amundsen gave his approval and negotiations for the purchase of the airship got under way, the project once again being financed by Lincoln Ellsworth. It met with considerable opposition from some factions in the Italian Government and in particular from General Balbo, the famous aviator, who did not take kindly to the idea that the honour of being the first to reach the Pole by air should fall to a team of Norwegians, backed by an American. In the end, as a compromise, it was agreed that although Amundsen would remain as expedition commander, Umberto Nobile would command the airship and its operations. Those who knew both men saw possible trouble ahead; Amundsen possessed a violent temperament and so did the Italian, and there were likely to be times when the two would be pulling in opposite directions. Nevertheless, the resulting contract produced a favourable result from the financial point of view; Ellsworth would now be required to put up only one-third of the money, the remainder being provided in equal amounts by the Italian Government and the Norwegian Aero Club.

On 29 March, 1926, the N-1 was renamed *Norge* at an impressive ceremony in Rome. She was 350 feet long, with a capacity of 653,000 cubic feet, and her three 250-hp Maybach engines gave her a top speed of 70 mph. She was essentially a functional craft, with no living quarters as such and very few refinements.

The *Norge* took off from Ciampino on 10 April, heading north-westwards for her first port of call: the airship station at Pulham, in Norfolk. Carrying a crew of sixteen, she reached her destination at 3 pm the following day, and was moored alongside the British rigid airship R-33 until 13 April, when weather conditions were favourable for the next leg of her flight — to Oslo. Leaving Pulham at 11 pm, she crossed the North Sea in the darkness and slipped over the Danish coast early the following morning, arriving over Oslo at 11.30 a.m.

The weather was still favourable, and it was decided to continue on the next stage — to Leningrad — as soon as the airship had been replenished. Taking off at 1.20 am on 15 April, she arrived over the Russian city at 6.16 that evening, but now the weather was closing in rapidly and there seemed to be little prospect of continuing the flight until it cleared again. But it was three weeks before the north Russian weather obliged, and the airship was forced to remain at Leningrad until 5 May, when she was at last able to continue to Vadsö, on the northern tip of Norway. She stayed there a few hours before setting out on the final leg to King's Bay, Spitzbergen.

She reached her destination at 6 am on 7 May, and the expedition team immediately began preparations for the Polar flight. The *Norge* was thoroughly overhauled and the necessary equipment stowed on board, after which the airship's fuel tanks and hydrogen cells were topped up.

Then, on 9 May, while preparations were still under way, the Amundsen expedition received a bitter blow. At 4.30 pm, a three-engined Fokker VIII-3m monoplane, fitted with skis, appeared out of the northern sky and touched down at King's Bay. The two-man crew climbed stiffly from the cockpit; they were Commander Richard Byrd, United States Navy, and his pilot, Floyd Bennett. With them they brought the news that they had become the first men to see the North Pole from the air.

Byrd and Bennett had already been at King's Bay when the *Norge* arrived, and a race had developed between the two teams in an endeavour to get off first. The skis fitted to the Fokker Tri-motor had presented one of the biggest problems for the two Americans; several pairs had been tested, and each pair had fractured under the strain of landing. By the night of 8/9 May they were down to their last pair, and with Amundsen's team almost ready to depart the Americans decided that it was now or never.

So, at thirty minutes past midnight in the morning of 9 May, 1926, the Tri-motor — named *Josephine Ford* — took off into the Arctic twilight, for at this time of year there was no night in these regions. Some way into the flight one of the aircraft's oil tanks developed a leak, but the crew decided to take a risk and press on; in any case, memories of the unfortunate experiences with the skis deterred the men from risking a landing. Fortunately, the leak grew no worse.

At 9.04 am, GMT, the Fokker reached the North Pole, according to the calculations of the two crew. The aircraft circled the area until 9.18, and Byrd threw out an American flag before they set course for Spitzbergen, conscious that they still had an eight-hour flight in front of them. They encountered trouble not long afterwards, when the bubble sextant slid off Byrd's chart table and was broken. At these latitudes, so close to the Magnetic North Pole, an ordinary magnetic compass was useless, but fortunately Byrd had brought a standby sun compass with him, and with this he managed to navigate them safely home while Bennett concentrated on flying the aircraft.

Disappointed though he was, Amundsen was the first to shake Byrd and Bennet by the hand and congratulate them. Then, on the morning of 11 May, it was his turn at last.

At 9.55 am, the *Norge* lifted away from the snow of King's Bay and climbed steadily towards the north. Weather was poor throughout the day, the airship running through patches of thick fog, but this presented no undue navigational problems and the navigator, Hjalmar Rijser-Larsen, held a steady course for the Pole. At 1.20 am on 12 May he made the last few minute corrections designed to bring the *Norge* as precisely as possible over the target. As members of the crew stood by to drop Norwegian, Italian and American flags, he knelt by an open window and took several sightings with his sextant. Suddenly, he called, "Ready with the flags!" and a moment later, "Now — we're here!"

The Norwegian flag went down first, fluttering on its aluminium staff towards the crinkled expanse of snow and ice which, according to the navigator's careful calculations, was Latitude ninety degrees North. Despite a stiff breeze the flag landed upright and stood firmly implanted in the snow; it was followed a moment later by the flags of the other two nations involved in the expedition.

Wordlessly, Roald Amundsen turned and shook hands with his coxswain, Oscar Wisting. Fourteen years earlier, on 14 December 1911, these two men had also planted the Norwegian flag at earth's other pole. It was a moment of great pride.

The *Norge* cruised on, heading for Nome, in Alaska, bombarded with radio messages congratulating the crew on their success. Their high spirits, however, were soon dampened by bad weather, and by 8.30 am the airship was nosing her way through dense fog. Ice began to build up on parts of the airframe and also on the propellers; chunks of it flew off like shrapnel and punched holes in the lower part of the envelope, giving the crew serious cause for concern. They succeeded in patching up the worst of the damage, however, and by evening the worst of the weather was behind them.

The ship flew on in steadily improving visibility, and at 6.45 am on 13 May there was great excitement on board when land was sighted off the port bow; all the crew felt that the worst was now behind them, and when Rijser-Larsen announced a few minutes later that the landfall was Point Barrow, they knew that the navigator had brought them across the unexplored Arctic wastes with astonishing accuracy. They were only a few miles off their intended track, and a few hours later the airship droned over a small settlement which Amundsen identified as Wainwright. He and Lieutenant Oskar Omdal — who had accompanied him on the ill-fated Dornier expedition to the Pole the previous year, and who was now also on board the *Norge* — had stayed there briefly in 1922.

The Arctic weather, however, was to have the final word. In the early hours of 14 May the *Norge* was battered by a short but savage gale, and when it blew itself out it was replaced by more dense fog, blowing the ship off track and forcing Nobile to take her up to higher altitude in order to avoid colliding with the rugged peaks of the mountainous terrain. Rijser-Larsen found it impossible to navigate accurately; the best he could do was to follow the coastline along the Bering Straits, visible through infrequent rifts in the murk. After a while, no longer certain of his position, he agreed with Amundsen and Nobile that the *Norge* would have to land soon; the gale was blowing again and there was a danger that it would drive the airship out over the Straits. Moreover, all crew members badly needed a rest; they had been on duty for seventy hours, with only a few fitful snatches of sleep, and cold and fatigue were taking their toll.

At 7 am on 14 May, the airship's crew sighted an expanse of fairly flat ground ahead, with a cluster of houses beside it. As Nobile brought the *Norge* steadily down towards the clear patch, people came running out to watch the landing. The wind was gusting badly, and with no ground crew to assist in the mooring operation Nobile needed all his skill to prevent a disaster. Every member of the crew tensed as he brought the airship in, riding the gusts, ready to jump overboard into the snow if the impact was hard enough to collapse the flimsy aluminium framework. Then, when the airship was only seconds away from making contact with the ground, the wind suddenly dropped to a dead clam. The ship touched down with scarcely a jolt, the crowd running forward to catch the trail ropes that the crew threw down to them.

The time was 7.30 am, GMT. The *Norge* had touched down at Teller, Alaska, only fifty-five miles short of her planned destination at Nome. In completing the first aerial traverse of the Arctic ice-cap, she had covered more than 3,000 miles non-stop. In some ways, it was a miracle that she had made the journey safely; before deflating the airship's envelope, the crew had to remove over 2,000 pounds of accumulated ice from it. If the ice build-up had been only marginally greater, the ship might have been too heavy to climb over the worst of the Alaskan terrain.

Sadly, the achievement of the *Norge* and her crew was marred to some extent by a childish squabble that developed between Amundsen and Nobile afterwards, as both men fought for a bigger share of the limelight. Nobile returned to Italy an angry man, determined to launch his own Polar expedition; he found himself to be a public hero, and funds to build a new airship were soon forthcoming from the Italian Government and the people of Milan.

The new ship, named the *Italia,* was approximately the same size as the *Norge,* but her useful lift was increased by 2,900 pounds and there were a number of internal improvements which made her — in theory at least — more adequately suited to exploration than her predecessor. She was powered by three 240-hp engines, giving her a speed of 70 mph.

The *Italia* flew for the first time in March 1928, and afterwards underwent a short series of successful test flights. Nobile decided that she was sufficiently proven to attempt a Polar flight, and at 1.55 am on 15 April, 1928, she took off from Milan and headed north towards her first port of call, the old German airship station at Stolp, in northern Germany. There were twenty people on board; most were Italians, but one — Dr. Malmgren, a scientist who had also been on the *Norge* expedition — was Swedish, and a Czech scientist named Behunek was also travelling as a passenger.

The first leg of the *Italia's* flight was beset by appalling weather, the airship encountering rain, fog, snow, hail, strong winds and thunderstorms. By the time she reached Stolp at 7.50 am on 16 April, all her ballast had been used up and one of her fins had sustained storm damage. This, however, was soon repaired, enabling the flight to be resumed on 3 May. The airship took off from Stolp at 3.28 am, heading for Vadsö in Norway in the teeth of a strong northerly wind. To conserve fuel only two engines were used during most of the flight. Navigation was made difficult by fog, but despite this hazard the ship moored safely at Vadsö at 9.10 am on 4 May.

The leg of the flight from Vadsö to King's Bay, begun at 8.34 pm the following day, was hampered by bad weather, and as the *Italia* approached Spitzbergen she encountered high winds and driving snow. The airship therefore stood off until the wind dropped on the morning of 6 May, eventually coming down to land on two engines — the third having broken down — at 12.45 pm.

The airship remained at her moorings for four days while the faulty engine was changed. Nobile and the crew put the delay to good use by putting the final touches to the exploration programme, which involved two flights over the Pole as well as undertaking a survey of unexplored areas of Greenland and Nicholas II Land. The *Italia* finally took off at 7.55 am on 11 May to carry out the survey of Nicholas II Land, but she was forced to turn back because of bad weather and she returned to her moorings at 4.10 that afternoon.

Soon afterwards it began to snow, and for the next two days layers of snow piled up on the airship's envelope faster than the crew could remove it. At one point Nobile feared that the weight would break the *Italia's* back. Luckily a thaw set in before any damage was caused, and at 1 pm on 15 May the airship once again left her mooring mast for Nicholas II Land. She carried a load of twelve tons, most of it made up of scientific instruments and survival gear, and 1,500 gallons of fuel, enough to keep her airborne — in still air conditions — for 4,300 miles. Sixteen people were on board.

The weather at first was almost perfect and the crew were able to obtain some excellent photographs of Nicholas II Land before the airship pushed on to her next objective, an uncharted area known as Gillis Land. Here the crew encountered fog and snowstorms, but Nobile perservered with the flight and completed this part of the survey progrmme. The *Italia* eventually landed back at King's Bay at 10.20 am on 18 May; she had spent sixty-nine hours in the air and had carried out the most comprehensive aerial survey flight up to that time, covering a total of 15,400 square miles.

Preparations now went ahead for the first of the Polar survey flights. At 4.28 am on 23 May all was ready and the airship took off, once again carrying 1,500 gallons of fuel and sixteen passengers. Two and a half hours after leaving Spitzbergen the *Italia* ran into dense fog; this persisted all through the morning, but by 1.45 pm it had cleared sufficiently for the crew to obtain sightings of the Greenland coast off their port bow and make appropriate course corrections for the Pole. The wind was behind the airship and she made good progress, arriving over the Pole at 12.20 am on 24 May. Nobile threw down an Italian flag and a wooden cross given to him by the Pope before the expedition left Italy, then circled the spot for two hours while the crew made various scientific observations. The airship was equipped with a waterproof gondola and Nobile's intention had been to land on the ice, but the wind proved too strong and he was forced to abandon this plan. At 2.20 am, he reluctantly set course for Spitzbergen.

With the wind now against her the airship made slow progress, and to add to the problem she once again encountered dense fog — accompanied this time by severe icing. By 8 am on 25 May, Nobile was forced to admit that the *Italia* was lost; Spitzbergen should have come into sight some time ago, but when the anxious crew scanned the southern horizon they saw nothing but pack-ice, shrouded in swirling fog.

The icing got worse. Suddenly, at 9.25 am, the coxswain at the helm shouted that the elevator was solidly jammed. Nobile at once gave orders for the engines to be shut down while the trouble was investigated. Drifting now without power, the *Italia* rose rapidly to a height of 3,000 feet, where she burst out into welcome and warming sunlight. Crew members chipped ice from the elevators and they were in operation again by 9.55, whereupon Nobile restarted the engines and brought the ship back down to 1,000 feet. While the *Italia* had drifted above the fog the crew had been able to take some sun shots, and the airship's position was now calculated to be 180 miles north-east of King's Bay. Assuming that this was correct, estimated time of arrival at base would be about 4 pm.

The *Italia* had been cruising on her new heading for less than thirty minutes when disaster struck. The coxswain reported that she was becoming stern heavy, and that it was impossible to hold her steady. Moments later, she began to slide stern-first towards the ice. There was no time to re-trim, or to use power to get her out of trouble.

At 10.30 am, the *Italia* impacted on the ice with a force that smashed open the control car, scattering occupants and equipment in all directions. Relieved of this weight, the ship bounded back into the air with six people still on board, quickly disappearing into the fog. Neither the airship nor these passengers were ever seen again.

The collision with the ice had produced one immediate fatality: a mechanic who had been working on No. 3 engine was thrown clear and killed. His body was discovered later. The nine survivors were all injured to some degree; Nobile had a broken arm and leg. Still stunned by the disaster, those who could still function began to collect the equipment that had been scattered in the crash; fortunately, it included a tent, sleeping bags and — miraculously — a radio transmitter that still worked.

The transmitter was operational by four o'clock that afternoon and the crew lost no time in sending out distress calls, but it was not until 29 May that a fragmentary message was picked up by the expedition's depot ship *Citta di Milano,* anchored off King's Bay. For some unaccountable reason, however, this signal was thought to be a hoax and was disregarded. A big air and sea search had meanwhile begun, but the searchers were hampered by the fact that they had no real idea where to look. Then, on 3 June, a Russian radio amateur in the Archangelsk area picked up a complete message from the survivors on the ice-floe. Four days later a further broken signal was received at King's Bay, and at 5 pm on 8 June two-way contact was at last established between King's Bay and the survivors. The position of the latter was now tentatively fixed at 80°30′ North, 28°00′ East. More air searches were undertaken, but these failed to locate the stranded party.

Meanwhile, three of the survivors — Malmgren, Mariano and Zappi — had set out to trek across the ice in a desperate attempt to find help. Malmgren, a sick man even before cold and exhaustion took their toll, collapsed after three days and could go no further. He begged his companions to leave him and save themselves; they did so reluctantly, knowing that he was dying, after leaving him as many of their scant provisions as they could spare.

Mariano and Zappi were incredibly fortunate. On 12 July, after suffering terrible hardships, they were sighted and picked up by the Russian ice-breaker *Krassin,* one of the ships taking part in the rescue operation.

In the meantime, the other survivors on the ice-floe had been finally located on 20 June by an Italian pilot, Umberto Maddalena, flying a Savoia S-55 floatplane. He dropped supplies to them and fixed their position accurately. In the evening of 23 June, Lieutenant Lundborg, a Swedish pilot, landed on the ice-floe in a ski-equipped Fokker CVD and flew out the badly injured Nobile and one other passenger: Nobile's dog Titina, the only passenger on the *Italia* to have escaped unhurt. Lundborg returned at 4 am the next day, only to suffer an engine failure; he crashed while attempting a forced landing on the ice-floe and was injured. He was brought out on 5 July by another Swedish pilot named Schyberg, flying a de Havilland Moth.

By this time, a remarkable number of aircraft were taking part in the rescue operation, Besides Maddalena's Savoia, Lundborg's CVD and Schyberg's Moth, these included two Junkers G-24s (pilots Nielsen and Chuknovsky) one Dornier Wal, two Heinkel He 5 floatplanes, two Hansa-Brandenburg floatplanes, two small Italian Macchi-18 flying boats, a Russian Junkers J-13, two Norwegian Sopwith Baby floatplanes and another Junkers J-13, named *Turka* and belonging to Finnair. This aircraft made several supply-dropping flights to the ice-floe, and on 13 July it landed to rescue two men — an Italian Alpinieri captain named Sora and Van Dongen, a Dutch coal-miner — who had been trying to reach the *Italia*'s survivors over the ice by dog-sledge and who had themselves run into trouble.

The biggest machine to take part in the search was a French flying boat, the Latham 47, which left Caudebec-en-Caux on 16 June, bound for Spitzbergen. It carried four crew: French Naval Commandants Guilbaud and Cavelier de Cuverville, flight mechanic Brazy and wireless operator Valette. When it arrived at Bergen, in Norway, at 9.45 that evening two passengers were waiting for it: Roald Amundsen and Leif Dietrichsen. Characteristically, now that Nobile's expedition was in trouble the Norwegian explorer had shrugged aside their former differences and was hurrying to be of assistance.

The Latham — carrying the serial N-02 on its nose — reached Tromsö at 6 am on 18 June, and with the six men on board took off in poor weather for Spitzbergen at 4 pm that same day. It never arrived. Somewhere beyond North Cape, in the freezing waters of the Arctic Circle, it vanished — though not quite without trace. Much later, two of its fuel tanks and one float were washed ashore and recovered; these tragic relics of the fate of some very gallant men are now preserved in France's Musée de l'Air.

The survivors of the *Italia* were finally picked up by the icebreaker *Krassin* on 17 July. The rescue came only just in time, for their ice-floe was breaking up and was almost completely under water. The Russian vessel transferred the men to the *Citta di Milano*, and they arrived at Narvik on 26 July.

The *Italia* tragedy marked the end of airship development in Italy. A disillusioned Nobile, accused of neglect, resigned from his post in the Italian Air Force and went to the Soviet Union, where he was deputy director of an airship research programme for a time. Returning to Italy in 1935, he was appointed Professor of Aeronautical Construction at Naples University. In 1939 he went to the United States, where he stayed before returning to Italy late in 1942 via Spain. After the war he played a leading role in Italian politics, helping to shape the country's new constitution.

There was one other Arctic exploration flight in 1928, and although this did not pass over the North Pole it was a very important aerial survey mission indeed. On 15 April, five weeks before the *Italia* set out on her ill-fated flight, a Lockheed Vega monoplane equipped with a single 200-hp Wright J-6 engine took off from Point Barrow in Alaska and set out over the unexplored regions of the western Arctic. The navigator and flight commander was the Australian explorer Hubert Wilkins; the pilot Carl Ben Eielson, an American.

Their first landfall was Grant Land, which they kept on their starboard side before altering course to take them roughly parallel to the north coast of Greenland. The first part of the flight was made in good weather, but after they had been airborne for thirteen hours they ran into thick fog and the temperature dropped to minus 46 degrees centigrade. There was no radio on board the Vega, but its navigation equipment comprised five different types of compass and two sextants, so dead reckoning navigation did not present undue problems. After 20 hours and 30 minutes in the air, the Vega landed at Doemansoeira, in the north of Spitzbergen. It had covered a total distance of 2,187 miles at an average speed of 106 mph, and the maximum altitude reached had been 6,000 feet.

A violent snowstorm kept Wilkins and Eielson confined to the aircraft's cockpit for four days. It was a frustrating time, for only fifty miles away, at Green Harbour on the south-east tip of Spitzbergen, a ship was waiting to take them and their aircraft to Norway. They eventually managed to dig themselves out on 20 April, and after a perilous take-off reached their destination in safety.

Despite the *Italia* tragedy, the idea of using airships for further Arctic exploration remained very much alive, and in 1928 the ideal craft for such exploration seemed to be the big German *Graf Zeppelin*, which had proved herself with a series of record-breaking flights. Two years earlier, the Norwegian explorer Fridtjof Nansen had proposed the setting up of an international organisation to explore the Polar regions using airships, and towards the end of 1928 he got in touch with Hugo Eckener, director of the Zeppelin Company, for discussions on how the *Graf Zeppelin* might be employed. Sir Hubert Wilkins was also deeply involved in these discussions; he proposed to take a submarine under the Arctic ice-cap and break his way through to make rendezvous with the *Graf Zeppelin* at the North Pole.

This venture, which at that time almost seemed to fall within the realms of science fiction, was backed by the newspaper millionaire William Randolph Hearst, who agreed to pay 150,000 dollars if airship and submarine met as planned at the Pole and exchanged passengers and mail, and 30,000 dollars if they made rendezvous elsewhere in the Arctic.

Unfortunately, Wilkins' scheme was beset by technical troubles from the very start. The submarine he was to use for the attempt, an obsolete United States Navy type, broke down several times during trials, and although he managed to get it across the Atlantic to Norway it broke down again in Trondheim harbour. It was now the early summer of 1931, and if the attempt was to go ahead it would have to be made before the end of July, when Arctic weather conditions would start to deteriorate.

The weeks went by, and it soon became clear that Wilkins' submarine — named the *Nautilus* — would not be repaired in time. (In fact, it was to be twenty-seven years before a submarine successfully traversed the Arctic under the ice: that was the second *Nautilus,* the US Navy's first nuclear-powered submersible. She made the journey in August 1958, travelling the 1,800 miles from Point Barrow to the Greenland Sea in 96 hours). It was therefore decided that the exchange of passengers and mail would take place between the *Graf Zeppelin* and the Russian icebreaker *Malygin,* which was scheduled to begin a scientific expedition to Franz Josef Land early in July.

The *Graf Zeppelin* took off on her mission from Leningrad at 9 am on 26 July, 1931, having arrived at the Russian city the day before from Friedrichshafen via Berlin. Carrying 650 pounds of mail and enough fuel for 130 hours' flying, she set her course over north-west Russia towards the Barents Sea. She altered course over Archangelsk, turning due north to head for the fringe of the Arctic icefield, encountering steadily decreasing temperatures as she flew on.

At 5 pm GMT, on 27 July, she made rendezvous with the *Malygin* in Quiet Sound, which was part of Franz Josef Land, Hugo Eckener — who was commanding the mission — bringing the airship down to land on the water close to the icebreaker. The *Graf Zeppelin* took off again thirty-seven minutes later after exchanging her mail — rather hastily, for Eckener had spotted several large ice chunks drifting in the airship's direction and he was afraid that one of them might damage her.

The next stage of the *Graf Zeppelin's* Arctic flight was a survey of Franz Josef Land and Severnaya Zemlya. The airship carried several geographers, and as a result of their observations existing maps of the area were completely revised. Upon making landfall on the coast of northern Siberia, at the mouth of the Yenisei, Eckener altered course again to head for the northern tip of Novaya Zemlya, which was sighted at 2 am on 29 July. After a flight along the island's barren coastline, the airship nosed out over the Barents Sea, heading back towards Leningrad. Arriving over the city, Eckener found that even after ninety hours in the air the *Graf Zeppelin's* fuel tanks still contained enough reserves of fuel for a direct flight back to Friedrichshafen, so he decided to press on — although, in fact, he called in at Berlin-Tempelhof on 30 July in response to a radio request that informed him of large crowds awaiting a sight of the airship.

It was to be five years before further aerial surveys of the Arctic regions were once again carried out, and this time it was the Russians who were at the forefront. On 29 March, 1936, two Polikarpov P-5 biplanes — civil versions of the military R-5, equipped with skis for this venture — set off from Moscow for Anderma in Siberia, which they reached on 31 March by way of Archangelsk. Their pilots were named Vodopyanov and Makhotkin.

The Russian's flight was hampered by poor weather and they did not reach Novaya Zemlya until 7 April. More storms grounded them at Cape Desire for a fortnight, but the weather cleared at last on 20 April and Vodopyanov flew on to Tikhaia Bay, Franz Josef Land, followed by Makhotkin the next day. Both pilots staged through Graham Bell Island.

There is very little information about this flight, but its principal objective seems to have been to carry out a survey of the Polar route with a view to establishing an air link with the United States. The mission failed, apparently because of bad weather; Makhotkin crashed on Franz Josef Land, wrecking his aircraft, and Vodopyanov returned to Moscow after making a few survey flights over the Arctic regions in the vicinity of 83° North and landing on Rudolf Island. Each P-5 aircraft, which differed from the R-5 in having a completely enclosed cockpit, also carried a mechanic and was fitted with radio.

The next Russian Arctic survey flight was made by three Soviet Air Force personnel — pilot Valery Shkalov, second pilot Georg Baidukov and navigator Aleksandr Belyakov — flying a long-range Tupolev ANT-25 monoplane, powered by a 950-hp AM-34 engine. Carrying a maximum fuel load, this aircraft took off from Moscow at 5.45 am on 20 July 1936 and, after making an aerial reconnaissance of Franz Josef Land and Severnaya Zemlya, it flew over the estuary of the River Lena before setting course for Petropavlovsk, Kamchatka, which it overflew at 3 am on 22 July. Altering course again, it then crossed the Sea of Okhotsk, heading for Kharbarovsk, but it encountered severe weather en route, and this — together with the fact that the crew were worn out with hours of flying at high altitude — made them decide to cut their journey short. Crossing the northern tip of Sakhalin, they made a night landing in pouring rain at Nikolayevsk-na-Amure. All three crew members were suffering from severe eyestrain; most of the flight had been made within the USSR's Arctic regions, and at that time of the year there was no sunset. Despite dark glasses, the constant glare of the sun on ice and snow had caused the crew severe discomfort.

Altogether, the ANT-25 had been in the air for a remarkable fifty-six hours, covering a total of 5,843 air miles. Later, after resting, the crew returned to Moscow in more leisurely fashion, following the Trans-Siberian Railway in easy hops.

During the 1936-37 period, as part of the plan to set up a commercial air route over the Pole between Moscow and San Francisco, the Russians placed considerable emphasis on setting up a scientific and meteorological station near the North Pole. A provisional camp and landing strip were established at Rudolf Island, some 500 miles from the Pole, by an expedition under the orders of the Russian scientist Papanin, and on 22 March 1937 five aircraft — four four-engined Tupolev ANT-6s and one twin-engined ANT-7 set out from Moscow for this destination. The aircraft were flown by Vodopyanov, Molokov, Mazuruk, Alexeyev, and Golovin, and they carried a total of forty-two scientific personnel led by Professor Otto Schmidt.

On 21 May, Vodopyanov took off from the Rudolf Island base with a number of scientists on board and landed on an ice-floe within a few miles of the Pole. During the days that followed, an air shuttle service landed a total of twenty-seven men and their associated equipment at the spot; their task was to set up a camp for the four scientists (Papanin, radio operator Krenkel, hydrologist Shirshov and meteorologist Fedorov) who were to spend several months on the ice. Preparations were completed and the camp established by 25 June, and the four men remained there through the long Arctic night until they were picked up on 19 February, 1938.

Meanwhile, on 18 June, 1937, the old team of Shkalov, Baidukov and Belyakov had set out from Moscow — in the same ANT-25 aircraft that had carried them on their long-distance flight the previous year — with a dual mission: to reconnoitre the proposed commercial Polar route from Moscow to San Francisco, and also to try and break the record for distance flown in a straight line, which had been held by the two Frenchmen Rossi and Codos since 1933.

The Russians reached the Pole at 5.10 am on 19 June and overflew it in good weather, but not long afterwards they ran into very poor visibility and a strong headwind. The weather grew steadily worse until the crew decided to abandon the flight and touched down at Portland, Vancouver, at 11.25 am on 20 June. The ANT-25 had been airborne for 63 hours 19 minutes and had covered a straight-line distance of 5,363 miles, landing 750 miles short of its goal.

The distance record was in fact broken a month later by a second Russian crew, Gomov and Yumachev (pilots) and Danilin (navigator/radio operator) in another ANT-25. Named *Triumph*, this aircraft took off from Moscow at 22 minutes past midnight on 12 July and flew over Rudolf Island at 9 pm that day; at 3.40 am on 13 July it crossed the Pole in a violent snowstorm and a temperature of minus 8 degrees centigrade, the pilots maintaining an altitude of 9,000 feet in a bid to escape the worst of the weather. At 8.45 am on 14 July it overflew Portland and reached San Fransico at 9.28, continuing its flight southwards until, at 2.30 pm, lack of fuel compelled Gomov to set it down in a field near San Jacinto, south of Los Angeles.

The ANT-25 had flown an air distance of 7,187 miles, and the FAI confirmed a straight-line distance of 6,780 miles, beating the previous French-held record by 652 miles. The flight, a magnificent achievement by anyone's standards, had succeeded in no small measure thanks to the navigational and weather information supplied by the Russian station near the Pole. Everything seemed set fair for the inauguration of the first commercial trans-Polar air service between the Soviet Union and the United States.

On 12 August, 1937, another ANT-25 flown by a Russian pilot named Levanevsky and carrying five passengers took off from Moscow to follow the same route as its predecessor. It crossed the North Pole at 5.54 pm the following day, and a radio message from it was received by the Soviet Polar Station when it was about 250 miles from the coast of Alaska. Nothing more was heard from it; it simply vanished without trace.

Its disappearance launched an international rescue operation on a hitherto unparalleled scale, involving dozens of aircraft and crews of different nationalities. They included Sir Hubert Wilkins, who took part in the search in the first series-production Consolidated PBY-1 flying boat, travelling north from San Diego on 19 August. Later, at the request of the Russians, Wilkins continued the search in a ski-equipped Lockheed Electra, purchased by the Soviet Government.

The search was co-ordinated as far as possible by the Soviet Polar Station, and lasted for a long time; it was known that Levanevsky and his companions had carried sufficient provisions to last them a hundred days. Two flights of ANT-6s, commanded by Captains Vodopyanov and Shevelev, and based on Rudolf Island, flew thousands of miles over the Arctic wastes, vainly combing the missing aircraft's route from the Pole to Alaska. The Wilkins search team carried on until March 1938, when they finally gave up and returned to New York; Wilkins himself had spent a total of 284 hours 35 minutes looking for the missing airmen, often in the most appalling weather conditions, and had covered a total distance of 43,750 miles, 31,250 of them inside the Arctic Circle.

The loss of Levanevsky and his crew was a bitter blow to Russian hopes of establishing a safe trans-Polar air route, but the Arctic tragedy was not yet over. On 6 February, 1938, the Russian airship V-6, commanded by Major Gudovantsev and en-route with supplies to the Soviet Polar Station, crashed into a hill in north Russia. Thirteen of the nineteen people on board were killed. Supplies were flown to the station ten days later by a STAL-2 aircraft, fitted with skis and operating from the ice breaker *Murman.* On a subsequent supply mission this aircraft had to make a forced landing on the ice, but its pilot was rescued by another aircraft from the icebreaker *Taymir.*

The following year, the even greater tragedy of the Second World War brought a halt to further Polar exploration by air. It began again in 1945, when aircraft of the RAF and USAF began to make regular flights to the Polar regions for mapping and meteorological purposes.

On 24 February, 1957, two DC-6B airliners of the Scandinavian Airlines System, one flying from Copenhagen to Tokyo and the other in the opposite direction, passed one another over the North Pole on the first regular scheduled service between Europe and Japan by way of the Arctic. At last, the old dream had become reality.

Chapter Seven
The European Connections

Belgium

Civil aviation in Belgium had its origins in the First World War, when Commandant Georges Nélis, head of the Belgian Air Corps' technical staff, began to lay the foundations for a civil air fleet which was to begin operations as soon as possible after the end of hostilities. Nélis received a great deal of encouragement in his aims from King Albert, who was keenly interested in aviation, and organised a pool of military pilots who were prepared to assist in the development of civil flying.

Early in 1919, a group of influential Belgian businessmen gave their financial support to an embryo commercial air transport organisation known as SNETA (Syndicat National d'Etudes du Transport Aérien), which had Nélis in charge of flight operations. Its first aircraft were acquired in the spring of 1920; these were three Breguet XIVs (O-BLON, O-BLOC and O-BROC), three de Havilland DH9s (O-BEAU, O-BELG and O-BIEN) and three Rumpler C.IVs (O-BORD, O-BRUN and O-BUIS). With these machines, the company began experimental mail flights between Brussels, London, Amsterdam and Paris, and these were considered to be successful enough to justify rapid expansion during the next two years.

SNETA acquired a further thirty-one aircraft by the summer of 1922, including some Farman Goliaths (two of which were registered O-BRUN and O-BLAN), DH9s, Bleriot-Spad 33s, Ansaldo A-300Cs, and six Levy-Lepen flying-boats. The latter were among the company's most important purchases, for in July 1920 they were used to inaugurate the first sector of SNETA's route between Kinshasa and N'Gombe, in the Congo, which was extended to Lisala in March the following year (see Chapter Five).

Early civil aviation in Belgium owed much to the forward thinking of HRH King Albert, seen here (left) on a tour of SNETA's facilities.

SNETA's fleet in the early 1920s. The aircraft are DH9s, Rumpler CIVs and Breguet XIVs.

On 23 May, 1923, with the Congo services and European air mail services now well established, the Belgian government stepped in and took over the assets of SNETA, establishing a new company called SABENA (Société Anonyme Belge d'Exploitation de la Navigation Aérienne). This took over SNETA's fourteen remaining aircraft, seven having been destroyed in a hangar fire in September 1921 and the others having either been destroyed in air accidents or disposed of in other ways. The initial inventory of SABENA therefore comprised one Farman Goliath, four Bleriot-Spad 33s, one Ansaldo A-300C, three Rumpler C.IVs, one DH4 and four DH9s.

Operations by the new air company began on the day of its formation, with a mail flight by a DH9 from Brussels to Lympne, in Kent, by way of Ostend. Plans were now made to extend the Company's routes, but before this could be done it was clear that new equipment was needed; neither the single-engined nor the twin-engined types then in service were capable of operating safely over water, so SABENA opted for a machine with three engines — the first airline to do so — and in May, 1924 it

Sabena's SABCA S-2 at Haren Airport, Brussels. (SABCA).

O-BEBE was the registration allocated to the first aircraft entered in Belgium's infant register of commercial aircraft on 19 March, 1920.
On the same day nine other aircraft belonging to SNETA were also added to the register. There were three De Havilland DH-9, three Rumpler C IV and three Breguet XIV. Their identification letters were easy to remember – O-BLON, BLOC, BROC, BEAU, BELG, BIEN, BORD, BRUN and BUIS.

took delivery of its first Handley Page W.8e, which could carry ten passengers and was powered by a combination of the most reliable engines of the day: a 360-hp Rolls-Royce Eagle IX in the nose and two 240 ph Armstrong Siddeley Pumas mounted on struts between the two wings.

SABENA's first W.8e was registered O-BAHG and it was followed by four more, all built under licence by the SABCA aircraft construction company and registered O-BAHJ, O-BAHK, O-BAHL and O-BAHM. With these machines the airline inaugurated several new routes, the first on 14 July 1924, when O-BAHG flew from Rotterdam via Brussels to Basle, in Switzerland. Other routes went from Brussels to Strasbourg and Amsterdam, and in 1926 one was opened between the Belgian capital and London.

Meanwhile, in April, 1925, SABENA had received the first example of an improved version of the Handley Page, the W.8f, which differed from the earlier model principally in having a cabin heating system. All of these, which were registered O-BAHN to O-BAHZ, were licence-built by SABCA, and most were used on services in the Congo. In the mid-1920s the airline's earlier W.8es also underwent some modifications, having their nose engines deleted and the two outboard Pumas replaced by Rolls-Royce Eagle VIIIs.

These machines bore the brunt of SABENA's services until 1929, when the airline acquired the first of thirty Fokker F.VIIb/3ms. These were a good 40 mph faster than the Handley Pages, and although they carried the same number of passengers they enabled route times to be cut drastically. Seven of these machines were sent to the Congo in 1931, where they were later joined by four six-seat Westland Wessex aircraft and six Junkers Ju52/3ms, the latter arriving in 1938.

By this time, SABENA airliners were flying to points in England, Austria, France, Czechoslovakia, Holland, Scandinavia, Germany and Switzerland, and in 1936 the trans-Africa route from Brussels to Leopoldville — which had been inaugurated with the Fokker F.VIIs — was greatly improved with the entry into service of the first of thirteen Savoia-Marchetti S.73 airliners. Three of the faster S.83s were also delivered in the following year, and in 1939 the airline received two Douglas DC-3s, which could carry 21 passengers over a distance of 1,500 miles. Other modernisation plans were interrupted by the war, when all SABENA's aircraft except a few were able to escape to England; these were later sent to the Congo to join other machines already operating there, and SABENA went on to support the Allies in Africa for the duration of hostilities.

Czechoslovakia

The original airline in Czechoslovakia was CSA (Ceskoslovenske Statni Aerolinie), which was founded on 28 July 1923, and enjoyed a monopoly until 1927, when a rival airline called CLS (Ceskoslovenska Letecka Spolecnost) began operations. The first type of aircraft used by CSA was the Aero A-14, which could carry only one passenger, and 23 people were carried over the airline's Prague-Bratislava route between 29 October 1923, the opening date of the service, and the end of the year.

By 1928, six Farman Goliath twelve-seaters, built under licence by Avia and Letov, were also in service, and in three years that followed other types added to CSA's fleet included Aero A23s, A32s and A35s, de Havilland DH50s, a Junkers F.13 and a Ford Trimotor. By 1937 the airline's equipment had been greatly modernised, and its inventory now included three Savoia-Marchetti S.73s, four Airspeed Envoy IIIs, seven Fokker F.VIIb/3ms, a Saro Cloud amphibian, one Avia-built Fokker F.IXd, seven Aero 35s, one Aero 38, one Letov S218, four Letov S32s and a Caproni Ca97. With this material, CSA inaugurated a network of external routes from Prague to Paris, Brussels, Venice and Trieste via Klagenfurt and Bratislava, to Rome and Bucharest via Brno, and to Susak on the Adriatic coast of Yugoslavia via Bratislava.

CSA's rival, CLS, although smaller, had more modern equipment in the shape of three Douglas DC-2s and one Douglas DC-3, as well as two Fokker F.XVIIIs, six F.VIIb/3ms and an Avia 25. It also operated in co-operation with foreign airlines on external routes; on weekdays, for example, it

Fokker F.VII of SABENA at Croydon.

ran the 'Blue Danube Air Express' from Rotterdam to Budapest via Prague and Vienna in conjunction with KLM. This service was extended to Croydon in 1938, from which CLS and KLM flew alternately to Budapest with their DC-3s.

Other CLS facilities in the late 1930s included a Prague-Marseille service via Munich, Zurich and Geneva, and other services to Vienna and Berlin in co-operation with the Austrian airline Austroflug and Deutsche Lufthansa.

Both CSA and CLS ceased operations in the spring of 1939, when Germany invaded Czechoslovakia, and their resources were taken over by Lufthansa.

Finland

Finland's civil airline has the distinction of being one of the oldest in the world. Known as Aero O/Y, it was founded on 1 November, 1923 by Consul Bruno Lucander and started its first service, across the Gulf of Finland from Helsinki to Tallinn, Estonia, on 20 March 1924 using a solitary Junkers F.13 floatplane, purchased for around £400. On 2 June, a second route was inaugurated between Helsinki and Stockholm, this service being undertaken in co-operation with the Swedish airline ABA. In the following year the Helsinki-Tallinn service was extended to Königsberg with a Junkers G.24, which was replaced in 1932 by a Junkers Ju52/3m equipped with floats — as were all Aero O/Y's machines in the early years, for Finland, dotted with innumerable lakes, had no airfields. It was not until 1936 that aerodromes were built at Helsinki and Turku, and in 1937 domestic services were started with two recently-purchased de Havilland Dragon Rapides. These initially flew on the Helsinki — Viipuri and Helsinki-Tampere routes, the latter eventually being extended to include Vaasa, Oulu and Kemi in northern Finland.

Aero O/Y's fleet in the mid-1930s comprised seven Junkers F.13s, the lone Junkers G.24W, the Ju52 and the two Rapides. The latter were registered OH-BLA and OH-BLB and were named *Salama* (Lightning) and *Lappi* (Lapland). By 1939 the airline was operating a service to Berlin through Tallinn, Riga, Königsberg and Danzig in conjunction with Deutsche Lufthansa, and eight Finnish towns also had the benefit of an internal air service.

Aero O/Y's operations continued virtually unchecked following the outbreak of the Russo-Finnish War of November 1939, although the Helsinki-Viipuri service had to be abandoned after the Russians captured the latter town. During the Second World War, when Finland was Germany's ally in the fight against Russia, civil operations continued until 1944, when the armistice brought a halt to all flying in Finland until the following year. The airline's name was later changed to Finnair.

The Farman 301, typical of the designs that were produced in France to meet the growing demand for feeder liners in the early 1930s.

The Farman Goliath, used by many European airlines in the early 1920s. This example is an Air-Union machine, F-ADDS.

France

Before the 1914-18 War, France had been both the cradle and hub of civil aviation. After the war, although the widespread destruction of surface communication led to the rapid establishment of air mail services, with half a dozen different companies all involved, France's attitude towards civil aviation seemed to be one of attempting to recapture former glories. Her aviators had led the world in the days before 1914; her air aces had been legends throughout the world before 1918, and the two combined to exercise a strange psychological effect on those responsible for furthering French aviation during the years that followed. Everything, it appeared, was geared up to create more heroes, with huge funds allocated to record-breaking attempts by intrepid young men in stripped-down ex-military aircraft; there was no attempt at co-ordinating civil flying, as there was in beaten Germany and elsewhere.

So, in the years immediately after the war, a rash of commercial air companies sprang up in France, most of them equipped with modified versions of wartime combat aircraft. One early company, for example, the Compagnie des Messageries Aériennes, was equipped with the Spad 27, a civil variant of the wartime Spad XX with an open cockpit for the pilot and an enclosed cabin in the rear fuselage for two passengers. With this aircraft, CMA inaugurated one of the first services between Paris and London in 1920.

The type in most widespread use for carrying mail in France, immediately after the war, however, was the Breguet XIV, about 150 examples of which served in a civilian role. The biggest user by far was the Lignes Aériennes Latécoère, which began its first service from Toulouse to Barcelona on 25 December 1918 and subsequently extended it to Africa (see Chapter Five). The Breguet XIV was also

A LVG C VI biplane of Deutsche Luft Reederei bearing film star Hans Albers.

used by CMA on the company's first mail and freight service from Paris to Lille on 18 April 1919; later, additional mail services were inaugurated from Paris to Brussels, London, Amsterdam and Marseille.

Generally, early French airlines were the creations of France's aircraft constructors; CMA, for example, resulted from a consortium of the most famous names in French aviation, Louis Blériot, Louis Breguet, René Caudron, Henry Farman, Louis Renault, Robert Morane and Louis Saulnier. Henry Farman broke away in 1919 and set up his own company, Les Lignes Farman; in May 1920 this became La Société Générale de Transports Aériens (SGTA). Before that, on 8 February 1919, a

A high-wing Sablatnig P III monoplane of Lloyd Luftverkehr Sablatnig.

An AEG N 1 biplane of Deutsche Luft Reederei.

Farman Goliath had carried eleven passengers from Toussus-le-Noble to Croydon on what was probably the first commercial international passenger flight, and the following day a converted Caudron C.23 bomber had inaugurated a passenger service to Brussels from Paris. On both occasions, the pilot was Lucien Bossoutrot, Farman's chief test pilot, who was later to make a series of pioneer long-range flights to Africa.

The Farman FF60 Goliath, designed originally as a bomber, was one of the mainstays of early French commercial aviation. It was powered by two 260-ph Salmson radial engines, had a span of 87 feet and a cruising speed of 75 mph at 6,500 feet. It could carry twelve passengers over a distance of

A Rumpler Ru C 1 biplane of Rumpler Luftverkehr.

about 250 miles, seated in relative comfort in wicker chairs. By June 1922 thirty-four Goliaths were in service with the various French airlines, the main operators being the Lignes Farman and CMA.

On 1 January, 1923 a new airline, Air-Union, was formed by the merger of CMA and another company, Grands Express Aériens, and this employed some fifteen Goliaths. On 27 January, 1926, one of these machines, flown by Paul Codos, demonstrated the possibility of flying passengers by night between Paris and London, having already carried out a number of pioneer night flights along other routes on the continent.

The formation of Air Union was a step in the right direction to bring about some order in France's confused civil aviation industry, but until the foundation of Air France in 1933 France's European services suffered undeniably from this diversification, even though French airmen achieved amazing successes in long-range pioneer flights to Africa, the Far East and Latin America, exploits which are described in other chapters. One result of the lack of a coherent civil aviation programme and a shortage of financial support was that French designers tended to concentrate on the development of short- and medium-capacity aircraft; large commercial designs rarely received government backing, although when such aircraft proved successful French governments were not slow to exploit them for propaganda purposes. When the big six-engined flying-boat *Lieutenant de Vaisseau Paris* flew the Atlantic via the Azores on 30 August 1938, for example, much was made of the fact; yet no appreciable payload was carried, and in any case the British and Americans had already done it.

The formation of Air France by the fusion of the various existing aviation lines in August 1933 was in the nature of a determined attempt by the French Air Ministry to streamline France's sprawling and unwieldy civil aviation network. The new airline, for which the State put up most of the capital, had an initial fleet of about 270 aircraft, half of them single-engined short-range types which were quite unsuitable for the kind of operations envisaged for the future, and so Air France embarked on a programme of standardisation, as well as issuing new specifications to the various aircraft constructors.

In 1936, with equipment on order, and Air France's financial position growing steadily more healthy, the airline was regularly serving sixteen routes. Apart from those overseas, discussed elsewere, the European routes included Marseille-Barcelona, Paris-Strasbourg-Prague-Vienna-Budapest-Belgrade-Bucharest, Prague-Warsaw, Paris-Brussels-Amsterdam, Paris-Cologne-Berlin, Brussels-Hamburg-Copenhagen-Malmö-Stockholm, Paris-London, Paris-Lyon-Marseille, Marseille-Cannes, Paris-Bordeaux and Paris-Toulouse. This network was altered somewhat following the outbreak of the Spanish Civil War in 1936, when some of the routes crossing Spanish air space or ending at terminals in Spain had to be abandoned or changed.

The aircraft available to Air France during this period were as follows:

Eighteen Fokker F.VIIb, mostly gleaned from the fleets of the previous companies. These were used mainly for mail and freight transportation, mainly overseas, and were gradually withdrawn from use from 1937 onwards.

Nineteen Potez 620 and 621. These twin-engined machines, which entered service with Air France in 1933 and were derived from the military Potez 54, carried ten to fifteen passengers at 175 mph and were mainly used on the European routes, although a few served in Latin America.

Sixteen Wibault 282T and 283T. These aircraft, which flew for the first time in 1931, could carry twelve passengers at a cruising speed of 125 mph over long ranges. Their three-engined reliability made them suitable vehicles for use on the Paris-Dakar run. Two of them, F-AKEL and F-ANBN (both 283Ts) were modified for use as special long-range transports and were capable of carrying two passengers over a distance of more than 1,250 miles.

Five Breguet 393T. These elderly trimotors, capable of carrying ten passengers, were all in service overseas: three in Africa and two in South America.

Three Dewoitine D-333. Also three-engined designs, these were among the fastest and most modern airliners in service with Air France. Capable of carrying eight passengers at a cruising speed of 162 mph, they were pressed into service on the African and South American routes.

Twenty-nine Dewoitine D-338. A development of the D-333, the D-338 was an elegant design which entered Air France service on the Paris-Cannes route in mid-1936. Later, it became the mainstay of the airline's fast long-range services. Passengers carried, ranged from 22 on short routes to 12 on long-range sectors.

Eleven Lioré-et-Olivier H.242/1. In service on the Mediterranean routes since 1934, these four-

Fuelling a Lufthansa Junkers F 13 in 1926. Nearby is a Fokker F III.

engined flying-boats carried up to 15 passengers at a cruising speed of 120 mph. Their primary route was from Marseille to Tunis, flying time 5 hours 42 minutes.

Two Breguet 530 'Saigon'. Three-engined flying-boats, civil versions of the B-521 'Bizerte', these machines carried ten passengers at 125 mph between Marseille and Algiers.

In addition to these aircraft, nineteen others were held in reserve; these were four CAMS-53, four Potez 25, five Latécoère 28, four Farman 190, one FBA-17 HMT2 and one Farman 302. Six further machines — two Farman 2200, one Bleriot 5190 and two Latécoère 301 — were all in service on the South Atlantic route.

With the exception of the Dewoitine tri-motors, all Air France equipment of the late 1930s was outdated. Yet only one new landplane design was on the horizon; this was the Bloch MB-220, which was also a three-engined design developed from the MB-210 bomber. It entered service with Air France in the latter part of 1937, five aircraft being acquired initially these were followed by another five in 1938. The MB-220 was first used on the Paris-Marseille route, and on 27 March, 1938 it went into use on the Paris-London service. By the end of that year, MB-220s were flying to Amsterdam, Prague, Bucharest, Stockholm and Zurich, replacing the ageing Potez 62s and Wibault 282s on all Air France's main European routes. In the summer of 1939, MB-220s were flying an hourly service between Paris and London, and this continued up to the outbreak of the Second World War.

In 1939, Air France — for lack of suitable indigenous designs — was beginning to look to the United States as a potential source of future airliners, and in that year it acquired a solitary Douglas DC-2 for evaluation. This aircraft, registered F-AKHD, was eventually used as a VIP transport by the Vichy Government after the collapse of France in 1940.

Deutsche Lufthansa AG, inaugurated a regular passenger service when this Dornier Komet III first flew the Berlin – Halle – Stuttgart – Zurich route on 6 April, 1926.

Ten examples of the Focke-Wulf Möwe (Seagull) were delivered to Lufthansa for use during the late 1920s and early 30s. Photograph shows the prototype, named 'Bremen' which was used by Nord Deutscher Luftverkehr before joining the DLH fleet.

Germany

The first regular commercial air service in post-1918 Germany began on 5 February, 1919, when aircraft of Deutsche Luft-Reederei started carrying mail, newspapers and passengers between Berlin-Johannisthal and Weimar. DLR, which had been formed the previous year, had rapidly risen to the forefront among the spattering of embryo aviation companics that had come to the surface in Germany following the Armistice, and its expansion was rapid. In March 1919 it inaugurated a second service, between Berlin and Hamburg, and a third route was opened to Warnemünde in April.

By mid-1920, the DLR fleet comprised seventy-one single-engined aircraft, almost all of them ex-military types such as the LVG and AEG, and thirteen twin-engined Friedrichshafen FF45 and GIIIA machines, the latter capable of carrying up to six passengers as well as two crew, mail and cargo. In August that year, the airline inaugurated the first international route from Malmö to Amsterdam, via Warnemünde, Hamburg and Bremen, in co-operation with KLM and DDL, the Dutch and Danish airlines.

Further expansion took place in 1921, when the consortium of businesses involved in DLR — AEG, HAPAG, Zeppelin — formed a holding company called Aero-Union AG. In November, this, together with DLR, became joint owner and representative of a new Berlin-based airline, the Deutsch-Russische Verkehrs-gesellschaft DbH, also known as Deruluft. On 1 May, 1922, the company began services between Königsberg and Moscow. Two days later, DLR aircraft also began a regular service to Great Britain, landing initially in a meadow near Folkestone.

By this time, Aero-Union was feeling the severe effects of recession, and its aircraft fleet was reduced to 45 machines. However, it managed to survive while other, smaller companies went into oblivion, and by 1923 its only serious competitor in Germany was an airline owned by the Junkers Aircraft Company, Junkers Luftverkehr. Early in 1923, Aero-Union and its associated companies, together with Lloyd Luftdienst GmbH, joined their forces and resources into a single large company, Deutscher Aero Lloyd AG, which received considerable financial backing from shipping companies, banks and various industrial concerns; in October, the new company set up a base at Berlin's Tempelhof Airport, which was officially opened on 8 October, 1923 and which was also used by Junkers Luftverkehr.

During 1925, both Aero Lloyd and the Junkers concern existed mainly by virtue of considerable government subsidies, and in October that year the German Transport Ministry took over 80 per cent of the shares of Junkers Luftverkehr as a means of pressurising the two companies to merge. This step, inevitable in the prevailing climate of financial insecurity, led to the formation of Deutsche Luft Hansa AG (it should be noted that 'Lufthansa' was a later spelling) which began operations on 6 April, 1926. The first scheduled flight by the new airline was made by a

Beginning in 1935, Junkers Ju 160s operated as express aircraft on most domestic Lufthansa routes. The third machine in this picture is a Junkers F 24.

The world's first strut-free all-metal low-wing monoplane with a closed cabin, the Junkers F 13, was the work-horse of the Lufthansa fleet between 1926 and 1932. More than forty of them operated as landplanes when equipped with wheels or skis, or seaplanes when fitted with floats. The heated cabin provided four passenger seats equipped with safety belts.

Dornier Komet III, which flew from Berlin to Zurich via Halle, Erfurt and Stuttgart.

Luft Hansa operated initially over eight routes, most of which were inaugurated by the end of April. The aircraft types in use were the Junkers F.13, the Dornier Komet III, the Dornier Wal flying-boat, the Fokker F.II and F.III and the Junkers G.24, which was basically a scaled-up development of the F.13.

On 1 May, 1926, Luft Hansa began the world's first passenger night service from Berlin to Königsberg and cut the flying time to Moscow to fifteen hours. Two days later, the airline's Dornier Wals opened a flying-boat service from Stettin to Stockholm, and on 25 May a service was started from Berlin to Paris via Cologne in conjunction with the Lignes Farman and the Société Générale des Transports Aériens.

The fortunes of German civil aviation took a big upturn in the summer of 1926, when the 'London Agreement' of 1921 — which forbade the manufacture of aircraft in Germany, thus forcing

Probably the most aerodynamically advanced aircraft of its time, the Heinkel He 70 broke several world speed records in 1933 and was operated as an express mail carrier on Lufthansa's so-called 'Blitz Routes'. Some examples were used as fast reconnaissance aircraft in the Spanish Civil War.

constructors to set up factories in Russia, Denmark and Italy — was finally lifted. The Germans were at last able to centralise their resources, and with aircraft supply assured Luft Hansa entered into bilateral agreements with several European countries, negotiating new international routes. Ten new routes were agreed at the 16th conference of the International Air Traffic Association — of which the old DLR had been a founder member — that August in Berlin.

During the next three years, Luft Hansa airliners operated regular services to Czechoslovakia, Norway, Italy, Spain, Russia, Great Britain, Denmark and France, and in 1930 a regular air mail service was opened between Vienna and Istanbul via Budapest, Belgrade and Sofia. In the following year, the world's biggest landplane, the Junkers G.38, made its debut on the Berlin-Amsterdam-London route; it was the forerunner of a whole range of new types that would put Luft Hansa in the forefront of European commercial aviation.

The most famous of these was the Junkers Ju52, which entered Luft Hansa service in 1932; no fewer than 231 were eventually to pass through the airline's hands, although most of these would be operated on behalf of the Luftwaffe between 1939 and 1945. Thirty-eight were in service by the end

Loading mail into a Heinkel He111 – the aircraft that replaced the smaller He70 on some 'Blitz Routes' from 1936 and was later converted into one of the most famous bombers of all time.

The first Junkers G 31 delivered to Lufthansa was baptized "Hermann Köhl" in recognition of his pioneer crossing of the North Atlantic from East to West. When it put this three-engined Junkers G 31 into service, Lufthansa was the world's first airliner to serve food and beverage on board.

Parked Lufthansa aircraft at the Berlin-Tempelhof airport (about 1936). A Junkers Ju 86 is in the foreground.

of 1934, the year in which Luft Hansa began a scheduled service to Warsaw, and with these machines the average cruising speed on international routes was raised virtually overnight from 100 to 150 mph.

Much of Luft Hansa's revenue came from day and night air mail services, and in 1933 the search for a fast mail carrier produced the Heinkel He70, which was aerodynamically the most advanced aircraft of its day. Appropriately named *Blitz* (Lightning), it set up an impressive series of closed circuit speed-with-payload records; powered by a single 750 hp BMW engine, it had a maximum speed of 224 mph at 13,000 feet and a range of nearly 500 miles. Twenty-eight went into service with Lufthansa (as the airline was now known) and these began a series of *Blitz* routes on 16 June 1934, linking Berlin, Hamburg, Cologne and Frankfurt. Eleven such routes were in operation by the end of 1935.

In February 1935, Lufthansa made the first of a series of trial flights from Berlin to Cairo, using a Junkers 52/3m. The return flight took 16½ hours and was accomplished on the same day, 20 February, the aircraft flying via Budapest, Athens and Alexandria. At this stage in its development, Lufthansa probably led the world in night- and blind-flying techniques, including controlled descent through cloud.

In 1936, it was decided to liquidate Deruluft, its routes to be taken over jointly by Lufthansa and Aeroflot. Lufthansa took control of the Berlin-Danzig-Königsberg-Kovno-Riga-Reval-Helsinki sector in September 1936, but because of protracted negotiations with Aeroflot Deruluft actually remained in operation on other sectors until March 22, 1941 — exactly three months before the German invasion of the Soviet Union. In 1937, exploratory flights were made by Junkers 52s to Athens, Rhodes and the Middle East to see if it would be possible to open a route to Asia via Baghdad, Teheran and Kabul, but this and other expansion schemes were rendered impossible by the outbreak of war.

Interior of Imperial Airways Argosy. Armstrong Whitworth Argosy was used late 1920s, early 1930s.

Imperial Airways A.W. Argosy at Croydon with line up of I.A. vehicles. Circa late 20s, early 30s.

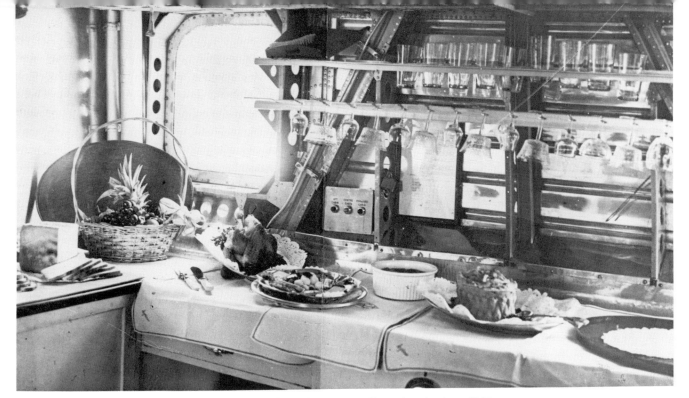

Imperial Airways Short 'Scylla' (landplane development of Kent flying boat), circa 1931.

Great Britain

Unlike their counterparts in some other countries, the small airlines that came into being immediately after 1918 did not have the benefit of state subsidies; their story is one of continual struggle to make ends meet, and few survived. The first British commercial aircraft company, in fact, was registered in the Autumn of 1916: this was Aircraft Transport and Travel Ltd. (AT & T) which was founded by George Holt Thomas, head of the Aircraft Manufacturing Co. which had produced such splendid designs as the DH4 and DH9. Other aircraft manufacturers such as Frederick Handley Page and A.V. Roe followed suit soon after the end of hostilities and began converting their wartime military designs to commercial machines.

Civil aviation in Britain took on a legal footing with the publication, on 30 April 1919, of the Air Navigation Directions, which set forth details of aircraft registration and maintenance requirements, crew licencing, rules of the air and so on. The following day the Air Navigation Act also came into force, and there was a rush to be the first to open a commercial service.

First off the ground was Flight Lieutenant Howard Saint, armed with the first commercial pilot's licence, and mechanic Bill Kelly, who took off in a DH9 of AT & T a few minutes after midnight on 1 May to fly a load of newspapers from Hendon to Bournemouth. However, what should have been the first British commercial flight ended in disaster when the aircraft crashed into a hill near Portsmouth. Saint received severe injuries, but Kelly escaped with shock.

One of Handley Page's big 0/400 bombers, converted into a transport, was more fortunate. Piloted by Lieutenant-Colonel Sholto Douglas, it set out from Cricklewood on that same night, carrying newspapers and eleven passengers, and reached Manchester three hours later. The next morning it took off for Edinburgh but was forced to turn back because of bad weather, and it was not until 5 May that the journey was completed.

In July, agreement was reached between the British and French governments for the establishment of civil air operations between the two countries, and on 25 August AT & T began the first regular service from Hounslow to Le Bourget and back, using DH4As and DH16s, while Handley Page Transport Ltd. also started services to Paris with their 0/400s. On 23 September, Handley Page also announced that they were starting a service to Brussels using the new W.8 airliner, developed from the 0/400. By this time, other companies were also getting in on the act; in October, for example, the steamship company S. Instone and Co. Ltd., bought a DH4A and hired a pilot to fly it, their intention being to fly shipping documents between London and the cross-Channel ports with the minimum delay.

The landplane version of the Kent, G-ACJJ 'Scylla' was used on Imperial Airways' Croydon-Paris service together with its sister aircraft, G-ACJK 'Syrinx'.

The initial euphoria, however, was destined to be short-lived. Poor weather in the autumn and winter of 1920 led to many cancelled bookings, and with no relief funds forthcoming from either the Government or industrial sponsors both Handley Page and AT & T were soon in deep financial trouble. By mid-December, AT & T had gone bankrupt, Instone had laid up its aircraft for the winter, and only Handley Page continued to operate on a sporadic basis. But it, too, ceased all air transport operations in February 1921, closely followed by Instone.

However, with the onset of finer weather — and the first hint that subsidies might become available from the Government at long last — Handley Page resumed operations to Paris in March 1921, and two days later Instone also re-opened their cross-Channel service, using Vickers Vimy Commercial G-EASI. What was left of AT & T, too, had been resurrected by the Daimler Hire Co. Ltd., and formed into Daimler Airways, starting operations initially with a de Havilland DH18, four of which were eventually also operated by Instone.

The civil aviation companies continued their uncertain course for the next two years, suffering financial tribulations and not infrequent accidents; on 7 April 1922, for example, one of Instone's DH18s collided with a Farman Goliath of Grands Express Aériens, all on board being killed. But finance continued to be the main problem, and by the end of 1922 the British Government at last recognised that something would have to be done if the airlines were to survive, so in January 1923 the Civil Air Transport Subsidies Committee was appointed to consider the whole question of subsidies and to advise on the best method of subsidising future cross-Channel air operations.

The Committee's report led directly to the founding, in 1924, of Imperial Airways, a national airline which incorporated all the previous operators and which was to be allotted a government subsidy of £1 million, spread over ten years. Operations began in May, with Handley Page W.8bs and DH34s flying the routes set up by the earlier companies, but because of Britain's preoccupation with

The Fokker F.VII replaced the earlier F.III in KLM service.

her Empire the European routes were always fated to take second place behind the long-range routes to the Middle and Far East and to South Africa. In 1927, in fact, only five European services were being operated — to Paris, Zurich, Ostend, Brussels and Cologne — compared with the seven that had been flown by the earlier companies. Aircraft procurement, too, was dictated by the longer routes, and it was not until 1928 that Imperial Airways invited tenders from all British manufacturers for new 40-seat, multi-engined airliners for service on the continental routes.

The design selected was the Handley Page HP42, which had the added attraction that it could also be used on the Empire routes overseas. However, the first proving flight from London to Paris was not made until 9 June, 1931, by *Hannibal,* and in the meantime Imperial Airways' European services were maintained by its fleet of Armstrong Whitworth Argosy and Handley Page W.8 aircraft.

The introduction of the HP42 brought a new air of organisation and efficiency to Imperial Airways' continental routes; it would never be relinquished, but in the spring of 1933, following several accidents and a sudden growth in traffic demands, the airline found itself desperately short of landplanes. Short Brothers filled the gap by building a landplane version of the Kent flying-boat; two examples were produced, named *Scylla* (G-ACJJ) and *Syrinx* (G-ACJK), and both went into service in 1934 on Imperial Airways' summer schedules from Croydon to Paris, Brussels, Basle and Zurich, supplementing the HP42s.

Meanwhile, during the early 1930s, a spate of small charter and air taxi companies had burst out over the British commercial aviation scene, equipped with a wide variety of aircraft. They included Highland Airways, Hillman's Airways, Jersey Airways, Railway Air Services and London, Scottish and Provincial Airways. From 1933, however, these small concerns began to standardise on a new and commercially successful feeder liner, the de Havilland DH84 Dragon. The DH89 Dragon Rapide was an uprated version, while another de Havilland machine — the DH86 — was evolved in 1934 to meet an original requirement for an aircraft capable of operating the Imperial Airways/Qantas route sector between Singapore and Brisbane. The DH86 was used by Imperial Airways on some of its continental services and also equipped two new companies, British Airways and United Airways, both registered in 1935.

Unlike Imperial Airways, none of these new airlines was restricted to buying British aircraft; British Airways' equipment, for instance, included a Junkers 52, a Lockheed 10A Electra and a Fokker F.VIII, and this choice gave it a decided advantage on the European routes over Imperial Airways, for in the mid-1930s there was no medium-sized British airliner that could compare with the leading foreign types. To remedy this situation, Imperial Airways ordered five examples of the new de Havilland Albatross, and these were delivered from October 1938 as G-AFDI *Frobisher,* G-AFDJ

Six Fokker F.VIIIs served KLM's European routes from 1928.

Falcon, G-AFDK *Fortuna,* G-AFDL *Fingal* and G-AFDM *Fiona.* From January 1939, these machines operated the Imperial Airways service from Croydon to Paris, Brussels and Zurich. In 1940, following the outbreak of war, they were used by the newly-created BOAC on services to Lisbon and Shannon.

Italy

The first steps to create an Italian national carrier were taken in 1928, when state-owned capital was used to form the Societa Aerea Mediterranea (SAM), which — with proper organisation and modern equipment — was ultimately to put Italy into the commercial running alongside Imperial Airways, Lufthansa and Air France. Operations began on 1 January, 1928, with a service between Brindisi and Valona, and in April a second route was added from Rome to Cagliari, a service that was later extended to Tunis. By 1930, the SAM fleet comprised nine flying-boats, nine Savoia S.55s, one

The Fokker XVIII was the last machine to follow Fokker traditional three-engined design. Five were delivered to KLM from 1933.

KLM was the first European airline to order the famous Douglas DC-3, in July 1936.

S.59 and one Cant 22, and its operations had proved sufficiently encouraging for the Italian Government to begin a cautious expansion by amalgamating other, smaller, operators with it. The first of them was Transadriatica, which was taken over in 1931, and in that year the company also inaugurated some new overland routes to Vienna, Munich and Berlin, using newly-acquired landplanes such as the Savoia S.71 — six of which were delivered — and the Junkers F.13. By 1932, SAM aircraft were flying on scheduled services to Cagliari, Tunis, Palermo, Bari, Brindisi, Tirana, Salonika, Florence, Venice, Vienna, Munich, Berlin, Aquila, Pescara and Ancona; its fleet had now grown to ten Savoia S.55s, one S.66, six S.71s, six Junkers F.13s, three Junkers G.24s and two Fokker F.VIIs.

In 1934 SAM took over three more Italian airlines, SANA — which already had an established network of flying-boat services to Africa, using Dornier Wals — SISA and Aeroespresso Italiana, and on 28 October that year it was formed into a new company named Ala Littoria, Italy's first national flag carrier. This did not mean that it had a monopoly, for another carrier — Avio-Linee Italiane, which was owned by the Fiat Company — retained its independence and continued operations with a mixed fleet of aircraft that included Fokker F.VIIs.

In March 1935, Ala Littoria absorbed another Italian concern, Società Adria Aero Lloyd, and took over that company's routes in Albania and North Africa. From then until 1939 the airline was responsible for carrying most of Italy's civil air traffic; in 1939 it opened its last service before the outbreak of war — a route from Rome to Buenos Aires, using Cant Z.506 flying-boats.

Netherlands

When it came to founding the basis of a civil aviation network after 1919, Holland enjoyed two big advantages. One was Anthony Fokker, builder of the renowned range of combat aircraft that had equipped the German Flying Corps; the second was a young lieutenant in the Dutch Army Aviation Service named Albert Plesman. In the summer of 1919, Plesman, together with another lieutenant, M. Hofstee, organised a very successful aircraft exhibition in Amsterdam. The interest shown by

Ten Fokker F - VII b/3m trimotors, built under licence by E. Plage and T. Laśkiewicz and powered by 240 h.p. Wright Whirlwinds, entered service with the Polish Airline LOT in 1930.

LOT was under some pressure from the Government to purchase Polish-designed equipment to boost the country's aircraft industry, and as a result evaluated various new types. These included the single-engined Lublin R-XI of which only the prototype was built, the R-IX, RWD-11, the eight-passenger PWS-20, the PWS-21, and the four-passenger PWS-24. None of these aircraft entirely satisfied the airline's rigid specifications and requirements, and only the PWS-24 was purchased and operated from 1 May 1933 on some of the company's domestic routes such as Warsaw-Poznań. The PWS-24 was a high-wing cantilever monoplane, powered by a single 240 h.p. engine. A later version, the PWS-24 bis was powered by a 420 h.p. Pratt and Whitney Wasp Junior.

Several Lockheed L.10 Electras were purchased by LOT from 1935.

people concerned with aviation from all over Europe encouraged Fokker, who had lost everything following Germany's collapse, to form a new company, while Albert Plesman toured Holland's business world and set about raising funds to fulfil a dream: the foundation of a Dutch civil airline. At last, with sufficient backing, he registered the new company on 7 October 1919 at The Hague; its title was Koninklijke Luchtvaart Maatschappij NV (KLM Royal Dutch Airlines), the 'Royal' having been granted by HM Queen Wilhelmina as a token of her confidence in the airline's future.

After seven months of preparation, KLM opened its first air service on 17 May 1920, when Jerry Shaw, a pilot working under contract, flew two passengers and a bundle of newspapers from London to Amsterdam in a leased de Havilland DH16. This aircraft, registered G-EALU, made the return flight on 18 May, inaugurating the first service from Holland to England.

The Lockheed L-14 "Super Electra", a bigger and more powerful version of the L-10 with seats for fourteen passengers, was added to LOT's fleet in 1938.

The first aircraft purchased by Plesman for KLM were two DH9s, soon followed by two Fokker F.IIs, and with this initial small fleet Plesman opened a new service from Amsterdam to Hamburg via Bremen on 1 September 1920 in co-operation with the German airline DLR. By the end of the year, KLM's four aircraft has flown over 50,000 miles and had carried 345 passengers, 48,500 pounds of cargo and 6,600 pounds of mail.

In 1921 Plesman purchased eleven new Fokker F.III aircraft, followed by a twelfth in 1922, and one of these machines — H-NABH — reopened the Amsterdam-Croydon service in April 1921, after a long and bitter winter had grounded the KLM fleet. In that year the airline opened its first air passenger and freight office in Amsterdam and also set up an aerial survey department, a diversification that turned out to be very profitable.

KLM now embarked on a progressive programme of expansion, opening new European routes to Brussels, Paris, Copenhagen, Malmö and Zürich, and in 1924 exploratory flight began to the Dutch colonies in the Far East (see Chapter Eight). By this time Plesman was beginning to replace his earlier Fokker F.IIIs with the much improved F.VII; three were ordered initially, the first of these entering service on KLM's London route in July 1924.

In 1927 the F.VII was followed by the F.VIII fifteen-seater, which was powered by two 440 hp Bristol Jupiter engines. The first aircraft of this type to be acquired by KLM was actually the prototype, which served only for a short time before being lost in a crash in August 1927, but during the following year six others were delivered for service on the airline's European routes. By 1929 these had been expanded to include Budapest, Istanbul, Baghdad, Karachi, Calcutta, Bangkok and Djakarta, and the KLM fleet now numbered twenty aircraft, all of them Fokkers. In 1930 services were also started to Athens, Cairo, Hannover, Belgrade and Rome, and in the following year KLM also opened some domestic routes, initially between Amsterdam and Groningen and then from Twente to Eindhoven. These, however, were not profitable and had to be carried on with the aid of large grants from regional authorities.

Lufthansa's four-engined Dornier Super Wal seaplane entered service in 1928 on the Lübeck-Copenhagen-Göteborg-Oslo and Berlin-Stettin-Kalmar-Stockholm routes.

Two types used by the first Spanish airline, the Compania Aerea de Transportes, in the late 1920s:
the Rohrbach RoVIII Roland I (M-CBBB) and a Junkers G.24 (EC-FFA).

In May 1930 KLM received the first example of a new Fokker airliner, the 20-passenger F.IX. However, only two were built, and they were quickly replaced by the F.XII, which was basically a three-engined development of the F.VIII. Eight of these were delivered to KLM in 1931-32 and continued in service until 1936, when they began to be replaced by the F.XVIII, the last machine to follow Fokker's traditional three-engined pattern. Five were delivered to KLM, the first in 1933.

The long association between KLM and Anthony Fokker's commercial designs, however, was fast coming to an end, for by the end of 1932 Albert Plesman was searching for a new and ultra-modern airliner that would serve KLM on both the Far Eastern and European routes into the 1940s. Fokker had new airline designs on the drawing-board, but they were no match for an American machine which, in 1933, was already flying; this was the Douglas DC-1, and its production version, the DC-2 entered airline service in the USA the following year.

Plesman lost no time in recognising the DC-2's potential and, in 1934, ordered the first of what was eventually to be a fleet of nineteen, three more also being acquired by KLM's subsidiary KNILM. The first of these aircraft, PH-AJU *Uiver,* was entered in the MacRobertson International Air Race from London to Melbourne in October 1934 and won first prize in the handicap section, a feat that gave a considerable boost to the DC-2's overseas sales.

By the late 1930s KLM was buying all its aircraft from American manufacturers. The DC-2 was followed, in July 1936, by the DC-3, KLM being the first European airline to operate this type. Two years later KLM also introduced the Lockheed 14 and European services continued to expand steadily; in 1939 a new route was opened between Amsterdam, Kristiansand and Oslo. By now the airline had 61 stations in 29 countries and its aircraft were flying more than 5 million miles every year, carrying 98,000 pasengers. It was universally respected and at the apex of its power; but Plesman's dream, which had come so far along the road to success since the embryo days of twenty years earlier, was soon to be tragically shattered by the German Blitzkrieg of 1940. Yet for KLM, it was not the end; those of its aircraft which managed to escape continued to operate throughout the war, flying from Bristol to Lisbon under charter to BOAC.

Poland

During the years between the two world wars, civil aviation development in Poland was among the most dynamic in Europe. It began in 1922, when the country's original airline, Polska Linia Lotnicza, began regular services between Danzig and Warsaw in conjunction with the German company Aero-Lloyd, using Junkers F.13s. In 1925 all German interests in Polish aviation were removed and the Polish airline adopted a new title — Aerolot.

During the next two years several domestic routes were opened, and in 1927 two new international routes were inaugurated, one from Puck to Copenhagen with a Junkers G23W floatplane and the other to Vienna via Brno, Czechoslovakia. Meanwhile, a second Polish airline had been founded in 1925 by the Poznan branch of the Union of Polish Airmen; this was Aero-Komunikacja Powietrzna, which started a service between Warsaw and Poznan using Farman F.70 biplanes.

On 1 January, 1929 these companies, and all civil aviation concerns in Poland, were taken under government control and a new state airline — Polskie Linie Lotnicze (LOT) was formed. This inaugurated more domestic routes, using Fokker F13s which had belonged to Aerolot, and in 1930 ten Fokker F.VIIb-3m trimotors were also purchased. In April 1930 a new international service was opened to Bucharest, and this was later extended to include Sofia and Salonika; a northern route to Riga and Tallinn on the Baltic was also inaugurated.

By 1937, LOT was flying regularly from Warsaw to Berlin, and had extended its southern route through Athens and Rhodes to Lydda, in Palestine. The airline now had the benefit of some of the most modern aircraft then in service anywhere in Europe, including three Douglas DC-2s and several Lockheed L-10s, which were purchased in 1935 and 1936; a single Junkers Ju52/3m also replaced the elderly F.13s.

In 1939, LOT's routes were further extended to Budapest, Belgrade, Venice, Rome and Copenhagen, while the Lydda service was pushed through as far as Beirut. By this time several Lockeed L-14s had been added to the fleet and the airline was casting its net around in search of a suitable airliner to undertake a transatlantic service, but all such plans were brought to an abrupt end by the German invasion of 1 September 1939.

Romania

The foundation of civil aviation in Romania may be traced back to 23 April 1920, and the formation of the Compagnie Franco-Roumaine de Navigation Aerienne, financed initially with money put up by a Romanian bank. Using SEA VII biplanes — civil conversions of the SEA IV observation aircraft — CFRNA began flights to Warsaw, Strasbourg, Prague, Budapest and Bucharest, extending the route to Constantinople in October 1921. By this time the company owned nearly 100 aircraft — SEA VIIs, SPAD 33s and 46s, and Potex IXs — and in 1924 seven-passenger Caudron C.61 trimotors were also introduced. The following year the company changed its name to the Compagnie Internationale de Navigation Aerienne (CIDNA), and this operated a miscellany of types until 1929, when it standardised on the Fokker F.VIIb.

In the meantime, the French Potez Company, which had strong associations in Romania, had founded an internal airline there known as SARTA; this was taken over by the Romanian Government in 1935 and a national airline, LARES, was founded. This operated services to Athens, Milan, Berlin and Warsaw until 1941, using aircraft that ranged from Douglas DC-2s to Savoia S.71s.

Scandinavia

Civil aviation in Denmark owed much to the Germans, for the first Danish airline, Det Danske Luftfartselskab (DDL) was founded with German aid in 1920 and operated jointly with Deutsche Luft-Reederie on the Malmö-Copenhagen route. Although relatively small, DDL retained modern equipment throughout the inter-war years, using Fokker F.VIIs during the 1930s. In 1938, the airline received two Focke-Wulf FW200 Kondors, and these entered service as OY-DAM *Dania* and OY-DEM *Jutlandia*. The two machines operated a scheduled service between Copenhagen, Amsterdam and Croydon for several months after the outbreak of war, OY-DAM finally being impounded by the British in April 1940 and impressed into BOAC service as G-AGAY *Wolf*.

Norway's inter-war airline, DNL, was created by Fred Olsen and other shipping companies and was purely a domestic carrier, serving Norway's far-scattered communities with a variety of landplanes and floatplanes, including — in the late 1930s — Lockheed 14s. Not until after the Second World War, however, did DNL begin to operate international services, using Junkers Ju52/3m floatplanes.

The largest of the Scandinavian airlines was Aerotransport AB of Sweden, which — like its Norwegian neighbour — relied on a mixture of landplanes and seaplanes. In 1924 ABA operated Junkers F.13s on a passenger service between Stockholm and Helsinki and these aircraft were later used on a night mail service from Stockholm to London via Malmö and Amsterdam. ABA also operated the Junkers G.23, G.24 and W.33, some of the G.24s being licence-built in Sweden, and in the 1930s the airline also acquired seven Junkers 52/3ms. The most modern equipment used by ABA before the outbreak of war was the Douglas DC-3, five of which were put into service on the neutral nation's international routes. It is interesting to note that, in 1938, ABA, DDL and DNL began talks aimed at an eventual merger; this finally came to fruition in July 1946, when the air transport resources of the three countries were pooled to form the Scandinavian Airlines System (SAS).

Spain

The first Spanish commercial operator was CETA (Compania Espanola de Trafico Aereo), which was set up in 1921 with British help and which, initially, used DH9s. The first pair were delivered on 19 September, 1921 and bore the registrations M-AGAG and M-AFAF. They were used to inaugurate a mail service between Seville and Larache, and sustained operations until the arrival of a Dornier Komet (M-AAIA) in October 1922. Aid was received during the remainder of the 1920s from both France and Germany, the former wishing to cultivate Spanish facilities for use by Aéropostale and the latter for use by airships. In 1927 all civil aviation concerns were taken over by the government and formed into a national carrier, Iberia, which continued operations on domestic and North African routes until 1936, when its amazing variety of aircraft were requisitioned by the government and put to use in an equally amazing variety of roles, some being used as bombers.

Soviet Union

Initial plans for a civil air fleet in the Soviet Union were drawn up in January 1921, and operations began the following May with four-engined Ilya Mouromets bombers, converted to the civilian role, flying passengers and mail over the Moscow-Orel-Kursk-Kharkov route. The aircraft were also used to carry passengers between Moscow and Nizhne Novgorod for a time in the summer of 1922.

On 17 March, 1923, an airline company named Dobrolet was formed, and this began regular services between Moscow and Nizhne Novgorod in July. Two other airlines were also founded in that same year: Zakavia, based at Tiflis, and Ukrvozdukhput, at Kharkov in the Ukraine. These two airlines later merged and inaugurated several important internal air routes.

In April. 1924 a Central Asian sub-division of Dobrolet was formed to operate services in the Tashkent-Samarkand-Termez area, and a seaplane service was also started between Sevastopol, Yalta and Yevpatoriya; during the next two years other internal services were opened to Kiev, Odessa and Rostov.

Until now, all international services had been undertaken by Deruluft, the joint Soviet-German air company, but in July 1926 Dobrolet initiated a service from Verkhne-Udinsk in Siberia to Urga in Mongolia, and in September that year another service was started between Tashkent and Kabul, in Afghanistan. Much attention was paid during this period to providing regular air services to various points in Siberia, where natural resources were beginning to be exploited on a large scale and where extremes of climate made surface transport difficult. From 1929, the principal feeder-liner used by Dobrolet was the nine-passenger Tupolev ANT-9, while Polikarpov U-2 three-seat light aircraft were used over short distances. Nevertheless, most of the aircraft used by Dobrolet up to 1930 were still of foreign origin.

On 25 February, 1932, all civil aviation activities in the Soviet Union came under the control of the Chief Directorate of the Civil Air Fleet, and on 25 March the State airline was renamed Aeroflot. New transport aircraft of indigenous design, such as the ANT-20 *Maxim Gorky,* were progressively introduced on to Aeroflot's internal routes, but in 1939 there were still no international services other than those to Mongolia and Afghanistan. Nevertheless, during the 1930s Soviet aviators and aircraft carried out important long-range pioneering work over the Arctic, and only the Second World War brought a halt to plans for a trans-Polar service to the United States (see Chapter Six).

Switzerland

The year 1919 saw the emergence of three commercial air companies in Switzerland: Aero-Gesellschaft Comte, Mittelholzer and Co, Avion Tourisme SA and Frick and Co, all of which undertook joy-riding and charter work with a mixture of aircraft ranging from Kondor E.IIIAs to Macchi M.3 flyingboats. The last-named company was reformed as Ad Astra AG in December 1919 and, over the next two years, took over the other two concerns.

More modern equipment was obtained from Germany in the form of two Dornier Komets, a C.II Dephine and a Junkers F.13, and with the latter aircraft Ad Astra began its first regular service from Geneva to Zürich via Nuremberg on 1 June 1922.

By 1925, foreign airlines were making inroads into Switzerland, and to counter this Ad Astra acquired four Junkers G.23s with which it hoped to recapture the Swiss sectors of the air routes. However, in September 1925 a serious Swiss rival materialised: the Basler Luftverkehrs AG, or Balair, which began operations in 1926 with five Fokker F.IIIs on routes to Stuttgart, Munich and Frankfurt. Balair standardised on Fokker aircraft, and by 1929 its services were reaching as far afield as Vienna, Marseille and Amsterdam. Ad Astra came back with a service from Zurich to Berlin, operated in conjunction with Luft Hansa, but this was not a commercial success; however, the airline managed to keep its head above water by carrying out some highly successful charter flights to North Africa, using some newly-acquired Fokker F.VII-3ms.

By this time, both Balair and Ad Astra were co-operating in certain spheres, and amalgamation was a logical step. On 26 March 1931, therefore, the two joined forces to become the Schweizerische Luftverkehr AG, or Swissair.

The airline's equipment on amalgamation comprised eight Fokker F.VIIbs, one Fokker V.IIa, two Dornier Merkurs, one BFW M.18D, one Comte AC4 and three Junkers F.13s. Later, in 1932, the company acquired two six-seater Lockheed Orion monoplanes and these were put into service on the Zürich-Vienna route, halving the previous flight time. Swissair now turned more and more to the United States for its equipment, purchasing a twin-engined Curtiss Condor and two Clark GA-43s in 1934, but the Condor crashed between Zürich and Berlin later that year when its wings folded up and all twelve people on board were killed. It was the first Swiss fatal air accident in thirteen years of operations.

In 1935 Swissair added four Douglas DC2s to its fleet, and with these the airline inaugurated a service from Zürich to Croydon via Basle. A fifth DC-2 was purchased later, and in 1936 a Junkers Ju86 was bought to operate a night mail service between Basle and Frankfurt. However, this machine experienced continual engine trouble and was returned to Junkers, along with a second example bought in 1937.

On the outbreak of war in September, 1939, Swissair's fleet comprised five DC-3s, three DC-2s a DH89 Dragon Rapide, a Comte AC-4 and a Fokker F.VIIa. All overseas services were suspended in August 1939, but some were resumed in the spring of 1940 and continued until 1944, when they ceased again until the end of hostilities.

Chapter Eight
In Search of Asia

1. The East Indies Route

By the Autumn of 1924, long-range pioneering flights had become not so much a question of individuals seeking to establish new records, but of airlines and governments seeking to establish links with distant possessions overseas, either for commercial or military purposes. The RAF's early long-range flights to India and South Africa were a good example of this trend, as was the French mail service to West Africa. However, it was Albert Plesman's Dutch airline KLM which became the first to explore and eventually to establish a full commercial service to colonies halfway round the world.

On 1 October, 1924, three months after the type first entered service on KLM's Amsterdam-London route, a Fokker F.VII took off from Schiphol on the first leg of a flight to Batavia, Java. Its pilot was Captain A. N. J. Thomassen à Thuessink van der Hoop; second pilot was Lieutenant H. van Weerden Poelman, and the flight engineer was P.A. van den Broeke.

Later that day, the aircraft landed at Prague after a flight of 520 miles, and from there it went on to Belgrade the next day. On the next stage, however, severe trouble was experienced when the water cooler developed a leak, with the result that the engine overheated and seized. Van der Hoop had to make a hurried forced landing at Plovdiv, in Bulgaria; there was no time to select a suitable field and the Fokker's undercarriage was smashed on rough ground. That was on 3 October, and it was a full month before the damage was repaired and the aircraft was able to resume its journey, reaching Constantinople on 3 November.

From there, its route took it to Karachi via Angora, Aleppo, Baghdad, Bushire and Bandar Abbas; it reached Karachi on 9 November and started the flight across India the next day, flying to Calcutta through Amballa and Allahabad. Then it went on to Akyab, Rangoon, Bangkok, Sengora and Medan, in Sumatra, where it arrived on 21 November. Only two stages now remained, from Medan to Muntok and from there to Batavia. This objective was reached on 24 November after a flight of 9,552 miles; the Fokker had left Amsterdam fifty-five days earlier, but because of the engine trouble in Bulgaria only twenty of them had actually been spent en route; flying time was 127 hours 16 minutes, and from Plovdiv onwards the aircraft's progress had been nothing short of remarkable, the successive legs of the flight being flown on an almost daily basis. Moreover, on arrival at Batavia both the Fokker and its replacement engine were found to be in excellent condition.

The aircraft and its crew returned to Holland in December, their round trip having given both KLM and the Dutch Government proof that not only were long-range flights to the East Indies feasible, but that they could be undertaken with existing equipment. However, it was decided that new airliners, with a greater seating capacity and preferably equipped with more than one engine for safety reasons, would be necessary before such flights could be undertaken on a regular commercial footing.

A further step towards the start of a regular Amsterdam-Java service was undertaken in 1927, when the American, W. van Lear Black, publisher of the *Baltimore Sun,* chartered an eight-seater Fokker VIIa from KLM to make the journey, which in fact was to be the world's first intercontinental charter flight. The aircraft left Schiphol on 15 June 1927, piloted by Captain G. J. Geysendorffer, with First Officer J. B. Scholte as co-pilot and K. A. Weber as flight engineer. Thirteen days later, van Lear Black and his valet were delivered safely to Batavia, the Fokker having flown by the same route as its predecessor, and the flying time was 86 hours 27 minutes. The return journey took fourteen days, the aircraft arriving back in Amsterdam on 23 July after an elapsed time of 97 hours.

In the summer of 1927 KLM received the first of its new three-engined Fokker F.VIIa-3ms, the aircraft designed to meet the airline's requirement for a transport with a greater carrying capacity that the single-engined F.VII, and one of these, H-NAEA, made a proving flight to Djakarta that autumn. This was followed by a second proving flight in the spring of 1928. After setting up base facilities along the route and making a further proving flight in October 1928, KLM inaugurated its first scheduled service to Djakarta — the longest in the world, covering a distance of 8,540 miles — on 12 September 1929.

Meanwhile, on 1 November 1928, domestic air traffic services had been started in the Dutch East Indies by a KLM subsidiary company, KNILM (Koninklijke Nederlandsch-Indische Luchtvaart-Maatschappij), which was initially equipped with Fokker F.VIIbs. Four of these had been purchased and two of them (H-NAFA and H-NAFB) arrived in September and October, but the other two were damaged during the delivery flight.

KNILM's inaugural flight was made by H-NAFB (now re-registered PK-AFB) which flew from Djakarta to Semarang on 1 November 1928 carrying the Governor-General of the Dutch East Indies, A. C. D. de Graeff. A second route was opened between Djakarta and Bandung, and in 1929 the Djarkarta-Semarang route was extended to Surabaya. Such was the success of KNILM's operations that a fifth F.VIIb was purchased in 1929, followed by two more in 1930. In that year a new route was opened to Palembang and this was soon extended to Singapore, the weekly service being inaugurated on 4 March.

By 1 November 1930, two years after it opened its first service, KNILM had carried 31,352 passengers and carried 377,000 pounds of freight, as well as over 20,000 pounds of mail. In the following year, the first proving flight was made to Australia, Fokker F.VIIb PK-AFC departing from Djakarta on 12 May 1931 and arriving at Wyndham, Western Australia, two days later. The aircraft, named *Abel Tasman* after the famous Dutch explorer, flew on across the Australian continent and visited Sydney and Melbourne, eventually flying back to Djakarta on 27 May. The crew on this flight were Captain M. P. Pattist, Jan Moll and Simon Elleman.

The year 1931 also saw some expansion within the KNILM fleet, with two Fokker F.XII trimotors (PK-AFH and PK-AFI) being taken on charge. These machines entered service initially on the Djakarta-Medan route. Despite these additions, however, no new routes were opened until 1935.

In the meantime, KLM had been cutting down the time on its Amsterdam-Djakarta route. Up to 1931 this continued to be served by the Fokker F.VII-3m; the Fokker F.IX, which could carry up to six passengers in sleeping accommodation, had been intended to augment it, but although one proving flight to the East Indies was made in 1930 the two F.IXs delivered to KLM were subsequently used on European routes. The aircraft that did replace the F.VII-3m on the Far East route was the F.XII, which — although smaller than the F.IX — had a greater capacity, being capable of seating 16 passengers. Eight F.XIIs were built for KLM, and these went into service on the Djakarta route in 1931.

The real breakthrough, however, came with the introduction of the Fokker F.XVIII, which was powered by three Pratt & Whitney Wasp engines. Five were delivered to KLM: these were PH-AIO *Oehoe*, PH-AIP *Pelikaan*, PH-AIQ *Kwartel*, PH-AIR *Rijstvogel* and PH-AIS *Snip*. On 18 December 1933, *Pelikaan* left Amsterdam for Djakarta, crewed by Captain Smirnoff, P. Soer, J. M. H. Grosfeld and C. H. van Beukering, and flew to Dkajarta in a record time of 4 days and 4 hours, returning in the same time.

Also in 1933, Fokker began design work on his latest airliner, the F.XXXVI, which would be able to carry 16 passengers at 155 mph in comfort on the Java route. By this time, however, Albert Plesman was becoming increasingly interested in the new generation of airliners being built by the Douglas Aircraft Company of Los Angeles; it seemed that the DC-2 would be the ideal vehicle for the Far East service, bringing with it a whole new dimension in speed and passenger comfort, and in November 1933 Plesman made the first moves to obtain licence rights from Douglas to manufacture the DC-2 in Holland — although who the Dutch manufacturer would be was by no means clear. However, Anthony Fokker, sensing which way the wind was blowing, made his own approaches to Douglas, narrowly beating Plesman's bid; the result was that Fokker Aircraft became the manufacturing and sales agent for the DC-2 (and also, later, for the DC-3) in Europe. Fokker ultimately were to sell 39 DC-2s to various customers, although none of the new airliners were in fact built in Holland.

The first DC-2 acquired by KLM was PH-AJW, which joined the fleet in August 1934 and, in October, took part in the MacRobertson Air Race from London to Melbourne, covering the 12,350 miles in a flying time of 71 hours 28 minutes. The aircraft captain on this flight was K. D. Parmentier, with Jan Moll as first officer and B. Prins as flight engineer, and three fare-paying passengers were also carried. This DC-2's career with KLM was destined to be short, however, for it crashed at Rutbah in Iraq on 20 December 1934. KLM's second DC-2, PH-AKG *Gaai,* was also unfortunate; entering service with the airline on 30 March 1935, it crashed at Piah San Giacomo on 20 July that same year.

Nevertheless, KLM purchased thirteen more DC-2s in April and May 1935, and some of these were pressed into service on the Amsterdam-Djakarta route, reducing the flight time to 57 hours. Their debut enabled KLM to combine passengers and mail satisfactorily and, in fact, began to deprive Imperial Airways of a good deal of traffic along the route sectors as far as Singapore, which led to a fierce competitive struggle that started in December 1934, when the first DC-2s entered service.

In July 1935, KNILM also bought three DC-2s (PK-AFJ, PK-AFK and PK-AFL),and these machines also entered into strong competition against the Qantas-Imperial Airways service from Darwin to Singapore, flying between Dkajarta and Singapore and effectively cutting down the flying time from seven hours to four. Also in 1935, KNILM acquired three DH89A Dragon Rapides, which it used for aerial survey work, mostly on behalf of the Netherlands New Guinea Petroleum Company.

In 1936, KNILM opened a new service with its DC-2s from Djakarta to Borneo; it was originally planned to extend this service to Manila, but this scheme was never realised because of difficulties encountered in negotiations with the Philippine and US Governments. KLM also acquired its first DC-3 in that year; this was PH-ALI *Ibis,* which joined the fleet in October 1936. It was joined by thirteen more in 1937, three more in 1938 and a further five in 1939. A DC-3 service to Djakarta was begun in October 1937, reducing the flight time from 57 to 55 hours.

On 30 April, 1922, a Fokker F III marked RR 1 became the first 'Deruluft' (German-Russian Airlines, founded 24 November, 1921) aircraft to land at Moscow's airport Chodynka. The second Fokker airplane, marked RR 3, arrived the following evening.

At the other end of the Amsterdam-Djakarta route, KNILM expanded further in 1938 with the purchase of five new Lockheed 14 Super Electras, which were registered PK-AFM to PK-AFQ. In July, these aircraft opened a new service to Sydney, and this extension made it possible for a traveller to fly from either Amsterdam or London to Sydney in just eight days. Another important route was inaugurated in August 1938, to Saigon; this was flown by the airline's DC-2s.

More aircraft were purchased early in 1940, for — even though the German attack on Holland in May had resulted in the cessation of operations by KLM — there was no reason to suppose at that point that the war would spread to the Far East, and it was envisaged that KNILM operations would increase. The new aircraft were two Grumman G-21As and two Sikorsky S-43 amphibians, with which the airline operated services to the Celebes Islands.

With the occupation of Holland, KNILM now assumed responsibility for KLM's affairs, which included responsibility for the Lydda-Djakarta sector of the route to the East Indies. Some KLM aircraft, including a trio of DC-3s, were taken on charge by KNILM, and so were two Douglas DC-5s which had been ordered by KLM but never delivered. These were flown direct to the East Indies from the USA, and in 1941 they were joined by two more which had been in use on KLM's West Indies services.

In December, 1941 war came to the Far East, and in February, 1942 KNILM's aircraft were used to evacuate women and children from Singapore and other points threatened with the Japanese advance. Afterwards, as many aircraft as could be saved were flown to Australia, where they were subsequently used in the military transport role. KNILM, which had become one of the most profitable of all pre-war airlines, was never resurrected after the war because of the confused and dangerous situation that prevailed in the Dutch East Indies; instead, in 1947, it was merged with KLM, which became responsible for the Indies air network until the Dutch East Indies became independent in 1949.

2. China and Japan

By 1925, pioneering flights by half a dozen nations had succeeded in linking Europe and Asia by a southerly route, running through the Middle East and India; but nobody had yet done so by flying the much more inhospitable and poorly-charted northern route across Siberia. It was perhaps appropriate that the honour of being the first should fall to a Russian expedition, organised jointly by the 'Friends of Aviation' and Dobrolet, the Soviet air transport company.

The purpose of the expedition, which set out in the summer of 1925, was to pioneer a route from Moscow to Pekin in sixteen stages, with support facilities — including a train which would follow the expedition as far as possible along the Trans-Siberian Railway — set up along the way. The flying element of the expedition was to consist of twenty persons — six pilots, six mechanics and eight passengers, the latter made up of photographers and press representatives. They would use a mixture of aircraft: two three-seater P-1 biplanes built by Aviakhim, two P-2s similar to the P-1s but powered by British Puma engines, an AK-1 monoplane fitted with a Salmson engine, and two Junkers F.13s.

The first leg of the flight, from Moscow to Nizhne Novgorod, was completed on 10 June, and a week later all the aircraft had arrived safely at Novo-Nikolayevsk, having flown 1,900 miles since leaving Moscow and crossed the Ural Mountains. This part of the route had been covered in six stages, varying in length from 200 to 400 miles.

On 24 June the six aircraft arrived at Irkutsk, on the shores of Lake Baikal, where the crews remained for a week before leaving on 1 July to fly the next leg — a 300-mile stretch to Urga, in Mongolia, the last civilisation before the wastes of the Gobi Desert. No-one had ever flown across the Gobi, which represented a distance of some 620 miles with only two stops, one at Ude and the other at Kalgan.

Only five aircraft arrived at Ude; the sixth, the AK-1, had been forced down in the desert with engine trouble and had been damaged on landing, although the occupants were safe. On 9 July, the other five machines flew on to Kalgan, where one of the Junkers unfortunately struck an obstacle on landing and was wrecked. Once again, the crew escaped unhurt. The remaining four left Kalgan on 13 July for the last 110-mile hop to Pekin, arriving without incident that same day. On the 17th they were joined by the AK-1, which had been repaired on the spot by a support crew.

Despite occasional setbacks the expedition was hailed as a success and a considerable propaganda achievement; one of its objectives had been to demonstrate the power of Soviet aviation to the

On 19 September, 1930, the German-Chinese airline "Eurasia Aviation Corporation" was founded. *Lufthansa participated by providing equipment and staff. This airline, equipped, at first, with Junkers F 13s and Junkers W 33s, and later with Junkers Ju 52s, spread a well-functioning network across China.*

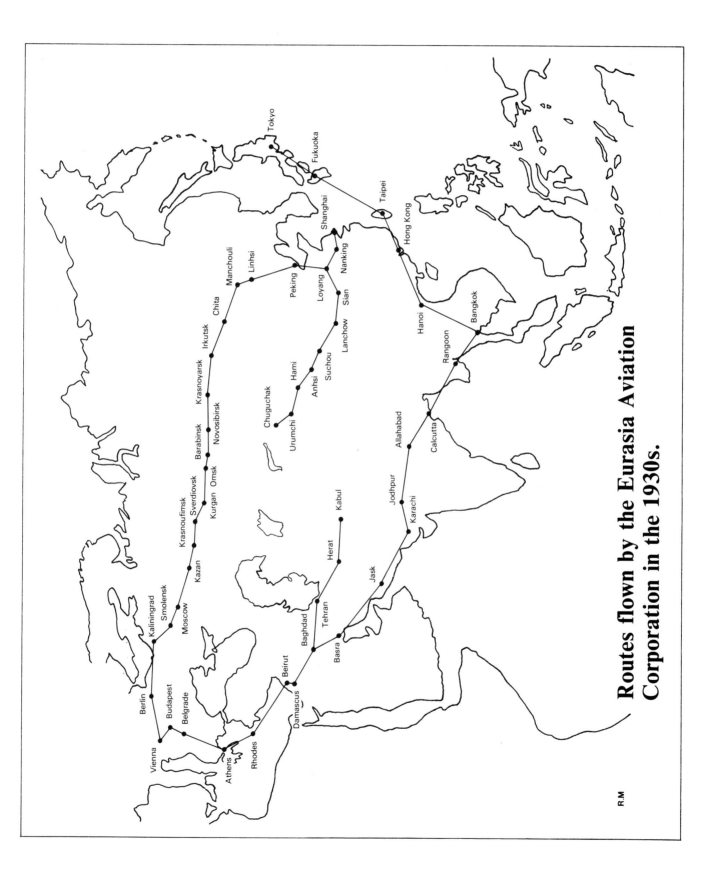

Routes flown by the Eurasia Aviation Corporation in the 1930s.

R.M

The record-breaking KLM DC-2 'Uiver', PH-AJU, and the crew who came first in the transport class and second (to the DH.88 Comet) in the speed class in the 1934 MacRobertson air race from England to Australia.

The Handley Page HP42 enabled Imperial Airways to establish regular, well-served landplane routes to Asia and Africa.

Mongolian tribes and also to the Chinese, and there is no doubt that it created the desired impression in those quarters. The flight, which had covered a total of 4,375 miles, had lasted a total of forty-four days.

Only eight days after the Russians' arrival in Pekin, two more aircraft set out on a remarkable flight from Asia to Europe. Both carried Japanese insignia and their crews were Japanese, but the machines themselves were French-built Breguet XIX-A2s, powered by 400 hp Lorraine-Dietrich engines. The expedition commander was Captain Abe, who was accompanied by his mechanic Shinohara; the pilot of the second machine was named Kawatchi, and his mechanic Katachiri. The flight had been organised by the Japanese newspaper *Asahi,* with the help of public subscriptions.

The two Breguets left Tokyo on 25 July and reached Harbin, Manchukuo, on 2 August. From there they followed the Trans-Siberian railway through Irkutsk, Krasnoyarsk, Achinsk, Berkresk, Novo-Nikolayevsk, Kurgan and Kazan to Moscow, where they arrived in 23 August. They stayed there for three weeks while both aircraft and engines were overhauled, then on 15 September flew on via Königsberg, Berlin, and Strasbourg to Paris, reaching the French capital on 28 September. During their stay there, the Japanese airmen paid a visit to the French aviator Pelletier D'Oisy, who had flown to Japan fifteen months earlier in an abortive attempt to fly around the world. After their machines had been thoroughly checked by Breguet and Lorraine-Dietrich, the Japanese crews visited London, Brussels, Lyon and Rome before returning home.

The Soviet and Japanese flights did much to stimulate interest in developing the northern air route to Asia, but it was to be another year before anyone proved that such a route had definite commercial possibilities. Then, at midnight on 23 July, 1926, two all-metal Junkers G.23 trimotors belonging to the new German airline, Deutsche Luft Hansa, set out from Berlin-Tempelhof to fly to Pekin. The expedition was a joint Soviet-German affair, with two German pilots (Schnabel and Poldi) and two Russian (Kozlov and Kudruansev). There were also two flight engineers, a meteorologist and a Dr. R. Knauss, who was in command of the venture.

Each aircraft carried enough fuel for $7\frac{1}{2}$ hours' flying as well as everything that might be required during the flight, from spare parts to sleeping bags. Knauss and another Luft Hansa representative, Herr von Winterfeld, had been responsible for planning the flight and for setting up ground support facilities along the route. It had not been easy; for example, the Russians had indicated that they might not be able to provide high-octane fuel for the Junkers, so their engines had to be modified to burn ordinary petrol — with a resulting performance drop of 90 hp per engine. Also, to save weight, all excess equipment — including radios — had been taken out of the machines. Nevertheless, the Junkers were basically ordinary airline machines, unlike the 'flying fuel tanks' which had made such long-range flights before them.

The expedition reached Moscow on 24 August, having flown via Königsberg and Smolensk, and then continued through Kazan to Krasnoi Ufinsk, which was reached on 25 August. The whole of the next day was spent in carrying out survey flights over the Urals, and when the aircraft tried to take off on the next leg of their flight the following day they encountered their first real problem. The 1,500-foot airstrip at Krasno Ufinsk was simply not long enough to permit the take-off of a heavily-laden aircraft; one of the Junkers, D-903, tried it and hurtled over a ditch to come to rest in a cornfield. The pilot of the second machine, D-901, waited until the sun had dried the rain-soaked ground before making his attempt — but when he started his take-off run his wheels broke through a thin crust of baked earth and sank into the mud beneath. Russian workers toiled all night to extend and firm up the runway, and the two Junkers managed to take off the next morning after some of their equipment had been off-loaded. However, more time was lost when D-901 again ran into soft ground at Kurgan, the next stop, and had to be dug out.

At night, navigation could be difficult, even when following the Trans-Siberian Railway. Sometimes the crews were lucky; at Barabinsk, they were guided to their objective, a tiny strip near a spur of the railroad, by the glare of a big forest fire.

At Irkutsk, the expedition was delayed for a fortnight while it awaited entry permits from the Chinese, which had proved impossible to obtain before the start of the flight. They duly arrived — but the documents did not cover the two Russian pilots on the team. This resulted in a further delay of nine days while diplomats tried to sort out the problem, but in the end the Junkers took off on the next leg of the flight from Irkutsk without the Russians. The two aircraft arrived in Pekin on 30 August to a massive reception and flew home via the same route on 26 September. Despite all the delays en route, the expedition had been a success; the two aircraft had linked Berlin and Pekin in a flying time of only six days, compared with the seventeen that it took a traveller on the Trans-Siberian Railway.

Nevertheless, the flight also showed that many difficulties had to be overcome before there could be a regular air service across the vastness of the Soviet Union. Airfields were too primitive, there were no telephones or telegraph and no emergency landing strips or weather forecasting facilities. Worst of all was the Soviet brand of bureaucracy, which proved obstructive at almost every turn.

Negotiations did in fact begin between Luft Hansa and Dobrolet with a view to setting up a Berlin-Pekin route after this proving flight, but they ran into financial difficulties. However, in 1928 the two airlines began a Berlin-Moscow-Irkutsk mail service; the Moscow-Irkutsk sector ran twice weekly between 1 August and 1 October. On 23 August, a Luft Hansa Junkers W.33 *Ural* set out from Berlin to survey the possibilities of a Berlin-Moscow-Siberia-Shanghai air mail link with the co-operation of Deruluft and Dobrolet; the aircraft stopped at Kazan, Sverdlovsk, Kurgan, Omsk and Krasnoyarsk, landing at Irkutsk on 30 August. The return flight began on the same day, the Junkers reaching Berlin on 2 September. Later that year, between September 18 and October 18, another Junkers W.33 — named *Europa* — flew from Berlin to Tokyo in ninety hours.

In 1930, Deutsche Luft Hansa and the Chinese Transport Ministry reached a ten-year agreement for the creation of a joint air mail company named the Eurasia Aviation Corporation, with its headquarters in Nanking. The company's technical director, Herr Schmidt, had been laying the groundwork since 1927. The company, which employed twenty German personnel — Luft Hansa holding one-third of the shares and supplying aircraft and equipment — achieved a level of co-operation with the Chinese, both with the central government in Pekin and with the regional authorities, that was quite remarkable. At the beginning of 1931, a Junkers F.13 and three Junkers W.33s were assigned to operations in China, and on the last day of May a regular air mail service was started over the Shanghai-Pekin-Linse-Manchuli route, the mail being flown from Berlin to Shanghai in seven to eight days.

However, the dangers attending mail flights over Chinese Inner Mongolia soon became apparent. On 31 July, 1931, a Junkers W.33 crewed by Johannes Rathje and Otto Kölber, flying over the sensitive border triangle between China, Russia and Mongolia, encountered heavy ground fire from Mongolian troops and both men were wounded. Rathje managed to land the aircraft, which was surrounded by a large number of soldiers with fixed bayonets, and the two airmen were arrested and taken to the nearest settlement, where they were accused of espionage.

Kölber was in bad shape, having had his leg amputated under primitive conditions, and Rathje was subjected to interrogation after interrogation before a travesty of a trial sentenced both him and his colleague to death by firing-squad. Fortunately, diplomatic channels had been hard at work, and the release of the two men was secured just in time. After this incident, however, the mail route terminated at Pekin.

During the next two years, the Germans opened up much unexplored territory in the underdeveloped west of China and initiated some interesting sidelines, such as aerial sightseeing trips along the Great Wall of China. Two Junkers W.34s were added to the fleet in 1933, followed in 1934 by the first Junkers 52 to visit the Far East. This aircraft was delivered via the southern route, which took it through Egypt, Baghdad, Jodhpur, Rangoon, Bangkok, Hanoi and Canton. On arrival in China it undertook a series of demonstration flights, carrying local dignitaries on night flights over Shanghai. Three Ju52s were assigned to Eurasia in 1935, and by the end of the following year these aircraft were flying nearly threequarters of the company's scheduled services.

In 1936, Lufthansa began exploratory flights over the central Asian route to China. In June, a Junkers 52 flew over the Hindu Kush and Pamir mountain ranges, and meteorological facilities were set up in Afghanistan. More flights were made in the summer of 1937, when the Ju52s set out from Berlin for Kabul. From there, they climbed over the Wakhan pass between Pamir and Karakorum to the Chinese town of Ansi. On the return flight, one of these aircraft, D-ANOY, commanded by Captain von Gablenz, had to make an emergency landing at Lob Bazar in Chotan on 28 August. Civil war was raging and the Junkers came under heavy small-arms fire as soon as it landed; the crew, miraculously unhurt despite having had their cockpit shattered by bullets, climbed down and were taken prisoner by Chinese troops of the 36th Tunganese Division. They were imprisoned in Chotan and repeatedly interrogated and beaten until, unexpectedly, the order for their release came; it

The Junkers G.38 was the biggest landplane of its time when it entered Lufthansa service in 1931. Two were built and registered D-AZUR and D-APIS. The former was lost in a crash on take-off at Dessau in 1936.

seemed that a friendly general had gained the upper hand in the local conflict. The Junkers had been stripped by looters, but the crew were able to make it airworthy and it reached Kabul on 27 September.

Lufthansa began a mail and freight service on the Berlin-Athens-Baghdad route on 29 October 1937, and this was later extended to Teheran and Herat. At the same time, in an attempt to extend Eurasia's domestic Chinese routes to link up with Air France's Indo-China services, the company extended its Sian-Kunming route to Hanoi. By now, however, the bitter Sino-Japanese conflict was forcing Eurasia to alter almost all its Chinese routes, and routine civil operations were becoming increasingly hazardous. On Friday, 13 April 1939, for example, a Eurasia Ju52 was attacked by Japanese fighter-bombers while on a flight from Hanoi to Kunming and forced down by machine-gun fire, after which it was bombed. The pilot, Captain Rathje, had a broken arm and foot and had to be carried by the other crew members, who trekked through the jungle until they reached the Hanoi-Kunming railway. Eurasia officials later organised an expedition to repair the damaged machine, which lay on its belly on a mountainside, and hundreds of coolies were recruited locally to dig out an airstrip. The machine was successfully repaired and Captain Leiding made a hazardous take-off, reaching Yunnan Airport safely despite a defective engine.

An aircraft renowned for its safety and economy, the tri-engined Junkers Ju52, nick named "Aunt Ju", was put into Lufthansa service in 1933. Initially, it flew on routes within Europe, later to East Asia and across South America to Santiago de Chile.

By the summer of 1940, the conflict in China had made Eurasia's operations virtually impossible. In November, all services were suspended on the orders of the Chinese Government and Kunming, the company's main base, evacuated. All German personnel had left China by the end of the year, and Eurasia's surviving aircraft were taken over by the Chinese.

Meanwhile, in 1938, Lufthansa had extended their Asian wings still further with a flight from Berlin to Tokyo by a Focke-Wulf Fw200 Kondor. The aircraft, D-ACON *Brandenburg,* left Berlin on 28 November and landed at Tokyo's Tachikawa Airport on the 30th after a record flight of 46 hours 18 minutes, with refuelling stops at Basra, Karachi and Hanoi. This achievement was marred when the aircraft ditched in the sea off Manila on the return flight, but all the crew escaped.

In April 22, 1939, Lufthansa made a second Tokyo flight, this time with a well-proven Ju52/3m commanded by Freiherr von Gablenz. The journey lasted until 22 May, the aircraft flying via Bangkok, Hanoi and Taipeh. In Tokyo, von Gablenz negotiated an air traffic agreement with the Japanese, aimed at establishing a regular through service from Berlin to Tokyo by way of the southern route through Asia. The first proving flight on this route began on 8 August 1939, when Ju52 D-AGAK left Berlin on the first stage of its long journey. Five days later it arrived in Bangkok on schedule, having flown via Beirut, Baghdad, Basra, Jask, Karachi, Jodhpur, Allahabad and Rangoon. At Bangkok, the aircraft was checked over before setting out for Tokyo, with refuelling stops at Hanoi, Hong Kong, Formosa and Kyushu. The flight was an unqualified success, and Lufthansa publicity agents were already preparing brochures to advertise the new route when the Ju52 arrived back in Berlin on 27 August, 1939. Three days later, German forces invaded Poland.

During the 1920s, Europe had enjoyed a substantial lead over the United States in pioneering long-range commercial routes, so it was hardly surprising that the Germans had been the first to exploit the Chinese market. The Americans, however, were not slow to realise China's huge commercial aviation potential; after all, in a country without railways, where the principal arteries were rivers and dirt roads, flying seemed a logical development.

The first American to make inroads into China, from the commercial aviation point of view, was Clement M. Keys, who owned the Glenn Curtiss Company and who, during the 1920s, had founded several aviation enterprises in the USA, Europe and Latin America. His business enterprises, in fact, were a constant thorn in the side of Pan American's president, Juan Trippe, who was also turning his attention to the Asian market.

Keys, however, got there before his rival. In 1929 he sent a team of aviation experts to China, headed by Major William B. Robertson, to found an airline; this emerged as China Airways and, flying Loening Air Yachts, was soon carrying mail between various points. However, the really lucrative mail routes were sewn up by the Germans, and China Airways' operations quickly became characterised by a struggle against China's bureaucracy. A series of fatal crashes, followed by the great Wall Street Crash in the USA, all but wiped Keys out and he lost control of Curtiss-Wright. His fellow directors, faced with severe financial burdens at home, now looked for someone who might take over China Airways and make a profit out of it, and that someone was Juan Trippe.

Trippe sent an emissary, Harold M. Bixby, to Shanghai to try and sort out the muddled fortunes of the airline, which had now been renamed China National Aviation Corporation (CNAC). After some exploratory survey flights. Bixby decided that the company's salvation lay in opening several new routes; one of these, from Shanghai to Canton, had already been negotiated by the previous administration: the problem was that, under the terms of the contract, it had to be inaugurated by 8 July 1933.

In the nick of time, a Pan American expedition arrived in Shanghai on 26 June, equipped with two Sikorsky S.38 amphibians, and one of these set off for Canton, where it arrived on 6 July. However, the contract stipulated that the machine had to carry mail on the return flight — and no mail was waiting for it. In desperation, Bixby, who was on board the S.38, sought out the local postmaster, who was a European, and persuaded him to hand over two sacks of mail which were duly flown back to Shanghai — much to the consternation of the Chinese Minister of Communications, who had withheld the mail in the first place in the hope of obtaining a bribe from the Americans.

Bixby soon found that bribery was an accepted way of life in China, but he and Juan Trippe stubbornly refused to enter into such arrangements. Instead, they stood their ground and insisted on a legitimate agreement with the Chinese authorities. In the end the Chinese gave in, an agreement was signed and, on 24 November 1933, a Sikorsky S.38 took off from the Whang Poo River on the first

Sikorsky S-38 flying-boats were used by Pan American's subsidiary, the China National Aviation Corporation.

passenger flight from Shanghai to Canton. A few minutes later it was back again, its pilot, George Rummel, having encountered thick fog over Hangchow Bay. He tried again later that morning, only to run into fog again. This time, it closed in so quickly that he lost sight of the water, and in trying to make an emergency landing on a strip of beach he mushed into a hilltop, completely wrecking the aircraft. Fortunately, no-one was seriously hurt, but it was a sorry start to CNAC's passenger operations.

The company battled on with the remaining S.38. But things became steadily worse, not just from the financial viewpoint, but also because of the adverse effect the primitive conditions in China were having on the crews and their families. The wife of one pilot jumped to her death from the top of an apartment building, holding the hands of her two little children.

Then, one day, the surviving S.38 took off from Shanghai for Canton and was never seen again. Lesser men might have given up there and then, but Harold Bixby was determined to make a success. Expecting no real help — other than financial — from Trippe, who was now preoccupied with other routes, he brought about a complete reorganisation of the company, invested in new aircraft and ground equipment, and started all over again. The recovery was nothing short of miraculous; in 1935 the company made a small profit for the first time in its existence, and this increased in 1936.

CNAC now had a new manager, William L. Bond, which left Bixby free to negotiate deals and generally to act in a liaison capacity. By the summer of 1937 the company had in operation, or on order, eighteen aircraft, and there were thirty-four pilots and co-pilots. Four of the aircraft were DC-2s, which flew fast mail and passenger services to twenty major Chinese cities. Morale was high, and prospects were excellent. Then, in July 1937, Chinese and Japanese forces clashed near Pekin; fighting spread rapidly, and soon the Sino-Japanese War burst in its full fury over the country.

In the United States, Juan Trippe's first inclination was to close down CNAC, fly its aircraft to safety in Manila and freeze all the company's assets until the war was over. Bond, who was in the USA on leave, talked him out of it and returned to China, only to find that CNAC's aircraft had been requisitioned by the Chinese Air Force. Bond went to see a Colonel Lem, who had been placed in charge of CNAC's fleet, and tried to get the aircraft back; it was hopeless. So he decided to wait and let matters run their course.

The outcome was inevitable. Some of the Chinese who now flew CNAC's aircraft had worked as co-pilots with the company, but they were only partly trained and knew little about maintaining schedules or administering an airline. Before long, the aircraft stopped flying. Eventually, after passing through all sorts of official channels from the Chinese Prime Minister downwards, Bond got his aircraft back again.

Operations soon restarted, and although there was no longer any possibility of flying the old routes — the Japanese advances had brought an end to that — this was one of CNAC's busiest-ever periods, for its aircraft were always filled with diplomats, journalists and official delegations of one kind or another. Not unnaturally, the work had its attendant hazards. On one occasion, DC-2 *Kweilin,* bound for Chungking with fourteen passengers on board and piloted by Captain Hugh Woods, was attacked by Japanese fighters only a few minutes out of Hong Kong. The Japanese machine-gun fire killed nine of his passengers and, with his aircraft badly damaged, Woods ditched in a river. The Japanese continued to machine-gun the DC-2 as it floated and there were only three survivors, including the pilot. The aircraft was pulled out of the river and repaired, only to be caught in a strafing attack on Chungking just as it was about to take-off for Hong Kong. The machine was set on fire and eight of the thirteen passengers killed, together with the pilot, Walter Kent, who was hit in the back by a 20-mm cannon shell.

Hugh Woods, who had so narrowly escaped with his life on the previous occasion, now had another close brush with death when he was again attacked by Japanese fighters, this time while flying a DC-3. He managed to land and evacuate the crew and passengers, but the fighters continued to strafe the aircraft and destroyed its starboard wing.

Bond, in Hong Kong, was determined to salvage the damaged DC-3; every aircraft was precious. The problem was that there was no spare DC-3 wing in the whole of China. There was, however, a spare DC-2 wing. No-one knew whether a DC-3 would fly with a DC-2 wing on one side, but it was decided to try it. The spare wing was duly flown to the stranded aircraft, lashed to the fuselage side of another DC-2, and fitted to the stub of the DC-3's wing. Then, with Hugh Woods at the controls, the hybrid aircraft made the 860-mile flight back to Hong Kong, and the pilot reported that the asymmetric wings had made hardly any difference to its flying characteristics. That particular machine passed into aviation legend as the one and only 'DC-2½'.

CNAC continued to operate, in spite of all the hardships and dangers. It was still flying when the Japanese attacked Hong Kong in December 1941. In the ensuing holocaust Bond managed to evacuate some of his aircraft and 275 people, including all of his crews, before Hong Kong fell. The airline continued to operate throughout the war in the transport role, and in fact did so until 1949, when the communist victory in China finally brought operations to an end.

Ironically, it was the Sino-Japanese conflict, which destroyed so many European and American aspirations in China, that gave impetus to the establishment of Japan's first national carrier. Several small airlines had been in service in Japan since the early 1920s, carrying mail and some passengers on domestic routes, and in 1928 these were absorbed into a single entity known as the Japan Air Transport Company. This used mainly foreign aircraft, including Fokker F.VII-3ms. In 1938, mainly to serve the needs of Japan's overseas expansion into China, the Japanese Government founded the country's first government-owned commercial airline, Greater Japan Air Lines (Dai Nihon Koku K.K.), and an extensive programme was launched to modernise its equipment. Nakajima obtained rights to build the Douglas DC-3 under licence, and in 1938 Mitsubishi began the conversion of twenty-four G3M2 bombers to commercial transport standard, with seating for eight passengers. These were operated on domestic services, and also on routes to China, Formosa, Korea, Thailand and — at a later date — Pacific islands captured by the Japanese. Another G3M2, J-BACI *Nihon,* was purchased in 1938 by the Mainichi Shimbun newspaper group, and between August and October 1939 this machine undertook a world tour to Alaska, Canada, the USA, Central and South America, French West Africa, Casablanca, Rome, the Middle East, South-East Asia and Formosa, covering a distance of 32,845 miles in a flying time of 194 hours.

The expansion came too late to present a serious threat to other commercial operators in the Far East. Greater Japan Air Lines operated throughout the war, and was disbanded by the Allied Occupation Forces in 1945.

Chapter Nine
Aviation in the Americas

Just as they had done in China, the Germans — mainly because of extensive business interests in that part of the world — became the first to introduce commercial aviation to Latin America. The story of their involvement dates back to December 1919, when the Sociedad Colombo Alemana de Transportes Aereos (SCADTA) was founded at Barranquilla, capital of north-west Colombia, with German personnel and aircraft — two Junkers F.13 floatplanes.

Thousands of people gathered on the banks of the Rio Magdalena, Colombia's main waterway, to watch the inaugural flight on 5 December by one of the F.13s, piloted by Helmuth von Krohn and carrying two passengers, together with their baggage. In the hot and humid conditions, however, the aircraft refused to take off until all the luggage had been off-loaded. It finally staggered into the air and set off along the river, but after it had been flying for an hour the radiator developed a leak and von Krohn had to make an emergency landing. The hole was repaired and the aircraft flew on in a series of hops, the pilot landing on the river whenever the radiator boiled, and finally — much to the relief of the passengers — reached its destination at Girardot.

After several trial flights, during which the Germans learned a great deal about operating conditions in Colombia's climate, a regular service between Barranquilla and Girardot was opened early in 1921. Flight to the Colombian capital, Bogota, presented something of a problem, because the city lay on a high plateau and the F.13s could not reach it when carrying a worthwhile payload; it was to be 1929 before a regular service from the coast to Bogota was inaugurated, when new aircraft became available.

In its early days, SCADTA experienced severe financial difficulties, and it was not until Dr. Paul von Bauer, a wealthy Austrian geographer, gave the company his financial backing that it began to make real progress. In 1924, Deutscher Aero Lloyd AG and SCADTA established the Condor Syndikat in Berlin, the object being to study the viability of South American operations; Aero Lloyd's interest was to establish a Latin American terminal for its future air services across the South Atlantic, while SCADTA wished to set up an air network linking Colombia, Central America and the United States. As a result of this meeting, funds were made available to the Condor Syndikat for the purchase of two Dornier Wal flying-boats, to supplement the two F.13s already in service.

The two Wals, named *Atlantico* and *Pacifico,* were shipped in crates from Europe to Curacao. On 10 August, 1925, they took off from Barranquilla on a proving flight to Central America, calling at Costa Rica, Nicaragua, Honduras, San Salvador, Guatemala, British Honduras and Mexico. On 19 September they flew to Havana, and then went on to make trial flights to Key West and Miami, Florida. Despite the success of this flight, months of negotiations with the US Government over traffic rights came to nothing, even though several American businessmen were interested in financing the venture, and in 1926 the Condor Syndikat's proposed 'Interamericana' scheme was abandoned. Nevertheless, the same period saw further expansion in a different area, with the formation of a German-administered Bolivian airline company named Lloyd Aereo Boliviano (LAB); a Junkers executive was appointed head of operations and technical director, and the company operated Junkers F.13 aircraft.

In November 1926, the Condor Syndicate and Luft Hansa undertook a joint venture which was designed to impress upon the Brazilian Government the importance and feasibility of commercial air services in their country. Two Dornier Wals — the *Atlantico* and a new machine, the *Hai* — were shipped to Montevideo and flown from there to Buenos Aires for the start of a prestige flight to Rio de Janeiro. The expedition was known as the *Luther Flight,* because Dr. Hans Luther, the former Reichs Chancellor, was to accompany it. Unfortunately, the *Hai* collided with a jetty of Buenos Aires and so the *Atlantico* had to make the flight alone, taking off from Buenos Aires on 17 November on the first stage of a journey that took it to Montevideo, Pelotas, Rio Grande, Porto Alegre, Florianopolis, Sao Francisco and Santos, before it finally reached Rio de Janeiro to a tremendous

The Brazilian airline "Syndicato Condor Ltda." was founded on 1 December, 1927, in Rio de Janeiro, with participation of Lufthansa. It operated German aircraft exclusively, like this Junkers F 13 "Iguassu".

reception. The German party was welcomed by the Brazilian president, who was taken for a flight over the city.

Dr. Luther entered into negotiations with the Brazilian transport minister with the object of acquiring a scheduled air service licence, and on New Year's Day, 1927 agreement having been reached, the Minister was taken for a flight to Florianopolis to mark the official birthday of civil aviation in Brazil. On 26 January — *Atlantico* having in the meantime made several more much-publicized flights to various points in Brazil — the Condor Syndicat received full approval to begin passenger and mail operations on the coastal route between Rio de Janeiro and Port Alegre. This was followed, in September, by a further licence to operate a service from Rio to Natal.

Meanwhile, on 7 May, a local service carrier known as VARIG (Empresa de Viacao Aerea Rio Grandense) had been founded under the auspices of the Condor Syndikat to take over responsibility for the latter's Brazilian services. Its first aircraft was the faithful *Atlantico,* now registered P-BAAA, and a Dornier Merkur was added later in the year. One of the company's staff at that time was a 19-year-old ticket clerk and book-keeper named Ruben Berta; many years later, when VARIG's Boeing 707s and DC-8 jet airliners were flying to destinations all over the world, he was to become the airline's president. On 1 July 1927 the old Condor Syndicate ceased operations in Latin America and was replaced by a new company, the Syndicato Condor Ltda. In June the following year the Syndicato Condor received the first of three Junkers G24Ws, and this machine made a tour of northern Brazil, calling at towns which were to be added to the airline's schedule.

While the Condor Syndikat busied itself in Brazil, Junkers Luftverkehr had been working hard to set up a commercial aviation line in neighbouring Argentina. However, the first commercial air company in that country, the Compania Rio Platense de Aviacion, had already been founded in 1919 by a Major Shirley Kingsley, beginning operations in January 1920. In 1922 the company started its first scheduled passenger service from Buenos Aires to Montevideo, using a pair of DH16s, but after a promising start rising costs forced a suspension of operations in 1925.

It was at this point that Junkers stepped in, financing a new company, Aero Lloyd, at Cordoba. In the autumn of 1925 Aero Lloyd opened a route to Villa Dolores, on the other side of the Sierra de Cordoba; the Junkers F.13s could carry little payload other than mail over the 6,000-foot peaks, but they established the first rapid communciations across the mountain range. However, the company received no backing from the Argentine Government, and after a few months of operations Junkers decided that it was not a commercial success and pulled out.

It was left to the French company Aéropostale to develop civil aviation in Argentina, as a means of extending its mail routes on the western side of the Atlantic. In 1927, Aéropostale's principal director, M. Bouilloux-Lafont, allocated about £400,000 to the development of the Latin American route network, and on 14 November that year the company opened the first regular mail service between Natal and Buenos Aires. This was followed by exploratory flights to other points in Argentina, during which Aéropostale received invaluable advice from Captain V. A. Almonacid, a highly respected aviator and former fighter pilot, who had flown with the French Flying Corps during the 1914-18 War.

These survey flights led to the foundation of Aeroposta Argentina, a subsidiary of the parent French company, which began operations in January 1929 with a service from Buenos Aires to Asuncion, the capital of Paraguay, via Monte Caseros and Posadas, using Latécoère 25 monoplanes. At a later date, services were also started to Santiago, the capital of Chile, via Cordoba and Mendoza, and from Bahia Blanca to Comodoro Rivadavia, a distance of 600 miles. The latter was an extremely important development, because Comodoro Rivadavia was at the centre of a major oil-producing area and was extremely difficult to reach by land, most communications taking several days to make the journey by sea from Bahia Blanca. Aircraft operations in the inhospitable climate of southern Argentina were far from easy, the crews having to battle their way through severe winds, and in the early days there were no hangars to provide shelter for aircraft on the ground; but once adequate base facilities had been set up Aeroposta pushed its service 400 miles further south to Rio Gallegos, close to the Magellan Straits.

When Jean Mermoz and other French pioneers began their series of transatlantic proving flights in

The Sikorsky S-40 flying-boat was used by Pan American Airways and its subsidiaries on routes to Latin America.

1930, the future of Aéropostale's mail links with Latin America seemed secure; but then, in 1931, the company began to run into financial difficulties, and was eventually declared bankrupt. The backlash of this disaster was keenly felt by Aeroposta, which for lack of financial support was forced to discontinue its services to Asuncion and Santiago. However, the Rio Gallegos service was rescued by the Argentina Post Office, because by this time the mail route to southern Argentina was playing an indispensable part in the development of that area.

Further subsidies were received in 1934, enabling the company to purchase some Latécoère 28s to replace the 25s, which were now much the worse for wear, and the Argentine Government also agreed to supply petrol free of charge. Then, in 1936, Aeroposta was purchased by Sr. Ernesto Pueyrredon, head of a very wealthy business consortium, and he at once proceeded to tear the existing structure apart and replace it with a new and more efficient one. The first priority, he quickly realised, was to purchase new equipment, and so he approached the Syndicato Condor, which by now was also operating in Argentina, and asked its management if they could arrange for Lufthansa to supply a small number of Junkers 52/3ms and associated technical equipment on favourable terms.

Syndicato Condor had received a concession to expand its air mail services into Argentina two years earlier, in April 1934, and similar approval had been obtained from Uruguay later that year. In April 1935, it had opened an air mail route over the Andes from Buenos Aires to Santiago, and in that same year Lufthansa and Air France had pooled their resources to some extent on mail flights over the South Atlantic. The Germans were therefore by no means reluctant to bring Aeroposta into their expanding South American net, which is what the supply of German aircraft and equipment would virtually mean, and so they agreed to supply three 17-seat Ju52s, fully equipped for blind flying. With these machines, Aeroposta expanded its routes dramatically, starting a new service to Tierra del Fuego and increasing its volume of passengers and mail eightfold during the next few years. It continued to operate until 1949, when it was absorbed into Aerolineas Argentinas — surviving and flourishing, ironically, long after the German-controlled company that had supported it had ceased to exist.

One of Huff Daland's famous 'Dusters' which started crop-treating and passenger services in Peru in 1926.

First type used by Mexicana, the Mexican airline, on mail and passenger services was the Lincoln Standard in 1921.

In fact, German expansion throughout Latin America had continued at a rapid rate throughout the late 1930s. Following their concession in the Argentine, they had set up the Sociedad Ecuatoriana de Transportes Aereos (SEDTA) in Ecuador in July 1937; this was founded by Fritz W. Hammer, who had organized the Condor Syndikat's famous *Luther Flight* eleven years earlier. Equipped with two Junkers W.34s, chartered from Lufthansa, SEDTA began operations in 1938; flights with these aircraft and with two Ju52s continued until 1941, when operations were terminated.

A second German office was set up at Lima, Peru, by Lufthansa in 1938, and in May of that year a regular air mail service was started on the Lima-Arequipa-La Paz route. This service operated until 31 March 1941, and in fact was the last service to be run by the pre-war Lufthansa outside Europe. Also in 1938, Lufthansa extended a service from Buenos Aires to Santiago, in Chile, and later that year it opened another route from Natal to Rio de Janeiro via Recife and Bahia Blanca. Berlin was now linked to the furthermost corner of Latin America, and when a Focke-Wulf Fw200, on order for Syndicato Condor Ldta., flew across the Atlantic from Bathurst to Natal in 9 hours and 47 minutes on 27 June, 1939, it seemed to herald the great strides that would be made on the long-distance mail and passenger services during the next decade. Instead, that decade brought only war and misery to threequarters of the world.

*Fast mail and air taxi aircraft used by US operators in the 1930s: The Lockheed Air Express,
Lockheed Altair and Lockheed Orion.*

Pitcairn Aviation developed the Mailwing specially for fast mail carriage. Photo shows the Super Mailwing, which was larger and had a more powerful engine.

Predictably, the Americans were not long behind the Germans and the French in the race to open up the southern continent to commercial aviation. One of the first men to realise the enormous possibilities that existed south of the Caribbean was Ralph O'Neill, a 1914-18 fighter pilot who, in April 1929, founded NYRBA — the New York, Rio and Buenos Aires Line. O'Neill himself made the survey flight along the 7,800-mile route, flying a Sikorsky S-38, and on 28 August 1929 the airline opened its first South American sector, from Buenos Aires to Montevideo, using Ford Trimotors. Six weeks later, another service was inaugurated between Buenos Aires and Santiago, the Fords creeping through a convenient mountain pass whose altitude was 4,000 feet lower than the 20,000-foot peaks of the Andes. Each passenger was provided with an oxygen cylinder and tube, and was instructed to take a wiff if he found it hard to breathe.

O'Neill had decided to begin at the difficult end of South America, and gradually work his way northwards, opening new route sectors until he finally reached New York. His principal rival, an airline called Panagra, did just the opposite.

Panagra — short for Pan-American-Grace Airways — was a joint company founded in February 1929 by Juan Trippe of Pan American and W. R. Grace & Co., the giant trading company which dominated much of South America's commerce. Panagra's survey flights were undertaken by Charles and Anne Lindbergh and by other experienced pilots; NYRBA allowed them to use their base facilities until Panagra announced that it planned to start a weekly service from New York to Rio, whereupon attitudes changed sharply. On one occasion, a Panagra aircraft with engine trouble landed at a NYRBA base at Montenegro, Brazil; the pilot was confronted by a NYRBA official, who pointed a rifle at him and told him to take off immediately. The pilot did so, but his engine failed a few miles further on and he came down in the sea. He was rescued by a Pan American flying-boat.

By the end of 1929, NYRBA's fleet comprised four Sikorsky S-38s, three Ford Trimotors and one Consolidated Commodore flying-boat. The latter had a 100-foot wing span, could carry 24 passengers and had a range of 650 miles. The latter, however, developed serious splits in the hull, and time was lost while it was repaired. Trouble was also experienced with two more Commodores, delivered early in 1930; an engine tore loose from one while it was taking off from Fortaleza, Brazil, and the propeller tore through the fuselage, while the other had a bad fire in Dutch Guiana and had to have a wing replaced.

Despite these setbacks, NYRBA's first Buenos Aires-New York mail flight set off before dawn on 19 February, 1930, with O'Neill and L. C. Sullivan at the controls. All the mail carried was Argentinian; NYRBA had no contest with the US Post Office, and indeed had no authority even to carry foreign mail over US territory.

The flight was a fiasco. At Porto Alegre, the S-38 struck a harbour buoy, splitting open the hull and rupturing a fuel line. While Sullivan stayed behind to supervise repairs, O'Neill and the mail were transferred to a replacement S-38, brought in by William Grooch. As the latter approached to make a landing at Santos at the end of the next leg of the flight, there was a sudden loud bang as the hull struck a big wave; it was pitch dark, and O'Neill, thinking that Grooch had struck the roof of a house in the town, tried to snatch the control from him. Grooch struck his hand away and made a very heavy landing in rough water, and as he turned to taxi for the shore another big wave smashed over the aircraft. O'Neill, thinking they had capsized, kicked out the cockpit window and more water poured in. The aircraft was carrying two passengers, one of whom, a Portuguese panicked and drew a revolver, shouting hysterically; the flight engineer hit him over the head with a bottle and he subsided. Grooch managed to reach the shore, almost capsizing several times, and taxied out of the surf, whereupon the passengers jumped out of the machine and ran away into the night.

An inspection of the aircraft showed that both lower wings were badly damaged, and that the mail bags were floating in a foot of water in the cabin. Undeterred, O'Neill hired a car, drove all night with the mail to Rio, and boarded another S-38, which flew on to Bahia. There, the pilot, Clarence Woods,

Early air mail services in the USA were flown by ex-military machines such as the DH4, converted to single-seat configuration and with the front cockpit turned into a cargo compartment.

Warming up before a flight. This photograph shows a typical mail pilot's garb in the 1920s.

struck a sea wall, wrecking the machine. O'Neill eventually reached Miami on 25 February in yet another S-38 — only to be prevented from flying on to New York by the US postal authorities, who took the mail away from him.

Nevertheless, subsequent NYRBA mail flights went ahead, and were surprisingly successful, the aircraft flying an eight-day service from Miami to Buenos Aires and back. However, the company had committed itself to carrying South American mail at very low rates, and this proved its eventual undoing. By the middle of 1930 it was losing money at an unacceptable pace. In August, with bankruptcy staring O'Neill in the face, he sold out to Pan American.

Panagra, meanwhile, had opened a South American service in February 1929, flying to Mollendo in Peru with a Fairchild FC-2. Services were extended to Santiago in July, and to Buenos Aires in October. The company received a big boost with the acquisition of NYRBA's fleet, which consisted of fourteen flying-boats, mostly Commodores; it also inherited all the rights negotiated by O'Neill for operations along the east coast of South America. In September 1930, a subsidiary company called NYRBA do Brasil was created to undertake services south of Belem (Para) in Brazil; the name of this subsidiary was later altered to Panair do Brasil.

The services of Pan American and its subsidiaries along the South American coasts were flown by Sikorsky S-38 and S-40 flying-boats, and the Commodores, until 1934, when they began to be replaced by the luxurious 32-passenger S-42, which was capable of carrying a full load over a range of 750 miles — on average, 500 miles further than its predecessors. Later, routes were reorganized so that Panair do Brasil operated Brazil's internal services, while international links were maintained by Pan American. From 1935, the latter began using landplanes on its South American routes; these were DC-2s and Lockheed Electras, joined later by DC-3s and Boeing 307s, the world's first pressurized airliners.

Although Pan American became the greatest of the US carriers to operate the South American routes, it was not the first; nor, for that matter, was NYRBA. The honour of being first had already fallen to a company with the unlikely name of Huff Daland Dusters, founded by an enterprising man named C. E. Woolman and George Post, vice president of the Huff Daland aircraft manufacturing company of New York. Huff Daland Dusters was the first company in the world formed specifically for crop-dusting operations, and by 1926 it was equipped with 25 aircraft of various types, all equipped with chemical tanks. The biggest snag was that income was restricted to the harvest season, and so Woolman conceived that idea of moving operations during the non-productive months to Peru, where the seasons were reversed. He went there in 1926 with no knowledge of the language, taking with him films of crop-dusting activities. Some time later his aircraft arrived by steamship and he started operations in two valleys, working up to seven valleys within a year.

It was in Peru that Woolman first began to appreciate the value of air passenger services, and in 1927 he successfully secured rights to operate a Peruvian air mail service in the face of stiff competition from the Germans. He therefore became the first American airline operator south of the Equator in the western hemisphere, inaugurating a 1,500-mile route from Peru to Ecuador. However, the service was destined to have only a short life; in 1928, Peru was in the throes of revolution, and since there was a good possibility of his aircraft being seized by the military, Woolman sold them to a Peruvian company. He also sold his air mail route to Panagra, and then turned his attention to expansion in the north.

American Airways was a major US domestic mail and passenger carrier during the 1930s. Photographs show types in service: Ford Tri-motor

Ford Tri-motor

North America

Following the end of the 1914-18 War, aviation in the United States — military and civil alike — had slipped into the doldrums, mainly because of a steadfast refusal by Congress, under President Coolidge, to budget any funds for its development. Neither was there much incentive to develop new types of aircraft: after 1918 the market was flooded with thousands of surplus military machines, most of them in mint condition and crated ready for shipment overseas, and they were sold off to anyone who wanted them at ridiculously cheap prices. Some enterprising businessmen, with an eye to the future, bought several aircraft and made determined attempts to found an airline; in 1922, for

Lockheed Orion

Fokker Super Universal

example, Juan Trippe purchased seven Model 49B biplanes from the Philadelphia Navy Yard and, after using them to give joy-rides for a while, turned them into the nucleus of a company called Long Island Airways and started carrying passengers from Long Island to neighbouring holiday resorts in 1922. For the most part, however, civil aviation in North American in the early 1920s was dominated by stunt flying and barnstorming, with little attempt at organization, and anyone who did try to get an airline started had to contend with the privateers who flocked to the resorts in their ex-military machines, touting for trade.

As was also the case in Europe, the key to development in civil aviation during this period was mail. In the USA, no fewer than seven committees sat between 1918 and 1924 to investigate the possibilities of using aircraft as mail carriers; all of them had made favourable recommendations which had then been ignored. Then, in 1925, Congress finally passed the Air Mail Act — known as the Kelly Act after its architect and sponsor, Clyde Kelly — which turned over the carriage of air mail

The Lockheed 14 that revolutionized domestic air services throughout the world in the late 1930s

to private contractors. There was already a coast-to-coast air mail route, which was flown by military aircraft on charter to the US Post Office, but under the new Act bids were authorized for certain connections to this route. The most profitable and potentially worthwhile of these was the New York-Boston connection, for which there were two serious bidders; one was Eastern Air Transport, founded in September 1925 by Juan Trippe, and the other was Colonial Airlines, which was run by a consortium of influential investors. The two companies merged and became Colonial Air Transport, which was duly awarded the contract to fly on what the Post Office call Air Mail Route No. 1. Initially, the route was flown by Fokker Universals.

Meanwhile, in November 1925, another company called Western Air Express had been awarded a contract to carry mail between Los Angeles and Salt Lake City. Six Douglas M-2 biplanes — conversions of the military observation aircraft — were ordered, and operations with these began on 17 April, 1926. All flying was done in daytime and at low level; sometimes, to relieve the boredom, the pilots would make mock attacks on trains or stray animals, drop in for lunch with a friendly sheep farmer or land for a rendezvous with the pilot of a mail aircraft flying in the opposite direction. It was all very free and easy, and the schedule of eight and a half hours between Los Angeles and Salt Lake City allowed plenty of leeway for such diversions.

In May 1926 Western Air Express began to carry passengers whenever the mail load permitted, the trip costing ninety dollars. This provided welcome extra income, and in the first six months of operations the company showed a small profit — the only one of the original air mail carriers to do so. By the end of the year, Western was carrying 40 per cent of the country's mail and its directors were confident that they had a good chance of being awarded the contract for all or part of the coast-to-coast route. However, they were undercut by two other companies; the Boeing Airplane Co. got the San Francisco-Chicago section, while the Chicago-New York section was later awarded to National Air Transport — the only airline of consequence, apart from Colonial Air Transport, then operating in the eastern United States. Nevertheless, late in 1927 Western was awarded a valuable mail contract between Cheyenne, Denver and Pueblo; unfortunately, the unaugural flight ended in tragedy when the northbound aircraft from Denver crashed soon after take-off, killing the pilot.

In the east, following internal wrangling after Colonial Air Transport had failed in its bid for the Chicago-New York route against National Air Transport, Juan Trippe had left the company and was now bent on founding a new one. He gathered around him thirteen investors, all of them bankers, and on 2 June 1927 he incorporated the Aviation Corporation of America. At the same time, Trippe's board of directors authorized him to invest in a newly-formed New York corporation called Pan American Airways, Inc., which was in the running for a Key West-Havana mail contract that was shortly to be awarded.

Pan American's founders were all Army Air Corps officers. The principal architect was Major H. ('Hap') Arnold, who, seriously alarmed by German expansion in Central and South America, conferred with fellow officers Major Carl Spaatz, Jack Jouett and John Montgomery and determined to start a rival US airline that would operate from Key West to Havana, across to the Yucatan Peninusla, and then down through British Honduras and Nicaragua to Panama.

There was another American contender for the same mail contract over the Key West-Havana route. This was Atlantic, Gulf and Caribbean Airways, Inc., which had been incorporated out of Florida Airways — an embryo airline which had gone bankrupt in the spring of 1927. In the summer of that year, on learning that Pan American had been awarded the contract, Richard Hoyt, a Wall Street businessman who was interested in investing in Atlantic, Gulf and Caribbean Airways, attempted to take over Pan American and failed. He sought backing from Juan Trippe, who told him that if it proved possible to merge with Pan American and obtain the valued mail contract, then the new company would be known as Atlantic, Gulf and Caribbean Airways — but Trippe's Aviation Corporation of America would own the controlling interest, and the general manager would be Trippe himself. That was the price Hoyt would have to pay.

The mail contract had been awarded to Pan American on 16 July, 1927, and under its terms the service had to start by 19 October. But Pan American had no aircraft. On the other hand, Trippe, before he had left Colonial, had ordered several Fokker Tri-motors from the Fokker plant at Hasbrouck Heights, New Jersey; Colonial had not wanted these, which was one of the reasons for Trippe's split with the company, but production had gone ahead and the first two were nearing completion. It was a powerful lever with which to bargain with Pan American, and a deal was quickly

This photo taken at Pitcairn Field outside of Philadelphia shows a group of officials of Pitcairn Aviation, Inc. and the Ford Motor Co. entering a Ford all metal Tri-motor 12-passenger transport plane. Just before this picture was taken, Mr. Harold F. Pitcairn, President of Pitcairn Aviation, Inc. gave Mr. Leroy Manning of the Ford Motor Co. an order for 3 of these machines. The planes were used by Pitcairn on their New York-Miami passenger airline, the first unit of which started operations in the spring of 1930.

worked out. The merger would take place; control of all the merged companies would rest with the Aviation Corporation of America, which would hold 45 per cent of the stock. Atlantic, Gulf and Caribbean would hold 35 per cent, and Pan American 9 per cent.

On 13 October, 1927, Juan Trippe was elected president and general manager of Pan American. On 28 October, the new company's first Fokker Tri-motor made the inaugural flight from Key West to Havana, carrying 772 pounds of mail.

From then on, expansion was rapid. A new base was set up in Miami, and later in the year a new service was started to Nassau, in the Bahamas. Trippe's plan now was to encircle the whole of the Caribbean, forming a route that would pass through Mexico and into Texas; to do it Pan American needed an amphibian, and after carrying out trials with the Sikorsky S-36, which proved unsatisfactory, Trippe ordered the eight-passenger S-38, which entered service with the airline in October 1928. Before that, in July, Trippe bought out a rival company which stood in the way of Pan American's ambitions; this was the West Indian Aerial Express, which had begun services between Port au Prince, in Haiti, and San Juan in Puerto Rico in December 1927, using Fairchild FC-2 floatplanes. In January 1929 Trippe also purchased the Mexican airline Compania Mexicana de Aviacion (CMA), which had been operating since 1924 and which, five years later, was equipped with Ford Tri-motors, Fokker F-10s and Fairchild 71s.

By May 1930 Pan American's circle around the Caribbean was complete, and the airline now owned no fewer than 110 aircraft, comprising 38 Sikorsky S.38s, 29 Ford Tri-motors, 12 Fokker F.10s and 31 Fairchild 71s and FC-2s. It was an impressive foundation on which to base what was to become the greatest civil aviation enterprise in the world.

In the meantime, other American operators had been expanding too. Early in 1928, Western Air Express had opened another route along the California coast, using Fokker F.10s, and in June that

Pan American Airways in the 1930s.

year they had absorbed Pacific Marine Airways, which was then flying between Los Angeles Harbour and Catalina Island, twenty-two miles to the west. In January 1929, the company's ageing Douglas M-2 aircraft were replaced by four new Boeing 95s, and this was quickly followed by the purchase of another smaller company, West Coast Air Transport, which was then flying between San Francisco and Seattle.

Western Air Express was now one of the main contenders in the race to open a second coast-to-coast mail route, and new airports were built east of Los Angeles. On 2 June, 1929, the company opened a service that went as far east as Kansas City, and later that year a company that might have blocked the central part of the transcontinental mail route, Mid-Continent Air Express, which flew from Denver to El Paso via Albuquerque, was taken over.

WAE was now racing neck-and-neck with an eastern air company, TAT, to secure contracts on the central mail route across the USA, and both companies were losing money. Then WAE had to face some severe setbacks in 1930, with a series of disasters that robbed the airline of some of its most experienced crews, although mercifully no passengers were killed. On 10 January, 1930, a Boeing 95 went missing in the mountains of Utah; the wreckage was not found until June, with the body of the pilot, Maury Graham, lying about seven miles away. Dazed and shocked by the crash, he had apparently tried to walk to safety through a blizzard.

February 23, 1930, was the worst night, when three aircraft went missing. Jim Doles, with a co-pilot and steward, was missing on a flight from the east, while Fred Kelly — the company's first pilot — disappeared in Utah while flying the night mail. Another pilot, Bart Cox, crashed on take-off at Cedar City; another pilot set out to pick up the stranded pilot's mail and went missing too, although he turned up safe and sound the next day, having made an emergency landing en route. Kelly, however, had crashed and had spent the night huddled in his parachute; he was picked up the next day.

The third missing aircraft, an F-10, was not found until 7 March near Lake Arrowhead, west of Los Angeles. All three crew members were dead.

In April 1930 WAE moved into new base facilities at Alhambra Airport, and in that month it acquired the first four-engined transport to enter airline service in America, the 32-passenger Fokker F-32. In the following month WAE bought out yet another company, the Aero Corporation of California, together with its subsidiary, Standard Airlines, which was then flying east to Tucson and El Paso with air and rail connections to the east coast.

Finally, on advice from the US Postmaster, who had made it quite clear that only one airline would be awarded a new coast-to-coast mail contract, WAE and TAT settled their differences and merged, also bringing in the Pittsburgh Aviation Industries Corporation, which had pioneered some routes across the Allegheny Mountains. On 25 October, 1930, an all-air service from coast to coast was inaugurated by the new airline, whose name was now Transcontinental and Western Air — TWA. Twenty years later the name would be changed yet again, to Trans World Airlines.

By the early 1930s, civil aviation in the United States was firmly in the hands of massive conglomerates, and the US Postmaster-General, Walter Brown, was determined that the all-important mail contracts should stay with the big concerns, even though many smaller companies were striving to get into the market with lower bids. He was very probably right, but his attitude was the subject of a good deal of what would nowadays be called investigative journalism and a Senate Committee of Enquiry was set up to look into the whole business. Brown was cleared of any suspicion of fraud, but as a result of the enquiry Franklin D. Roosevelt, who had been elected President in 1932, ordered the new Postmaster-General, James Farley, to cancel all existing contracts and put the carriage of mail into the hands of the Army Air Corps. After a month of accidents and general confusion, however, it was decided to invite civilian tenders once more, and Farley called a meeting which was attended by 45 operators — but the big airlines could only take part if they agreed to sever their connections with the big businesses that had supported them.

The four big airlines that did attend the meeting were TWA, American, Eastern and United. Of these, TWA had strong links with North American Aviation, which now sold its shares in the

Douglas DC-2

company; American Airlines had been part of a holding company, the Aviation Corporation, which now relinquished its interest; General Motors had had substantial holdings in Eastern Airlines, and now pulled out as well; while the Boeing Aircraft and Transport Company, which had combined with several other firms to form the United Aircraft and Transport Company, also severed its ties. The measures were drastic, but they were necessary if the major airlines were to retain their transcontinental routes and survive. At the same time, the measures threw a lifeline to the smaller companies, enabling them to put their operations on a sounder footing. One such was the Delta Air Corporation, which had emerged from the old Huff Daland Dusters and which, in June 1929, had started passenger services from Dallas, Texas, to Jackson, Mississippi, with three Travel Air monoplanes. From July 1934, Delta was able to carry mail as well as passengers, and plans were made for expansion to meet the new demands. The company prospered and survived to become today's Delta Air Lines.

The measures had another consequence, too, in that they compelled the airlines to look elsewhere for new aircraft. Hitherto, airlines had been forced to purchase aircraft from the manufacturers who controlled them. If aircraft cost so much that they brought about financial losses, these were offset to some extent by higher mail subsidies, which could be obtained without undue difficulty by the big

The Boeing 247 was overshadowed by the DC-2 on American short and medium-range routes. This example was used by Mexicana, the Mexican airline. The type entered service in 1936.

corporations, and if the airline losses cancelled out the manufacturer's profit, it was a convenient method of ensuring that the parent corporation did not pay federal taxes. Now, with the airlines and the manufacturers both having to stand on their own feet, competition to produce and sell aircraft that would give an airline a lead over its competitors on the mail and passenger routes suddenly became fierce.

Predictably, however, the big airlines still turned to the manufacturers they knew and trusted, and it was in a bid to gain a firm leadership over his rivals that Frederick Rentschler, President of United Air Lines, placed an off-the-drawing-board order for sixty examples of a new Boeing design — the twin-engined all-metal Model 247, which was partly based on the B-9 bomber. The order was an astonishing gamble, for it involved a sum of $3\frac{1}{2}$ million dollars — in those days, a fantastic amount to tie up in an aircraft that had not even flown.

Production of the Model 247 began in the summer of 1932, and on 8 February 1933 the prototype — NX13301 — made its first flight. Boeing's Seattle factory worked around the clock, and by the end of June thirty aircraft had been delivered to United Air Lines. One of these, NC13308, made the 247's first scheduled coast-to-coast flight on 11 July 1933, flying from Newark Airport, New Jersey, to San Francisco in 20 hours 30 minutes, with seven stops en route.

Not only did the 247 cut eight hours off the trans-continental service; it also combined speed with a high standard of comfort. In its first month of service, it brought United a massive increase in ticket sales.

Then, on 10 October 1933, a 247 bound for Chicago exploded in mid-air over Indiana, killing all seven on board. The aircraft was not at fault — the disaster had been caused by an explosive item of cargo that had found its way on board — but, inevitably, the machine lost some of its passenger appeal as a result. Nevertheless, its future might have been assured if Boeing had been prepared to sell it to TWA, which wanted it badly; but at that time both Boeing and United were still controlled by the same board of directors, and they turned down TWA's application.

So Jack Frye, TWA's president, turned to another manufacturer — Donald Douglas. The result was the DC-1, prototype of the DC-2, the first of which was delivered to TWA on 14 May 1934. The DC-2 carried four more passengers than the Boeing 247 and was 25 mph faster; suddenly, the day of the Boeing airliner was over. From then on, although Boeing's name would be a synonym for long-range air transport, it would be Douglas machines that would dominate the domestic routes of the United States, and of half the world.

Photographic Acknowledgements

The Author
Page 1, 2, 3, 9, 25, 26, 27, 37, 38, 39, 41, 43, 44, 45, 46, 47, 48, 50, 51 Bottom, 62, 66, 67, 68, 69, 89, 91, 93, 107, 108, 109, 110, 111, 113, 126 Top, 133, 134, 135, 138, 141 Bottom, 145, 146.

Lufthansa Photos
Page 7, 10, 11, 12, 13, 14, 15, 16, 20, 21, 36, 94, 95, 97, 98, 99, 100, 101, 102, 103, 112, 120, 122, 125, 126, 131.

Short Brothers Ltd.
Page 18, 51 Top, 53, 56, 59, 106.

Pan American Airways
Page 22, 28, 29, 127, 132, 144.

Royal Air Force
Page 49, 52.

British Airways
Page 54, 104, 105, 126 Bottom.

Science Museum
Page 57.

E.C.P. Armees
Page 74, 75.

SABENA
Page 88, 90.

Roger Giraud Archives
Page 92.

American Airlines
Page 136, 137, 139, 140, 141 Top.

Eastern Airlines
Page 143.

Index

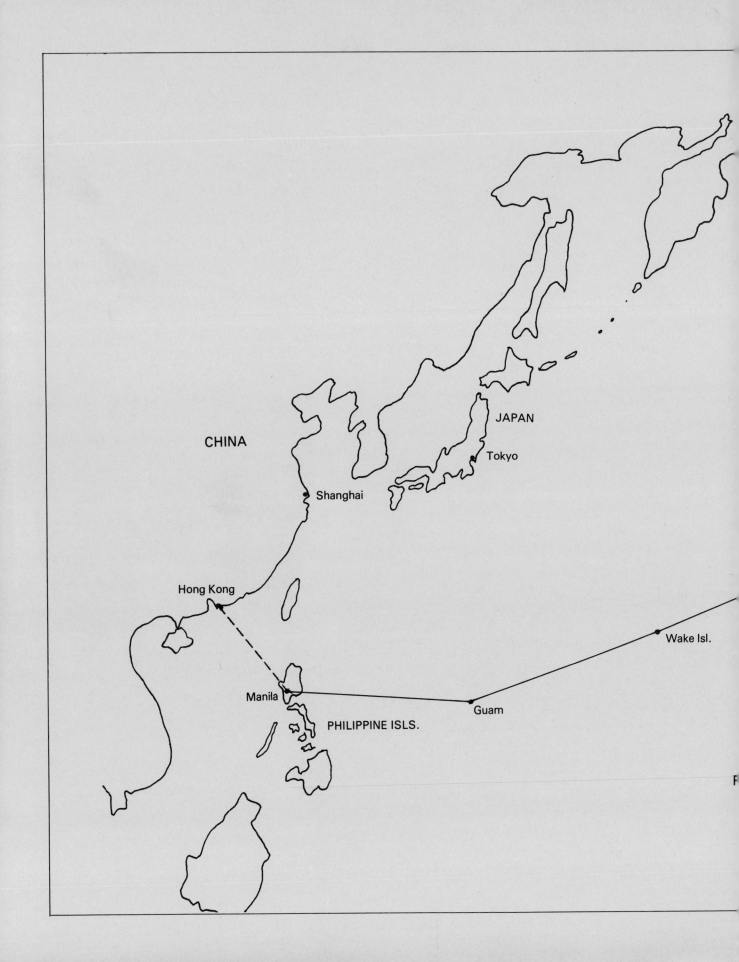